Transatlantic Encounters

Transatlantic Encounters

Europeans and Andeans in the Sixteenth Century

EDITED BY

Kenneth J. Andrien
and Rolena Adorno

UNIVERSITY OF CALIFORNIA PRESS
Berkeley   Los Angeles   Oxford

The publisher wishes to acknowledge the generous
assistance of the Program for Cultural Cooperation
Between Spain's Ministry of Culture and United States'
Universities in the publication of this book.

University of California Press
Berkeley and Los Angeles, California
University of California Press
Oxford, England
© 1991 by
The Regents of the University of California
Printed in the United States of America

1   2   3   4   5   6   7   8   9

**Library of Congress Cataloging-in-
Publication Data**
Transatlantic encounters: Europeans and Andeans
  in the sixteenth century/edited by Kenneth J.
Andrien and Rolena Adorno.
      p.   cm.
  Includes bibliographical references and index.
  ISBN 0–520–07228–6 (cloth: alk. paper)
    1. Indians of South America—Andes Region—
Government relations.   2. Indians of South
America—Andes Region—Cultural assimilation.
3. Indians of South America—Andes Region—
First contact with Europeans.   4. Incas.
5. Peru—History—Conquest, 1522–1548.
I. Andrien, Kenneth J., 1951–   . II. Adorno,
Rolena.
F3429.3.G6T73   1991
980'.013—dc20
                                       91–12232
                                          CIP

The paper used in this publication meets the minimum
  requirements of American National Standard for
  Information Sciences—Permanence of Paper for
  Printed Library Materials, ANSI Z39.48–1984 ∞

CONTENTS

PREFACE

The idea for this volume grew out of a Columbian Quincentenary Conference held at the Ohio State University, 9 to 11 October 1986, entitled "Early European Encounters with the Americas: Reciprocal Influences of Cultures in Contact." Inspired by that conference, we decided to address its theme of "reciprocal influences" for the single area of the Andes. Our hope is to serve both scholarly and pedagogical needs. Our goal and that of our contributors has been to synthesize current knowledge and to suggest directions for future investigation, by providing various disciplinary perspectives on Andeanist research and offering an anthology of essays that may be used profitably in the classroom. In most areas examined here—from the socioeconomic formation of the colonial state to the creation of a mestizo culture—much work remains to be done. The aim of this collection of essays is to point in some of those directions.

For the purpose of carrying out this project, we have received generous support from the Ohio State University College of Humanities and its Dean, G. Micheal Riley, as well as the Center for Medieval and Renaissance Studies and its Director, Christian A. Zacher. Both individuals facilitated this project with the same enthusiasm and generosity they devoted to the earlier conference. We acknowledge their support with gratitude. We would also like to extend our personal thanks to David S. Adorno and Anne Andrien for their support and assistance.

Collaborative scholarly ventures of this sort have the potential to allow the editors and collaborators to present a truly interdisciplinary perspective for interpreting the past. This is particularly important for a topic as multifaceted as the "encounter" between Europeans and Andeans in the formative years of the sixteenth century. We sincerely hope that our readers will profit from this volume as much as we have in preparing it.

Kenneth J. Andrien
Columbus, Ohio

Rolena Adorno
Princeton, New Jersey

INTRODUCTION

Kenneth J. Andrien and Rolena Adorno

Scholarly interest in the emergence of a distinctive colonial society in the Andes during the sixteenth century has led to an impressive output of interdisciplinary publications, particularly over the last twenty years. While earlier studies tended to focus narrowly on the centers of power at the viceregal and Spanish courts, most newer works have rejected this "creole scholarship" and dealt primarily with the Andean peoples in the rural zones and provincial capitals, where the majority lived their daily lives.[1] This trend has led scholars to supplement the traditional chronicles and accounts of high-level colonial administrators with materials drawn from a wide range of archaeological sites and provincial archives.[2] It has also involved employing new conceptual models, drawn from the Andean experience, rather than attempting to utilize uncritically Eurocentric social science theories.[3] The result has been a thorough reexamination of the Andeans' contributions to the colonial society emerging after 1532, and their concerted efforts to resist European domination.

The essays in this volume attempt to add to this burgeoning scholarly literature by defining a broad perspective, examining the influences of the European and the Andean peoples on the formation of colonial society. The essays in part I examine the influence of the Old World background in shaping those critical events in the early encounter period. The chapters in part II consider the interplay among the key forces of historical change in the Andes during the sixteenth century: the demands of the crown and the forces of mercantile capitalism, the interests of the European settlers, and the Andean strategies for resistance and survival after the fall of the Inca state (Tawantinsuyu). Finally, the essays in part III examine the use of Andean symbolism in Inca times and its hybridization afterward, illuminating aspects of the transition from Inca to *indio*. This collection of essays reflects two related but different types of scholarly inquiry. The essays in parts I and II utilize a variety of archival sources and secondary works, while the three chapters in part III rely on a close analysis of key cultural and artistic texts. Taken together, however, these essays attempt to demonstrate the importance of multiple disciplinary approaches to writing the history of the European/ Andean encounter.

PART I. THE OLD WORLD HERITAGE TO THE ENCOUNTER

The social, economic, and political structures of Castile on the eve of the Columbian voyage played a key role in shaping the nature of the Iberian expansion, leading to the Pizarro invasion. In their essay, William and Carla Phillips provide an overview of Spain in the late fifteenth century, explaining many of the factors shaping this expansionary drive. Despite its ties to Africa and the Islamic world, Spain was fully a part of the cultural, legal, religious, and economic traditions of Europe, and it is hardly surprising that Christopher Columbus found support for his ventures at the court of Ferdinand and Isabella. The military prowess arising from the long Christian reconquest of the peninsula from the Muslims, Spain's well-developed commercial links to the Mediterranean and Atlantic worlds, and the gradual emergence of a more unified monarchy under the Catholic kings all laid the groundwork for the invasion and settlement of the Indies. The men of the Pizarro expedition inherited the late medieval European legacies of town life, Roman law, militant Christianity, rigid social classes, entrepreneurship and economic production, long-distance trade, and military expansion, which they attempted to replicate in the Andes during the sixteenth century.

In his study of the methods of warfare employed by Europeans and Andeans, John F. Guilmartin, Jr., examines the role of technology, tactics, and strategy in determining the outcome of the European invasion of 1532. Guilmartin assesses the importance of European superiority in weaponry, horses, and political unity in overcoming a numerically superior enemy, despite the bravery, organization, and skill of the Andean forces. These factors, along with infectious diseases, the assistance of large numbers of Andean allies, and the political disunity in the Inca empire in 1532, all contributed to the stunning victories of Pizarro and his followers.

PART II. EUROPEAN AND ANDEAN RESOURCES
IN THE ENCOUNTER PERIOD

John V. Murra's essay indicates that the earliest chronicles of the encounter can still provide fresh insights into how the invaders perceived
the human and natural landscape of the Andes. According to Murra,
the early European observers had the opportunity to witness and describe the complex Andean world as a functioning socioeconomic system. From the earliest accounts of European explorers in the Pacific to
the chronicles of the first generation of European settlers, bureaucrats,
and priests, Murra shows how scholars can find information about previously neglected topics, like the apparently large-scale oceanic commerce
within Tawantinsuyu. Murra also urges investigators to be vigilant for
clues about the location of new source materials, perhaps even outside
of the standard archaeological sites or archives, which might add significantly to an understanding of the Andean world, before its radical alteration by Viceroy Francisco de Toledo in the 1570s.

Following the theme of European perceptions of Andean resources,
James Lockhart examines how the first Spaniards attempted to exploit
the wealth of the Inca empire. Lockhart attacks stereotypes of the "conquistadors" as professional soldiers or romantic adventurers. According
to Lockhart, the Spaniards were truly an advance guard of European
economic expansion, acquiring land and mines, engaging in all sorts of
trade, and changing the ecological and human landscape to meet their
needs. Even the religious zeal of the first clerics and laymen was tem-
pered by a strong sense of realism and hardheaded entrepreneurship.
Lockhart uses an old railroad metaphor describing how the Spaniards
established a central economic "trunk line," extending from the rich
silver mines of Potosí through the coastal city of Lima-Callao to its Atlantic terminus in Panama. From this main economic route, a number of
"feeder lines" developed, linking nearby centers of the Andean population, like Cusco, with distant provinces such as Quito and Chile to the
central trunk line.

Kenneth J. Andrien examines how the presence of an interventionist
colonial state, established primarily during the viceregency of Francisco
de Toledo (1569–1581), influenced the formation of the new Andean
socioeconomic order. Although Toledo's reforms managed ultimately
to wrest control of the Andes from the fractious conquistadors and establish royal control, he was largely unsuccessful in implementing his
more ambitious designs to plan and manage the emerging colonial society and market economy. Through his tax, labor, and resettlement

policies, Toledo hoped to redirect the flow of wealth from the Andean villages into royal hands. Such attempts to fashion a planned and centralized economy were undermined by the decline of the traditional Andean economy, the resistance of the Amerindian ethnic communities and the European elites, and the corruption and dishonesty of the colonial officials serving the crown. This gradual erosion of the colonial state began even before Toledo left the Andes and continued apace in the next century.

PART III. CULTURAL AND ARTISTIC ENCOUNTERS

Part III addresses the issues of how Andeans, before and after the arrival of the Europeans, interpreted their experiences past and present. In this section, the document and the artifact are seen as texts, that is, as material constructions that convey various types of symbolic meaning when reintroduced into the settings of social action in which they originally prevailed. The notion of the text that predominates here is much broader than the written record. The scholars who have contributed these essays use various types of cultural productions—chronicles, archival records, Inca textiles, ceramics, ritual objects, and European and colonial paintings—to illuminate the ways in which Inca symbolism was understood in its own time and how it was reinterpreted in the early colonial period. The transformations of the ideal and personal figure of the Andean lord emerge as the main theme of this section. We see first the Inca during his reign, then the heirs of the Inca and other dynasties in colonial times. The examination of iconographic symbolism associated with the Inca and the subsequent reinterpretation of those Andean symbols in relation to European ones provide insights into how the Inca present was ordered in its own time as well as how the Andean past was interpreted, indeed reconstructed, in the centuries that followed the fall of Tawantinsuyu.

R. Tom Zuidema opens this section with a remarkable essay on Inca royal dress. In contrast to the richness of Inca ornament commented upon by eyewitness Spanish accounts of the conquest, Zuidema provides a new, Andean focus: the ritual meaning of Inca attire and its role in imperial administration and social hierarchy. Thanks to Zuidema's investigation, we understand how the Inca's royal vestments functioned ("were read") as an indispensable feature of Inca administrative and ritual life. With a goal he describes as the "iconographic understanding of the Inca polity," Zuidema amasses and articulates an extraordinary range of evidence assembled from his vast knowledge of Andean civilization. Carefully analyzing early colonial written and pictorial chronicles and colonial paintings, he combines them with surviving textiles from Inca and postconquest times, as well as Huari ceramics, in order to reveal the myriad meanings of imperial Inca attire. Zuidema reconstructs a complex typology of pattern and meaning along ancestral, calendrical, and administrative lines, thanks in large measure to the pictorial record left by Felipe Guaman Poma de Ayala (1530s–1616?). Insisting that the extant examples of royal tunics offer much evidence for further investigation, Zuidema focuses on the type of dress worn by the Inca on a ritual occasion of great importance, the initiation of noble youths in Cusco at the December solstice. In this groundbreaking essay, Zuidema opens an avenue of exploration that brings to life with great vividness the lost world of the Inca.

Thomas B. F. Cummins's essay reflects upon this loss by taking up the theme of the artistic representations of the descendants of Inca and non-Inca lords in colonial times. Not content to examine these artistic productions exclusively for art's sake, Cummins relates them to the social and political consequences of their contemporary situation. He examines these silent portraits of Incas and local ethnic lords as crucial aspects of the transformation of their social and cultural identities in colonial times; he does so by highlighting their Hispanization and suppression of distinctive "otherness." The granting of status in Spanish colonial idioms of course masked the European usurpation of indigenous Andean power and prerogatives. Nevertheless, Cummins's research reveals that what he terms an "epistemological shift," which granted these images European evidentiary value, was used by their subjects to make claims and defend their rights within the Spanish legal system. Further, he shows how this Hispanicized iconography of the native lords came to identify them with direct Inca descent and to be disseminated widely among the native population due to their ritual use on *keros*, ceremonial Andean drinking cups. These new uses had new meanings, and Cummins concludes that these colonially controlled depictions of the Incas in artistic representations and ceremonial events had as their purpose the neutralization of Andean themes and subservience to Spanish colonial goals.

Rolena Adorno closes the volume by examining one further colonial transformation of the Andean lord, that is, as *indio ladino*, a term of identification used by the colonizers to describe native Andeans who were competent in the Spanish language and familiar with European ways. Most prominent among the written sources she employs is Guaman Poma, whose extensive commentaries on the subject suggest that the externally defined category *indio ladino* would be, from the colonized Andean's perspective, a pertinent topic of cultural historical analysis. Not confined to a single social status or type, the individuals called *indios ladinos* by the colonizers performed a great variety of public and domestic tasks in colonial society. Adorno presents a typology that enumerates the most readily documentable of these roles, discussing alternately *indio ladino* collaboration with and rejection of Spanish colonial enterprises. She emphasizes the ambivalent positions occupied by *indios ladinos* and the crises of identity and varying degrees of marginality to European-creole and Andean communities which such experiences produced. She concludes that the study of colonial society through the examination of *indio ladino* experiences can yield much further insight into the construction of colonial identities and the development of mestizo culture.

Overall, the collaborative scholarly venture undertaken in this volume reveals that the challenge of interpreting the past lends itself to ever more varied disciplinary and interdisciplinary pursuits. This is particularly so for an ancient American civilization of great complexity and the processes of cultural exchange and transformation that occurred between Andeans and Europeans in the sixteenth and subsequent centuries. It is our hope that this volume will help stimulate further questions about the Andean past of the periods before and after the European invasion. As any interest in the past is oriented by concerns formulated in the present, this volume is dedicated to the conviction that the past is relevant to the present and that both are pertinent to the future.

NOTES

1. Several review articles survey much of this important recent literature. See, for example, Leon G. Campbell, "The Historical Reconquest of Peruvian Space," *Latin American Research Review* 21, 3 (1986): 192–205; Steve J. Stern, "New Directions in Andean Economic History: A Critical Dialogue with Carlos Sempat Assadourian," *Latin American Perspectives* 12 (Winter 1985): 133–148; Brooke Larson, "Shifting Views of Colonialism and Resistance," *Radical History Review* 27 (1983): 3–20; Luis Millones, "Ethnohistorians and Andean Ethnohistory: A Different Task, a Heterodox Discipline," *Latin American Research Review* 17, 1 (1982): 200–216; Frank Salomon, "Andean Ethnology in the 1970s: A Retrospective," *Latin American Research Review* 17, 2 (1982): 75–128; Heraclio Bonilla, "The New Profile of Peruvian History," *Latin American Research Review* 16, 3 (1981): 210–224; Franklin Pease, "Historia andina: Hacia una historia del Perú," *Revista Histórica* 32 (1979–1980): 197–212; and John V. Murra, "Current

Research and Prospects in Andean Ethnohistory," *Latin American Research Review* 5, 1 (1970): 3–36.

2. Campbell, "The Historical Reconquest," 193.

3. John Murra makes this point forcefully in arguing against calling Tawantinsuyu "socialist" or "oriental" or a "hydraulic despotism." Murra, "Current Research," 15–18.

PART ONE

The Old World Heritage
to the Encounter

ONE

Spain in the Fifteenth Century

William D. Phillips, Jr.,
and
Carla Rahn Phillips

The conquest of Peru began with a dramatic and ultimately decisive event: the seizure of the Inca by the Spanish expedition at Cajamarca. The 168 men who captured Atahualpa in November 1532 came from a part of Europe that had known conflict across cultural frontiers for centuries and that had formed a strong and unified monarchy only half a century earlier. We will follow convention in referring to the conquerors of Peru as "Spaniards," but in the late Middle Ages, and even in the sixteenth century, "Spain" was more a convenient shorthand to designate the diverse regions of central and eastern Iberia than an irreversible reality.

The "men of Cajamarca," as their biographer has called them,[1] owed their ultimate allegiance to King Charles I of Castile, who also held the title Emperor Charles V of the Holy Roman Empire. While he was still a child, it was clear that Charles would be the most powerful ruler in Europe, through his inheritance of the combined legacies of the Trastámaras of Castile and Aragon and the Habsburgs of central Europe. Charles's grandparents, Ferdinand of Aragon and Isabella of Castile, had brought the diverse lands of Spain together through their marriage, but only with their grandson were the lands ruled by one individual. From Charles's other grandparents he had inherited the Habsburg possessions and responsibilities. With power based in several key cities, he ruled an empire that included a large portion of central Europe, the Low Countries (the Netherlands, Belgium, and Luxembourg of today), and the Spanish kingdoms with their possessions in the Mediterranean and on both sides of the Atlantic. When Charles was born in 1500, explorers and conquerors acting for Castile were establishing colonies in the Caribbean islands and making tentative forays farther toward the west. By the time he became king of Castile in 1516, it was widely suspected that the lands farther west formed part of a vast continent—perhaps two—rather than the mainland of Asia which Columbus thought he had found. A few years later Hernán Cortés and his six hundred men conquered the Aztecs in the Valley of Mexico; a decade thereafter, the 168 men of Cajamarca brought a similar fate to the Incas of Peru.

The astonishing speed of these events is sometimes lost on readers in the late twentieth century, when events of worldwide significance customarily move quickly. For the world of the fifteenth century, change customarily moved rather slowly. Then, in just fifty years starting in 1492, hitherto unknown continents and vast civilizations were encountered by Europeans, conquered, and shaped into a bureaucratic empire. We must understand the full context of the men of Cajamarca, and their counterparts elsewhere, to comprehend those fifty years of rapid change and the centuries of colonial empire that followed. In other words, we must understand Spain, the Spaniards, and Spain's position in Europe and the world.

SPAIN

Spain in the fifteenth century was undeniably part of Europe, although it maintained ties with the Islamic world and with Africa and the Atlantic islands. This has to be stated firmly at the beginning, because Spain is frequently neglected in general survey texts. Historians of Europe often ignore Spain or treat it as an afterthought, better suited to discuss with Latin America than with Europe. Historians of Latin America have enough to deal with already, however, and tend to treat Spain only as the distant home country of the early settlers. Both approaches often present fifteenth-century Spain as a unified country, though isolated from its neighbors and unprepared to deal with the New World that Columbus claimed for it. Such images distort reality so thoroughly that they make it impossible to understand how Spain could conquer several powerful empires and establish a bureaucratic, colonial, and commercial empire of its own within a few decades. In reality, fifteenth-century Spain, though just beginning to be unified, was linked through trade with all the Old World and well organized by history and inclination to rule over foreign lands. Moreover, even without its American empire, and before Charles I inherited his European empire, Spain was on the verge of becoming the dominant power in Europe.[2]

Our first task is to understand how and why this had come to pass.

First of all, there was no "kingdom of Spain" in the fifteenth century and would not be for centuries. Instead, four separate Christian kingdoms and one Muslim kingdom shared the Iberian peninsula: Aragon, Navarre, Castile, and Portugal represented the Christians, and Granada the Muslims. The words "Spain" and "España" are both derived from the Latin word "Hispania," which the Romans used to designate the whole peninsula that the Greeks had called "Iberia." The word "Spain" was commonly used in Europe in the fifteenth century to designate either Castile or the whole peninsula except Portugal.

Even after the marriage of Ferdinand of Aragon and Isabella of Castile, the Spanish kingdoms of Iberia remained divided among several smaller political entities, each one the product of geography, topography, environment, and history. The crown of Aragon in the east contained three separate units: Aragon, Catalonia, and Valencia. The kings of Aragon also ruled a Mediterranean empire, which included the Balearic Islands, Sicily, Sardinia, and the kingdom of Naples in southern Italy. Northwest of Aragon lay the small kingdom of Navarre. Dominating the center of the peninsula from north to south was the kingdom of Castile, an accumulation of territories acquired during the long reconquest of the peninsula from the Muslims during the medieval centuries. Castile included the northern coastal areas of Galicia, Asturias, Cantabria, and the Basque regions of Vizcaya, Guipúzcoa, and Alava; Leon and Castile (Old Castile) to the north of the central mountains, and La Mancha and Extremadura (New Castile) to the south; and the kingdoms of Andalusia and Murcia in the extreme south and southeast. The kingdom of Portugal lay to the west of Castile, formed in its own reconquest of territory from the Muslims. The kingdom of Granada in south-central Iberia was the last Muslim possession in Europe in the fifteenth century; in 1492 it was conquered by Ferdinand and Isabella and became part of the kingdom of Castile.

All of the 168 men of Cajamarca were subject to Charles I, and all but 4 of them were subject to him in his capacity as king of Castile. Two others were from the kingdom of Aragon, and the remaining 2 were Greeks who had settled in Castile. The largest number came from the western Castilian region of Extremadura (36 individuals), followed closely by the southern region of Andalusia (34 individuals). Old and New Castile contributed 17 and 15 men respectively. Another 15 came from Leon, and 8 came from Vizcaya.[3] This concentration of origins is striking, but easily understandable: conquests in the Americas were the legal possession of Castile, and Castilians made up the bulk of Spanish emigrants throughout the colonial period.

The legal separation of Castile's empire in the Americas and Aragon's empire in the Mediterranean reminds us that there was nothing inevitable about the creation of modern Spain through the amalgamation of Aragon and Castile. In medieval times, Castilian rulers had made as much effort to secure marriages with Portugal as with Aragon, and throughout the fifteenth century, Castilian and Portuguese monarchs arranged marriages between their children. Consequently, there could as easily have been a merger of Castile and Portugal as between Castile and Aragon. When Isabella died in 1504, Ferdinand married again—his new queen was Germaine de Foix, heiress of Navarre. Evidently, the merger of Castile and Aragon held no special place in his plans. He wanted to produce a new heir who would alone inherit his Aragonese possessions. Events made that impossible, but the eventual consequence of Ferdinand's second marriage was the absorption of the part of Navarre south of the Pyrenees into Castile. By the time Ferdinand died in 1516, the peninsular area his grandson Charles would inherit corresponded to a modern map of Spain, its territories divided and accentuated by the rugged topography that makes Spain the second most mountainous country in Europe. It included the crowns of Castile, Aragon, Navarre south of the Pyrenees, and Granada, where the Christian victory in 1492 marked the last act of the Reconquest.

The Christian reconquest of Iberia from the Muslims had lasted on and off for centuries. The Muslims had conquered most of the peninsula in the early eighth century as part of their rapid expansion over the Middle East and the Mediterranean basin. They built a brilliant civilization in Spain and made it an integral part of the wider Islamic world. In the beginning, the Muslims had failed to take all the peninsula, leaving enclaves of Christian strength in the mountainous north. These enclaves became the basis for the Christian kingdoms and counties of Asturias, Leon, Galicia, Navarre, Aragon, and Catalonia. The period known as the Reconquest lasted from the early eighth to the late fifteenth century, suggesting that Christian and Muslim Spaniards confronted one another with drawn swords for over seven centuries. In fact, open hostility and warfare alternated with periods of what the Spanish call *convivencia*, or living together. It it was not exactly peace, neither was it war. During the course of the Middle Ages, the Christian states grew in population and expanded southward when they could. This was possible only when the Muslims were disunited, but over the course of centuries Christian power extended slowly and inexorably southward. When Islamic Spain was strong and unified, there was little possibility of Christian advance, but in those periods the Christians learned much and benefited economically from the more advanced Islamic civilization across their southern frontiers. Gradually attitudes hardened on both sides of the border, however, and by the fifteenth century, there was a growing sense of implacable hostility between the two civilizations that shared Iberia.

The experience of the Reconquest was instrumental in shaping several Christian notions about the world. One notion was that there was wealth to be gained from the armed conquest of alien peoples. Another was that the security of Christian society and indeed its survival depended upon unity and a militant defense of the faith. Nonetheless, we must not draw the erroneous conclusion that the typical Spaniard of the fifteenth century was an armed professional warrior or minor nobleman, whose only interests were war, booty, and the oppression of non-Christians. Even among the men of Cajamarca during the invasion of Peru, few could be classified as full-time professional soldiers. Many more were artisans of one variety or another, merchants, or notaries and accountants.[4] The Reconquest shaped some of the attitudes of the Spanish population, but the social and occupational structure of the population was much like that in the rest of Europe.

THE SPANIARDS

A lack of demographic records before the sixteenth century in Spain, as in most areas of premodern Europe and the world, means that we know little about Spanish population in the formative medieval centuries. We have only estimates made from incomplete censuses, tax assessments, and other official documents. A safe guess for the total number of Spaniards in the late fifteenth century would be something on the order of 5,300,000. About 82 percent of the population and 76 percent of the land of Spain came under the jurisdiction of Castile, about 16 percent of the population and 22 percent of the land came under the crown of Aragon, and the remaining 2 percent of the land and people were in Navarre.[5]

In some respects, the men of Cajamarca were not representative of Spanish society as a whole, any more than they represented the peninsula as a whole. Most notably, as males they did not represent the female half of the population. This is hardly surprising, because the Spaniards at Cajamarca were a military vanguard, traditionally a male experience. Elsewhere in the Americas, Spanish women were already an important part of the colonial population, representing peninsular society. As we discuss the social and occupational structure of Spain, much of what we say would apply equally to women, who were often independent agents in control of their own lives and destinies.

The men of Cajamarca represented a society that was overwhelmingly rural. Like the rest of the preindustrial world, Spain depended for its food supply on the labor of a large majority of its population. Roughly four of every five persons in the peninsula worked on the land, but it is difficult to know what to call them. Most English-language studies call them peasants, a word whose origin refers to land or the countryside. Unfortunately, the terms "peasant" and "peasantry" have acquired pejorative connotations of poverty and oppression in the English language, especially in the late twentieth century. In other languages, the equivalent terms are not pejorative and give no clear indication of wealth. The terms are many and varied, but in general they denote persons who were neither nobles nor clerics and who did not live permanently in towns or cities. This relates closely to the word commonly used in Castilian, *campesino,* one who works on the arable land or *campo.* Ignoring the pejorative connotations, it would be easy to say that "peasant" is a good English translation of the Castilian word *campesino* and could serve to define those involved in farming or herding.

Unfortunately, the words "peasant" and even *campesino,* with their purely rural connotations, do not fully define a Spaniard who worked on the land. Those who farmed or kept livestock did not live in the countryside on isolated farmsteads. Instead, in the fifteenth century and thereafter, they lived in hamlets (*aldeas*), villages (*lugares*), and towns (*villas*), traveling back and forth to work their land and tend their flocks and herds. They might call themselves farmers (*labradores*) or livestock owners (*ganaderos*), but those terms described their occupations, not their dwelling place. For their residential status, they identified themselves proudly as citizens (*vecinos*) of the legal corporations of their hamlet, village, or town. Citizenship (*vecindad*) gave them a wide range of privileges and made them eligible for allotments of communal goods held in common for the use of all the *vecinos*: arable and grazing land, forest products, and water rights. Clearly their lives were very different from the lives of *vecinos* of large cities, many of whose inhabitants had lost their rural ties. Nonetheless, they shared the legal distinction of being part of an urban commune and defined themselves in those terms. This pattern of settlement had developed in part because people needed to cluster around the sources of fresh water on the dry plains of Castile. During the many centuries of Reconquest, they also needed to cluster together for protection and mutual aid. The strong identity of Castilians with the town and its legal and social structures would be implanted in the Americas almost from the moment that they arrived.[6]

No single word, either in Castilian or in English, can define the reality of the occupational, legal, residential, and social position of Spaniards who worked the land. The most likely words in Castilian refer too strictly to the rural milieu or to a specific occupation, and the most likely words in English are either similarly restrictive or pejorative in tone. It is better to rely on our initial functional definition: four out of five Spaniards worked on the land to produce the vegetable and animal products that society needed to feed itself. Their social and economic conditions varied widely. The last vestiges of serfdom, which bound people to the land and forced them to make payments to an overlord, had never been widespread in Castile and had been abolished by the end of the fifteenth century, but the population was hardly equal in wealth or status. Some individuals owned or leased large farms and employed others to work for them. They often lived very comfortable lives and could aspire to higher social status, even to the lower nobility. Others might own enough land to support one family or might own part of the necessary land and lease the rest. The land available for leasing was often owned by nobles or clerics, who allowed others to use it for terms ranging from a year or two to virtual perpetuity. Such wealthy landowners can also be counted among those who earned their livelihood from the land in Spain, despite their social and economic distance from those who actually worked that land. The owner of a plow team, with or without also owning land, was a cut above most others who worked the land, because draft animals represented a considerable investment. The same argument could apply to livestock owners. Those who owned neither land nor animals usually made a living by working for others, with no security in bad times. Some were *jornaleros,* who worked and were paid on a day-to-day basis. Others could arrange labor contracts for a season or a year.[7]

At the upper end of the social spectrum, urban and rural, was the nobility, whose ancestors had been given land and status in earlier centuries, usually for military service to the monarchy. This was not a closed caste in Spain, however; movement in and out of its ranks was common in the fifteenth century and thereafter. The standard threefold division of the nobility included as the lowest and most numerous category the *hidalgos*—loosely meaning "the children of some distinction"—whose only advantages were a certain amount of local prestige and exemption from ordinary taxation. Above them were lords (*señores*) with small territorial possessions (*señoríos*). At the top of the scale were the *títulos* or titled nobles, often called the *grandes*. The counts, marquesses, and dukes who made up this exclusive group were defined by their wealth and power, both of which were increasing in the fifteenth century.[8]

The holdings of the *grandes* were scattered, and the greatest among them owned or controlled towns and lands in several provinces. While each titled noble typically had a favored stronghold and various other fortresses, he did not usually reside on his estates. Instead, the Castilian nobility as a whole tended to be urban, with their spheres of action in the major towns and cities of the realm; the greatest nobles followed the royal court. In the towns and cities, nobles moved to dominate municipal governments and judicial positions by gaining supporters among lesser noble families through intermarriage and patronage. At the royal court they sought to establish hereditary control over important royal offices, such as the admiralty of Castile. They also exercised great influence on foreign commerce and over the administration of the Mesta, the crown-sponsored association of flock owners.

By inserting themselves into the highest levels of local and royal government, the Spanish nobility could secure and enhance their economic position, as well as their social status. By the mid-fifteenth century, fewer than two dozen families had amassed great amounts of wealth, land, titles, and political positions. The wealth of the high nobility rested on a common economic base: the land and its bounty. Whether they raised wheat, wine grapes, or olives, or derived their wealth from wool, meat, and hides from livestock, their primary aim was to secure the greatest possible return from their agricultural and pastoral pursuits. Nobles who lived along the coasts pursued analogous profits from the fishing industry, or from the export trade, either by controlling ports or by direct ownership of shipping. Nobles routinely engaged in business without losing either social status or their titles. One good example of a nobleman-capitalist was the Duke of Medina Sidonia in southern Spain. He was a shipowner in his own right and negotiated directly with the Commune of Genoa to sell the grain produced on his Andalusian estates. He also controlled the lucrative tuna fisheries of the Atlantic coast west of Cádiz, which earned him the popular nickname "The Tuna King."[9]

Another important source of wealth for the nobility came from political rewards, both for loyal service (particularly in time of war) and for promises of loyalty (particularly in time of political strife). This was just one way in which their political and economic positions were closely linked. The monarchs had at their disposal a vast array of material rewards to grant as *mercedes* (mercies or gifts). Royal offices, both in the central government and in the provinces and cities, were lucrative gifts, providing salaries and the potential for graft. Titles, most of them with more honorific than real value, were also bestowed as favors from the monarch. Grants of income based on royal taxes and customs revenues, outright monetary gifts and grants of vassals, towns and villages, and the rights to found *mayorazgos* or entailed estates were also bestowed on the nobility in return for their service and loyalty. Although very few of the high Spanish nobility migrated to America, they served as powerful role models for those who emigrated in search of increased wealth and status. Their military values, the way they dressed and spent their money, and their willingness to serve the crown in anticipation of substantial rewards all inspired Spanish conquerors in the New World. Landless laborers and the nobility occupied the extreme lower and upper ends of the social spectrum. Between them was everyone else, the middling sort who were represented by the vast majority of the men of Cajamarca.

The members of the Church formed a category all their own, legally constituting a unified group with collective rights and privileges, but actually mirroring all of society, with internal divisions and a well-defined hierarchy of wealth and status. In the late fifteenth century, the clergy as a whole represented some 2 to 5 percent of the population of the Spanish kingdoms. Members of the secular clergy, those who ministered to the spiritual concerns of the laity, ranged from rich and worldly archbishops to bishops in smaller cities, canons of cathedrals and churches, and priests in local parishes. The regular clergy lived in communes apart from secular society, governed by rules (*regula*) established by the founders of their particular monastic orders. They took vows to serve God through spiritual or charitable works; in Spain the most important of such monastic orders included the long-established Benedictines and Cistercians and the order of St. Jerome, founded in the late fourteenth century. The Jeronymites had their headquarters at Guadalupe in the hills west of Madrid, in the heart of the area that produced many early venturers to America. Consequently, the Jeronymites and the Virgin of Guadalupe had a great influence in Spanish colonies in the Americas. The late medieval orders of mendicant friars, the Franciscans and the Dominicans, flourished in the Spanish kingdoms as well. On a papal mission to France in the thirteenth century a Castilian nobleman had encountered the heretical movement known as Albigensianism or Catharism. He founded a new religious order to combat that heresy—the Dominicans—and was later sainted as St. Dominic. The Dominicans were represented at Cajamarca by the friar Vicente de Valverde, a native of Oropesa in New Castile.[10] The strength of the Catholic Church in

Spain helps to explain why religion was not only a powerful motivator for the Spanish conquerors but also a major force in early colonizing efforts.

Related both to the nobility and to the clergy were several important religious-military orders, originally founded in the twelfth century to aid in the Reconquest. Castile boasted the orders of Calatrava, Alcántara, and Santiago, and the crown of Aragon had the order of Montesa. In recognition of their crucial contributions to the success of the Reconquest, the military orders had received huge land grants from successive rulers of Castile in Extremadura, in La Mancha, and on the frontier with Granada in Andalusia. These grants included rich pasture lands eminently suited for winter grazing; as a result, the masters of the orders were intimately involved with the Mesta. The grand masters of the orders had jurisdiction over about one million people and enjoyed the privilege of bestowing nobility on some fifteen hundred individuals, the knights of the orders. They were roughly equivalent to the *señores* or middle ranks of the nobility. Along with the title of knight or *caballero* often went jurisdiction over tracts of land belonging to the order. The lands so granted were called *encomiendas* (from the verb *encomendar*), because they were commended to the care and protection of the knight, or *encomendero*. The military orders provided respected and influential positions for minor noble families and for the younger sons of great families. Their wealth and power, however, made the orders potential threats to the crown. From the fourteenth century onward, monarchs began to assert control over them, a process completed in the reign of Ferdinand and Isabella, when Ferdinand became the head of all three orders.[11] The pattern of granting *encomiendas* to hold newly conquered land was well established during the Reconquest, and it was also used during the Castilian conquest of the Canary Islands. With these historical precedents, the men of Cajamarca undoubtedly expected to be granted *encomiendas* for their service in the Americas.

Spaniards of all ages and both sexes who did not fall into the categories of nobles, members of the religious establishment, and workers on the land surely did not exceed 5 percent of the total. Almost exclusively urban, they ranged from wealthy merchants and town councillors to domestic servants and slaves. Slaves in Spain in the late fifteenth century were all of non-Christian origin. Some were Muslims captured in Mediterranean warfare, others were native-born Muslims, and still others were black Africans from south of the Sahara, brought to Spain by the Portuguese. The slaves were almost exclusively domestic workers, concentrated in a few large urban areas, especially Seville and Valencia.[12]

All these urban groups tend to be studied less thoroughly than the more familiar nobility and clergy, and a superficial view of early colonial Latin America might suggest that Spaniards were all warriors and clerics. If we turn again to the men of Cajamarca, however, their occupations will serve as an introduction to the wide variety of professions and occupations exercised by Spaniards in the fifteenth and sixteenth centuries.

Of the 168 conquerors of Peru, only 47 have left sufficient evidence to determine their occupations.[13] We might guess that most of those not identified worked on the land, but nothing is certain without evidence. Over a quarter of the men fully identified were notaries, notary-secretaries, or accountants (12 out of 47), a much higher representation than these groups would have had at home. Spain, as well as Europe generally, was experiencing a rise in economic activity from the late fifteenth century on, especially in long-distance trade. Economic activity over great distances and across linguistic and political boundaries required accountants who could keep track of business transactions and notaries who could certify the legality of partnership agreements and other matters. Modern accountancy and maritime insurance had been invented in the cities of northern Italy and had been transferred to the Iberian peninsula by immigrants from Genoa and elsewhere. In the business world, formal contracts, maritime insurance, and other legal arrangements were gradually replacing traditional ties based on family membership or geographic origin. The notaries who recorded those contracts emerged as part of the Roman legal tradition that was the basis for law in Mediterranean Europe. Not surprisingly, we know as much as we do about the men of Cajamarca because they drew up a legal contract to share the booty from the conquest of Peru.

There was also an important contingent of merchants and those of related occupations among the men of Cajamarca, whose occupations we know (13 out of 47). For a long period, the merchant tradition in Spain has not received due attention. Some historians have even assumed that being a merchant was incompatible with being a Spaniard, or at least with being a Castilian. That hoary misconception ignores the strongly developed merchant tradition in Spain as a whole, and in some regions in particular, as we will see later.

The largest contingent at Cajamarca with known occupations was composed of artisans (19 out of 47). Six tailors, 2 horse shoers, 2 carpenters, 1 cooper, 1 swordsmith, 1 stonemason, 1 crier, and 1 barber—all represented occupations to be found in any Castilian or Aragonese town. The 2 artillerymen and 2 trumpeters may have been professional soldiers. In a fair-sized town, artisans would have been organized in *gremios,* or guildlike brotherhoods. The guilds controlled materials, prices, and working conditions for the various artisans who supplied the town's basic needs for food, clothing and shelter, and services. The food trades were not well represented among the men of Cajamarca; in an ordinary town in Castile they would have included butchers, bakers, tavern keepers, and food sellers, to mention a few. The tailors at Cajamarca represented the clothing trades, which would have included shoemakers, mercers, dressmakers, and hatters, as well as a host of other specialties in large towns and cities. The carpenters and the mason represented a wide range of building trades; the others represented what we might call the service trades. Those occupations tended to be locally based everywhere. At the same time, there were other workers whose products were sold throughout the peninsula and exported abroad. For example, shipbuilders of the Cantabrian coast, western Andalusia, Barcelona, and Valencia produced vessels that were widely exported in the fifteenth century. Toledo and Segovia produced hats, and Toledo produced swords. Woolen cloth was manufactured for local use in many places, and high-quality cloth from the looms of Segovia, Cuenca, Zaragoza, and Barcelona found a much wider market, although Spain was never a major exporter of textiles. Iron deposits in the north gave rise to important mining and smelting operations. New Castile, Andalusia, and Murcia produced glass, and the ceramics of Andalusia and Valencia enjoyed broad fame.[14] The wide variety of artisan occupations in Spain and the highly urbanized character of human settlement ensured that Spanish colonial society could organize functional town governments and produce whatever was necessary to supplement shipments from home.

We should remember that the largest component of the Spanish economy remained the agrarian sector, with its production of food and animal products. Most of that production was used in Spain in the fifteenth century, but a considerable amount was exported, as we will see.

SPAIN AND EUROPE

Surveys of the Spanish background of Latin American history often content themselves with loosely defined generalities, searching for what might be called "the Spanish character" and fostering the impression that Spain was much different from the rest of Europe. National and regional distinctions surely existed, but Spain shared many characteristics with other European countries, not the least of which were a monarchical and bureaucratic form of government, the rule of law, and a well-organized Catholic Church. These Iberian institutions formed the basis for the institutional structure of Spain's colonies in the Americas.

In the fifteenth century, Spanish monarchs were working to extend the sway of royal law, like their fellow monarchs elsewhere in western Europe. Two legal developments proceeded on parallel courses in Castile and Aragon. One was the gradual adoption of Roman law as the primary law of the kingdom, and the second was the gradual imposition of royal law throughout the kingdom, a process still incomplete in the late fifteenth century. In the eleventh century the Italian legal scholar Irnerius had begun the academic study of the Roman legal code, and in the next two centuries knowledge and application of Roman law spread widely in western Europe, in part because it tended to bolster central authority. In the mid-thirteenth century, Alfonso X of Castile produced a new code for his kingdom, known as the Siete Partidas, which relied heavily on Roman law. Although it never fully became law in Castile, the Siete Partidas still had a significant influence on subsequent legislation in Spain, both for the home country and for the American colonies.[15] As the legal authority of the monarchy strengthened, so did the bureaucratic apparatus of councils and royal officials. In the sophistication of its governmental structure, Aragon was probably ahead of Castile. After the marriage of Ferdinand and Isabella, although their two kingdoms remained legally separate, Castile undoubtedly benefited from the close association with Aragon and began to refine the bureaucracy that would later be introduced in the American colonies. The well-defined hierarchy of authority enabled Spain to establish royal control fairly soon after the conquests of Mexico and Peru.

The Catholic Church in Spain had a great deal of power, as we have noted, but the Church in Europe as a whole had undergone major upheavals in the late medieval period. In the process of reestablishing its authority, the Church generally moved toward doctrinal uniformity and away from the relative toleration for unorthodox Christians and non-Christians that had characterized earlier times. In the early thirteenth century the Fourth Lateran Council established restrictive measures for the Jews of Europe, requiring them to live in segregated residential quarters and to wear distinctive clothing to set them apart from the Christian majority. These measures were not enforced in Castile for nearly two centuries, but they affected Jews elsewhere immediately. In the late thirteenth century Edward I of England expelled the Jews from his kingdom. France carried out its expulsion of the Jews early in the fourteenth century. Spain also had a large number of Jewish subjects and the only sizable Muslim minority in western Europe. During the fifteenth century, it became increasingly clear that relations among the several religions were worsening. At the end of the fifteenth century, Ferdinand and Isabella followed the path laid out by English and French monarchs two centuries before: they ordered the Jews to convert to Christianity or leave Spain. About half left, going mainly to North African cities and to Portugal. The rest converted. The Muslims were given a similar choice in 1500. With the exception of Muslims in the kingdom of Valencia, who were given several decades of respite, all had to embrace Christianity or leave Spain. Most chose to convert and remain. By the early sixteenth century, there were two large minority groups in the Spanish kingdoms: the *conversos,* Christians of Jewish origin, and the *moriscos,* Christians of Muslim origin.[16] Many so-called Old Christians resented and feared these New Christians, seeing them as a threat to religious unity that could tempt God's wrath. Both groups were considered notoriously bad Christians, and a religious inquisition had been in operation since 1478 primarily to enforce their Christian orthodoxy.[17] The growing militancy of Spanish Catholicism in the late fifteenth century shaped the response of Spanish conquerors to the native religions of the Americas. They would forcibly convert people to Christianity rather than see them outside the fold, endangering their own souls and the collective soul of the community.

We have already mentioned the connections between medieval Iberia and the Islamic world, which had helped to create Spain's religious militancy. Spain also maintained close relations with the rest of Christian Europe throughout the Middle Ages. Its ties to Rome were similar to those that linked the papacy with all parts of western Europe. Spanish cardinals resided in Rome, and Spanish clerics played a large role in the life of the Roman Catholic Church. The Dominicans—founded, as we have seen, by a Spaniard—became interested in education, and their colleges at the University of Paris and elsewhere attracted many Spanish students to study abroad. In the middle of the fourteenth century, Cardinal Gil de Albornoz, archbishop of Toledo, founded the College of St. Clement at Bologna. Popularly known as the Spanish College, it provided lodging and support for Spanish students of theology and law. A reciprocal movement brought foreign students to Spanish universities. The first university in the Iberian peninsula was at Palencia, chartered by Alfonso VIII in the early thirteenth century. The University of Salamanca, founded shortly thereafter, became the most prestigious in the peninsula, receiving royal support and attaining an international reputation quite early. Other universities appeared in Valladolid, Lérida, and Huesca.[18] A substantial proportion of young men of good family in sixteenth-century Spain attended university,[19] and in the Americas, universities would be established on European models very soon after the conquests.

In addition to intellectual ties, Spanish Iberia maintained political ties with the rest of Europe. The Castilian crown favored France and England alternately in its diplomatic orientation, and royal marriages periodically linked the Castilian monarchy with both kingdoms. In the twelfth and thirteenth centuries, the rulers of Catalonia controlled large portions of southern France. But Spain demonstrated its European connections most clearly through commerce. Because Aragon and Castile participated in different commercial networks, it is necessary to deal with them separately.

The Mediterranean empire of the crown of Aragon began in the thirteenth century, when the kings of Aragon took over the Balearic islands and Sicily. In the fifteenth century their descendants added Sardinia and Naples. Merchants from Barcelona, Majorca, and Valencia maintained a strong presence throughout Mediterranean and Atlantic Europe. They operated in a variety of trading networks, from the coast of southern France to northern Italy, from the islands of Corsica and Sardinia to Sicily, and into the Islamic Mediterranean, with enclaves in Alexandria and Damascus. They maintained a number of North African enclaves as well, in Tunis, Bougie, and Tlemcen, as well as other places. The North African connection provided access to tropical products and the gold of West Africa. Merchants from Barcelona and other cities in the crown of Aragon traded in northwestern Europe, with establishments in Bruges and later in Antwerp. They were also present in considerable numbers in Seville and Lisbon.[20]

On the Castilian side, foreign trade developed along with religious pilgrimages. For centuries, pilgrims had journeyed to the shrine of St. James (St. Jacques to the French, Santiago to the Spanish) in the northwest corner of the peninsula. Santiago de Compostela, with its large cathedral, was the goal of Europeans who traveled along the *camino de Santiago,* which began in Paris at the Tour St. Jacques.[21] Running southward through western France, the route entered Spain via the Pyrenean pass of Roncevalles. It then ran westward across northern Spain, passing through many famous towns and monasteries. From before the twelfth century, merchants had joined the pilgrims, and thus Castile had become linked commercially with France and the rest of Europe.

By the fifteenth century, commercial relations were highly developed, with merchant fairs integrating the interior and exterior trade of Castile.

Medina del Campo hosted the most important fair, which met for a total of one hundred days during two periods between May and October. Spanish merchants traveled to Medina from Seville, Burgos, Valencia, and Barcelona, joined by Flemings, Florentines, Genoese, Irish, and Portuguese. Medina was the kingdom's financial center in the second half of the fifteenth century.[22] The networks of trade developed by Aragon and Castile in the late Middle Ages encouraged Spanish interest in exploration and developed the commercial organization and business techniques that would be introduced in Spain's overseas empire. Remote as the Andean region was from Europe, Spanish merchants would establish regular trade there even before the region had been stabilized politically.

The foreign trade of Castile in the fifteenth century suggests the complexity of Europe's commercial networks, which had to be well developed or they could never have expanded to include the Americas. The Atlantic coastline defined one major circuit for Castilian merchants, a circuit that stretched from the Cantabrian ports to the Atlantic coast of France and to Flanders, the British Isles, and the North Sea. The driving force behind this trade was the inland city of Burgos, whose merchants grouped themselves into an association that became the Consulado of Burgos chartered by Ferdinand and Isabella in 1494. The organization settled internal disputes among its members, in addition to acting in their general interest to gain concessions from the crown and to keep trade flowing smoothly.[23] Burgalese enjoyed preeminence among all the merchants in northern Castile, and the city maintained a near monopoly on Castilian exports. It was the center of both the wool trade and the iron trade, and Burgalese merchants assured the regular transport of those goods by making agreements with mariners and shipowners on the coast.

The ability of the Castilian merchants to supply wool and other goods to the French, Flemish, and English markets depended upon the development of maritime transport. Shipbuilders and mariners on Spain's northern coast had a well-deserved reputation for competence, honed over the centuries. Like the merchants of Burgos, the mariners, shipbuilders, and owners had formed associations for their mutual benefit. One of them, existing by the late thirteenth century, later expanded to cover much of the northern shore. In the fifteenth century, this Hermandad de las Marismas determined the regulations binding the trading ports, judged disputes, and even conducted diplomacy, concluding treaties with England in 1351 and 1474. In return for royal favor, the organization furnished ships to the king for warfare and official missions. In general, the mariners of the northern ports served as transporters rather than merchants, contracting for the carrying trade with Castilian and foreign merchants.[24]

The port of Bilbao in the Basque province of Vizcaya grew from its foundation in 1300 to become a major center of shipbuilding and the export trade in iron and wool. Bilbao's hinterland provided timber and naval stores for the shipbuilding industry, and water and fuel for iron smelting. Iron mines in the coastal mountains from Santander to Vizcaya provided ore for the iron and steel industry. Around one third of Vizcayan iron was exported, usually in the form of bars, but occasionally as pure ore. Another third remained in the peninsula, used especially for the metal fittings in ship construction. The remainder was converted into hardware for export, including nails, anchors, artillery, armor, and weaponry. The region had difficulty producing grain in the hilly and damp environment, but this provided a further incentive for trade. With the profits from trade, wheat could be purchased in Old Castile or from the ports of western France.[25]

The trade in manufactured goods, iron ore, and various agricultural products was overshadowed by the export of raw wool. By the fifteenth century, Castile was one of western Europe's chief suppliers of high-quality wool. It had attained that position through a process stretching back to the eleventh century, when vast migratory flocks were developed to take advantage of the lands newly conquered from the Muslims. An expanding European market for cloth in the late Middle Ages provided a vigorous demand for raw material for the textile industry, especially in Italy and Flanders. When English wool exports suffered a decline in the fourteenth century, Castile was in an excellent position to supply foreign demand, as well as its own domestic need for raw wool. With ample pasture and careful breeding techniques, the Castilian Merino sheep became the new standard for quality. In the markets of Flanders, both for consumption there and for transshipment to central Europe, wool from Spain virtually replaced English wool, and Castile at times even sent wool to England. Because of this phenomenal growth, wool production and trade became the single most important element in the Castilian economy before the establishment of the American colonies.[26] Although the wool trade did not become part of Spain's transatlantic trade, the grazing economy and the organizational skills required for international marketing would play important roles in the economy of the American colonies.

The commerce with Flanders clearly outdistanced all other routes pursued by Castilians in the Atlantic. The primary exports from Castile to Flanders included iron, wine, and fruit, as well as wool. The primary imports to Castile were various types of Flemish cloth. Flanders was more than a manufacturing region, however. The major currents of European commerce met there as well: the Baltic trade of the Hanseatic League; the Italian, French, and English trades; and the Iberian trade from the south.[27] Merchants from Castile may have been in Flanders as early as the twelfth century; certainly they became important there from the thirteenth. In Bruges the Flemish authorities divided foreign merchants into "nations" according to their political allegiances. Thus, Castilians and Vizcayans originally were considered together as subjects of the Castilian king, but after lengthy disputes and litigation, King Henry IV of Castile in 1455 ordered them to separate into two distinct groups: Castilians and Vizcayans. The nation of Castile—or Spain, as it was usually called—included merchants from the cities of Burgos, Seville, Toledo, Segovia, Soria, Valladolid, Medina del Campo, Logroño, Néjera, and Navarrete, while Vizcaya included merchants from the areas of Vizcaya, Guipúzcoa, Alava, and the "coast of Spain." Despite the new arrangement, tensions persisted between the two groups well into the sixteenth century, and their rivalry often traveled across the Atlantic with them.[28]

Due to piracy and war, insecurity on the Castile-Flanders run was constant. Throughout the fifteenth century Castilian shipmasters often had difficulties with English naval vessels or with French and English pirates. Their response, with legislation passed in the Castilian Cortes (parliament) and with subsequent royal approval and support, was the creation of a convoy system in 1436, the precursor of the Flota of the Spanish Indies.[29] Despite the hazards, enough ships got through to Flanders to enhance the position of the Castilian community in Bruges and to allow the Castilian Cortes of 1453 to describe the transit taxes on exported and imported goods (the *diezmos de la mar*) as the largest single source of royal income in Castile.[30] War, piracy, and trade were intimately linked in the commercial networks of Europe in the fifteenth century. In fact, there was no clear distinction between them. Throughout the late Middle Ages and well into the early modern period there was no Castilian navy as such. Naval campaigns depended on impressed merchant ships. In that situation, merchant-mariners learned to confront armed attacks even as they practiced the more peaceful skills of commerce. The Castilian merchant marine with its military capabilities has often been called the strongest naval force in the region in the late Middle Ages. Whether this is true or exaggerated, the Castilian fleet was powerful, thanks in large part to its advanced naval technology and experience in high seas navigation. With this background, it is no wonder that Spanish commerce in the Americas was able to deal fairly effectively with the incursions of pirates, interlopers, and official enemy fleets during the sixteenth and seventeenth centuries.

Despite intermittent hostilities, especially during the era of the Hundred Years' War (1337–1453), England was the focus of much trade from the northern coast of Castile. Because Italian merchants dominated the foreign commerce of London and Southampton, most of the Anglo-Castilian trade centered on Bristol. In the winter months Castilian and English ships brought citrus fruits, figs, dates, raisins, honey, almonds, and vinegar to Bristol, mostly from the Cantabrian coast, but occasionally from Seville or other ports. In summer, the northbound freight would consist of iron and manufactured goods, from nails and combs to anchors and crossbows, plus olive oil and wine, soap and leather, alum for the cloth industry, salt for fisheries, and some raw wool and yarn. The return cargoes were woolen cloth and a variety of other items useful to Castile: herring and hake, grain and beans, lead and tin. The English even imported some Spanish wool and yarn. English and Spanish merchants used their own ships or rented those of their trading partners indiscriminately; by the end of the fifteenth century there was a roughly equal number of English and Spanish ships engaged in the trade.[31] Limited trade with Gascony and Bordeaux also formed part of the Atlantic circuit of Castilian trade.[32]

The other great area of Castilian trade was the Mediterranean, where merchants in Castile were active from the mid-fourteenth century onward. Seville and Cádiz on the southern Atlantic Coast of Spain and Cartagena on the southeastern Mediterranean coast were the most important ports involved in Castile's trade in the Mediterranean, with Seville predominating until the fifteenth century. Thereafter, even though Seville remained the financial capital, the increasing size of ships and the consequent difficulty of passage up the Guadalquivir River allowed Cádiz and Sanlúcar de Barrameda at the mouth of the river to seize the advantage. Such was the importance of the latter ports that virtually every Christian ship on its way through the Strait of Gibraltar stopped at one or the other. There was also a brisk exchange between Seville and Lisbon, where the Portuguese supplied apples, fish, and slaves from sub-Saharan Africa. The products of southern Castile—salt, wheat, barley, beans, peas, tuna, olive oil, wool, silk, and wine—generally sailed for Italy. The return cargoes were Italian manufactured goods, spices, and other Oriental products that the Italians obtained in the eastern Mediterranean.

For the most part Genoese and other Italians resident in Spain traded the products of the south in the markets of northern Europe. Local Spanish merchants participated in the trade, but they did not have the international connections of the Italians or of their compatriots in Burgos and elsewhere in northern Castile. Shortly after its reconquest in 1248, Seville had a Genoese quarter, and rich Genoese merchants intermarried with the local nobility. By the fifteenth century Genoese merchants were firmly entrenched in Seville, where they prospered as bankers and monopolized certain goods, among them mercury and cinnabar from the mines of Almadén; they shared domination of the wine trade from Jerez de la Frontera with the Florentines. Other foreigners in Castile's Mediterranean trade included Italians from Pisa, Milan, and Venice, Englishmen, Portuguese, and some Frenchmen, as well as other Spaniards—Catalans and above all Cantabrians.[33] Burgalese merchant families also maintained a strong presence in Seville, where they helped to organize the Castilian wool trade, among other ventures.

In governmental structure, legal forms, religious organization, intellectual orientation, and political relations, Spain in the fifteenth century fit firmly within the European context and was heir to centuries of development, not only in Europe but also in the Islamic world. That combined heritage would supply the background for the Spanish empire in the Americas. Several aspects of its commercial history would prove particularly useful in establishing and maintaining regular trade with the Americas: organizations of merchants and mariners to settle commercial disputes, a body of commercial law and maritime insurance, a tradition of shipbuilding and seafaring skills, experience with war and piracy in a commercial context, large ports such as Seville that could handle virtually every aspect of long-distance trade, a tradition of financing long-distance voyages, and linkages to the international banking community, to mention the most obvious. The Spanish background to Andean colonization combined broad European experience with a knowledge of the rest of the known world.

SPAIN AND THE WORLD

When Columbus brought his proposal for a westward voyage of exploration before the Spanish monarchs in the 1480s, he spoke to a court that was relatively well informed about the rest of the world. For two centuries before Columbus the cartographers of Mallorca had been producing detailed maps and atlases that depicted the Mediterranean and Europe with great accuracy and even included some reliable information about Africa south of the Sahara. Marco Polo's late thirteenth-century journey to China was certainly known in Spain, as were the fanciful tales of Sir John Mandeville. Well-informed Spaniards also knew of Francesco Pegolotti's fourteenth-century manual of commerce, with its description of Asian products and their origins. In the late fourteenth century, a Catalan writer produced a merchant's guide that revealed some knowledge of China. Moreover, early in the fifteenth century two Castilian embassies visited the court of the Mongol emperor Timur (Tamerlane) at Samarkand. Ruy González de Clavijo, a member of one of the expeditions, wrote *Historia del gran Tamorlán,* which contained geographical knowledge about the Middle East. In short, on the eve of the discovery of America, Spain knew as much about the rest of the Old World as did any of its neighboring countries.[34]

Spaniards were also voyaging into unknown portions of the Atlantic, and the first steps in Castilian overseas conquest had already been undertaken in Africa and the Canaries. Europeans had first entered the unchartered portions of the Atlantic in the thirteenth and fourteenth centuries, landing in the Atlantic islands of the Canaries and the Madeiras. Portuguese and Castilian ship captains had initially visited the islands for easily obtainable items such as wood and the red dye called "dragon's blood," the resin of the so-called dragon tree. Some occasionally used the islands as pirate bases. In time, Castilians had begun to claim the Canaries as their own, and by the end of the fifteenth century, they firmly controlled the islands.[35] Portugal established control over the Madeiras and the Azores.

Castilians developed a heightened interest in Africa after having established themselves in the Canaries, and their trade and commercial conflicts continued to involve both Africa and the Atlantic islands. In the last years of the fourteenth century, subjects of the king of Castile from the Basque region and Andalusia challenged the Portuguese for the goods of West Africa—gold, slaves, spices, marble, and dyes—which had formerly reached Europe via Muslim traders. Castile's monarchs also subsidized mariners to explore and exploit the coast of West Africa. By the mid-fifteenth century there was a regular route from Senegal through the Canaries to Cádiz for the transport of slaves, ivory, and especially gold. In Cádiz most of the gold passed into the hands of Genoese merchants, who maintained a virtual monopoly on the financial activity of the south. The Canaries provided several new products for the European economy, among them orchil (dyers' moss), algae native to the area, which produced a violet dye for the textile industry. Demand for this new industrial raw material increased greatly as dyes from the

eastern Mediterranean became scarce and expensive as a result of Turk-
ish expansion.[36]

European settlers introduced sugarcane quite early in the Canaries,
and from about 1455 sugar from the islands reached Iberia for sale or
reexport. Sugar production reached a peak early in the sixteenth century. The Welsers, a German banking family that often loaned money
to Charles I, owned four sugarcane plantations in Palma on Grand
Canary Island, before selling out in 1520. Sugar was used as an alternative currency in those years, which indicates its importance in trade and
in the local economy. Large plantations were worked by slave labor, first
using native Canarians and later using slaves imported from Africa. In
1526, near the peak of the Canarian sugar boom, there were twenty-nine
mills in the islands, compared to sixteen in Portuguese Madeira. The
Canaries acted as a way station for the expansion of Spanish sugar production and refining. Cane cuttings for the start of new plantations and
sugar-processing techniques were taken from the Canaries to the newly
discovered Caribbean islands and established there very early.[37]

Just as the Canaries served as a link in the history of sugar, experiences in the Canaries foreshadowed the relations between European and
native peoples in the Americas. In the Canaries slaves were used both
as laborers and as commodities for sale elsewhere. The first European
captains who visited the Canaries in the fourteenth and fifteenth centuries, armed with Castilian royal patents, found the islands inhabited
by natives who seemed related to the Berbers of northwest Africa. Because the Canarians did not know how to work metal before the Europeans came, their culture has been classified as Neolithic. Most of them
were primarily herders, although the people on Grand Canary Island
had developed an agricultural economy. They were organized into
bands; the Castilians made treaties with some of the bands and conquered others.[38]

In the initial phases of conquest, the conquerors needed quick profits
to pay for their expeditions, which were mainly financed on credit. The
sale of slaves offered a quick and easy way to generate profits to repay
the loans. According to medieval law, it was legal to enslave Canarians
who belonged to bands that resisted the Spanish incursion—in other
words, during a "just war." It was not legal to enslave members of bands
that submitted voluntarily. Members of allied bands who later rebelled
or refused to carry out the terms of their treaties could be enslaved as
"captives of a second war" (de segunda guerra). Conquerors and colonists
often circumvented the laws, however, given the profits to be made in
the slave trade. Canarians could use lawsuits to try to win their freedom,

but manumission was the most easily available path to freedom. Everything depended on the inclination of the master, and most masters demanded payment before they would grant a slave's freedom. Others demanded the promise of future payments or future labor service.[39] Many enslaved Canarians were sold in Spain or in Portuguese Madeira; others were kept in the islands and put to work, most frequently as household servants for Europeans. In 1529–1531 ordinances in the town of Las Palmas on Grand Canary even prohibited non-Canarian slaves from being used in the home. The conditions under which they lived resembled, not surprisingly, those of slaves in late medieval Spain.[40]

The island population of the Canaries was relatively small to begin with, and its numbers were diminished by epidemic disease after the European incursion. As we noted, members of many bands could not be enslaved legally, and those enslaved frequently attained manumission. In the early years of the sixteenth century, the Canarian slave trade to Europe ceased, as the remaining islanders were increasingly assimilated into European culture and intermarried with the colonists. For all these reasons, native workers never filled the labor needs of the Canarian colonial economy, and new sources of labor were necessary before the islands could be developed fully. Other workers, both slave and free, were therefore brought to the Canaries, including a number of free Castilian and Portuguese settlers. There was even a voluntary immigration of Moors and *Moriscos* from North Africa and Spain. Wealthier settlers brought slaves with them from the peninsula. Portuguese slave traders brought in black slaves from West Africa, and Castilian slave traders raided the coast for North Africans, Berbers, and other slaves to sell in the Canaries. Castilians in the Canaries also went directly to black Africa to obtain slaves. In the Cape Verde Islands they could purchase African slaves directly from the Portuguese resident there. Castilians in the Canaries also circumvented the Portuguese by going to Senegambia and the Upper Guinea coast to acquire slaves. This latter trade was illegal, however, until the union of the Spanish and Portuguese crowns in the late sixteenth century. The slaving expeditions to black Africa were always less frequent than expeditions to the Barbary Coast,[41] even if many of the Africans, especially the North Africans, were freed soon after their arrival in the Canaries. Following the first Spanish contact with the Americas, a few American Indians were sold in the Canaries as well, but the Spanish crown soon outlawed the slave trade in Indians.[42]

In the mode of its conquest, colonization, and economic organization, Spanish experience of the Canaries set many precedents that would later be repeated in the Americas. The initial search for quick profits, followed by the establishment of more lasting bases for the colonial economy, would characterize developments in both the Canaries and the Americas. In the Andean region, the need for predictable supplies of labor was solved less by importing slaves than by adapting the Incan system of labor service called the *mita,* and—increasingly over time—by the use of free wage labor.

Because of Spain's geographical setting, its previous history, its knowledge of the rest of the world, and its direct experience in Africa and the Canaries, it is not surprising that Christopher Columbus sought Spanish support for his scheme to sail westward to Asia, once he had been turned down in Portugal. The Iberian powers were ideally suited to lead the rest of Europe in expanding beyond the world they knew. Nor is it surprising that the Spanish in America replicated the traditions of town life, Roman and customary law, militant Christianity, agricultural and industrial production, local and long-distance commerce, and military expansion which they had known at home. All of these traditions sprang from centuries of development in Iberia in general and Spain in particular. Even though Columbus was not a Spaniard, he was heir to many late medieval traditions present in Europe as a whole, as well as in Spain. So were the 168 men of Cajamarca who undertook the conquest of Peru forty years later.

NOTES

1. James Lockhart, *The Men of Cajamarca: A Social and Biographical Study of the First Conquerors of Peru* (Austin, Tex., 1972). For a more recent work that examines the transatlantic ties of residents of Spain and its empire, see Ida Altman, *Emigrants and Society: Extremadura and Spanish America in the Sixteenth Century* (Berkeley, Calif., 1989).

2. There are several sound works in English on medieval Spain, including J. N. Hillgarth, *The Spanish Kingdoms, 1250–1516,* 2 vols. (Oxford, 1976–1978); J. F. O'Callaghan, *A History of Medieval Spain* (Ithaca, N.Y., 1975); Angus MacKay, *Spain in the Middle Ages: From Reconquest to Empire, 1000–1500* (London, 1977); T. N. Bisson, *The Medieval Crown of Aragon: A Short History* (Oxford, 1986). The best Spanish-language introduction to the late Middle Ages is Miguel Angel Ladero Quesada, *España en 1492* (Madrid, 1978); a new Spanish edition will appear soon and perhaps an English translation by 1992. That the late Middle Ages saw the rise of Spain flies in the face of conventional historical wisdom. See, for example, Henry Kamen, *Spain, 1469–1714: A Society of Conflict* (London, 1983), which argues that Spain was unprepared for the empire that was thrust upon it.

3. Lockhart, *Men of Cajamarca*, 28, 129, 377, 402, 414.

4. Lockhart, *Men of Cajamarca*, chart, 38; and scattered references.

5. Jorge Nadal, *La población española: Siglos XVI a XX* (Barcelona, 1966), 19–20; Ladero Quesada, *España en 1492*, 29.

6. For a stimulating analysis of the town's place in Castilian life, see Helen Nader, *Liberty in Absolutist Spain: The Habsburg Sale of Towns, 1516–1750* (Baltimore, Md., 1990).

7. For a current summary of late medieval rural society, see Paulino Iradiel Murugarren, "La crisis medieval," in *De la crisis medieval al Renacimiento (siglos XIV–XV)*, vol. 4 of *Historia de España*, directed by Antonio Domínguez Ortiz (Barcelona, 1988), 38–76; see also Ladero Quesada, *España en 1492*, 52–56, 67–78. A work of fundamental importance for the understanding of rural Spain in the sixteenth century is David E. Vassberg, *Land and Society in Golden-Age Castile* (Cambridge, Eng., 1984).

8. For the aristocracy, see Salvador de Mox, "De la nobleza vieja a la nobleza nueva: La transformación nobiliaria castellana en la Baja Edad Media," *Cuadernos de Historia* 3 (1969): 5–68; Marie Claude Gerbet, "Les guerres et l'accès à la nobless en Espagne de 1465 à 1592," *Mélanges de la Casa de Velázquez* 8 (1972): 295–325; Marie Claude Gerbet, *La nobless dans le royaume de Castille: Étude sur les structures sociales en Extrémadure de 1454 a 1516* (Paris, 1979); Miguel Angel Ladero Quesada, *Andalucía en el siglo XV: Estudios de historia política* (Madrid, 1974); Santiago Sobrequés i Vidal, *Els Barons de Cataluña* (Barcelona, 1957).

9. Richard Konetzke, "Entrepreneurial Activities of Spanish and Portuguese Noblemen in Medieval Times," *Explorations in Entrepreneurial History* 6 (1953): 115–120; Emma Solano Ruiz, "La hacienda de las casas de Medina-Sidonia y Arcos en la Andalucía del siglo XV," *Archivo Hispalense* 168 (1972): 85–172.

10. On the clergy, see Tarsicio de Azcona, *La elección y reforma del episcopado español en tiempo de los Reyes Católicos* (Madrid, 1960); José García Oro, *Cisneros y la reforma del clero español en tiempo de los Reyes Católicos* (Madrid, 1971); Antonio Linage Conde, *El monacato en España e Hispanoamérica* (Salamanca, 1977). For Valverde, see Lockhart, *Men of Cajamarca*, 201–207.

11. For the military orders, Derek W. Lomax, *Los Órdenes militares en la península ibérica durante la Edad Media* (Salamanca, 1976); Joseph F. O'Callaghan, *The Spanish Military Order of Calatrava and Its Affiliates* (London, 1975); Aurea Javierre Mur, "Fernando el Católico y las Órdenes militares," *Quinto Congreso de la Historia de la Corona de Aragón* (Madrid, 1962), 1: 287–300.

12. The classic work is Charles Verlinden, *L'esclavage dans l'Europe médiéval* (Ghent, 1955–1977); see volume 1, *Péninsule Ibérique—France*. William D. Phillips, Jr., *Slavery from Roman Times to the Early Transatlantic Trade* (Minneapolis, Minn., 1985), discusses slavery in Spain within a broad context; his book on slavery in Spain will be published by Editorial Playor in Madrid.

13. Lockhart, *Men of Cajamarca*, scattered references.

14. The standard guide to the Spanish economy has been Jaime Vicens Vives, *An Economic History of Spain*, translated by Frances M. López-Morillas

(Princeton, N.J., 1969), but it is inaccurate and out of date, especially those sections dealing with the crown of Castile. See J. L. Martín Rodríguez, *Economía y sociedad en los reinos hispánicos de la Baja Edad Media* (Barcelona, 1982); and the works by Ladero Quesada, *España en 1492,* and Iradiel Murugarren, "La crisis medieval," and the sources they cite.

15. For a general introduction to Spanish legal history, see Jesús Lalinde Abadia, *Iniciación histórica al derecho español* (Barcelona, 1970); in English, see E. N. Van Kelffens, *Hispanic Law until the End of the Middle Ages* (Edinburgh, 1968).

16. Yitzhak Baer, *A History of the Jews in Christian Spain,* 2 vols. (Philadelphia, 1966); Benzion Netanyahu, *The Marranos of Spain from the Late Fourteenth to the Early Sixteenth Century, According to Contemporary Hebrew Sources,* 2d ed. (New York, 1973); Julio Caro Baroja, *Los judíos en la España moderna y contemporánea,* 3 vols. (Madrid, 1962); José María Montalvo Antón, *Teoría y evolución de un conflicto social: El antisemitismo en la corona de Castilla en la Baja Edad Media* (Madrid, 1985); Angus MacKay, "Popular Movements and Pogroms in Fifteenth Century Castile," *Past and Present* 55 (1972): 33–67; Philippe Wolff, "The 1391 Pogrom in Spain: Social Crisis or Not?" *Past and Present* 50 (1971): 4–18; Henry Kamen, *Inquisition and Society in Spain in the Sixteenth and Seventeenth Centuries* (Bloomington, Ind., 1985); Bartolomé Bennassar, *L'Inquisition espagnole, XVᵉ–XIXᵉ siècle* (Paris, 1979); Antonio Domínguez Ortiz and Bernard Vincent, *Historia de los moriscos: Vida y tragedia de una minoría* (Madrid, 1978).

17. Recent work on the Spanish Inquisition has placed that institution in its legal and social context, dispelling many old myths about how it functioned. Jaime Contreras, *El Santo Oficio de la Inquisición de Galicia, 1560–1700: Poder, sociedad, y cultura* (Madrid, 1982); Ricardo García Carcel, *Herejía y sociedad en el siglo XVI: La Inquisición en Valencia 1530–1609* (Barcelona, 1980); Angel Alcalá, ed., *Inquisición española y mentalidad inquisitorial: Ponencias del Simposio Internacional sobre Inquisición* (Barcelona, 1984); *L'Inquisition espagnole XVᵉ–XIXᵉ siècle,* edited by Bartolomé Bennassar (Paris, 1979); Jean-Pierre Dedieu, *L'administration de la foi: L'Inquisition de Tolède XVIᵉ–XVIIIᵉ siècle* (Madrid, 1989). A multivolume work in progress is providing an up-to-date scholarly survey of the Inquisition as a whole: Joaquín Pérez Villanueva and Bartolomé Escandell Bonet, eds., *Historia de la Inquisición en España y América;* volume 1 is *El conocimiento científico y el proceso histórico de la institución (1478–1834)* (Madrid, 1984). Perhaps the most remarkable recent work is the attempt to analyze statistically every available inquisitorial proceeding from the mid-sixteenth to the late seventeenth century. The research to date is summarized in Jaime Contreras and Gustav Henningsen, "Forty-four Thousand Cases of the Spanish Inquisition (1540–1700): Analysis of a Historical Data Bank," in *The Inquisition in Early Modern Europe: Studies on Sources and Methods* (De Kalb, Ill., 1986), 100–129. The authors estimate the probable total cases at over 84,000 (see page 114).

18. C. M. Ajo González, *Medioevo y Renacimiento,* vol. 1 of *Historia de las universidades hispánicas* (Ávila, Spain, 1957).

19. Richard L. Kagan, *Students and Society in Early Modern Spain* (Baltimore, 1974).

20. Jesús Lalinde Abadia, *La corona de Aragón en el Mediterráneo medieval* (Zaragoza, 1979); C. E. DuFourcq, *L'Espagne catalane et le Maghrib aux XIIIᵉ et XIVᵉ siècles* (Paris, 1966); Mario del Treppo, *I mercanti catalani e l'espansione della corona d'Aragona nel secolo XV* (Naples, 1972).

21. Walter F. Starkey, *The Road to Santiago* (London, 1965); Marilyn Stokstad, *Santiago de Compostela in the Age of the Great Pilgrimage* (Norman, Okla., 1978); Vera Hell, *The Great Pilgrimage of the Middle Ages: The Road to St. James of Compostela* (1966).

22. For the fairs, the classic work is Julián Paz and Cristóbal Espejo, *Las antiguas ferias de Medina del Campo* (Valladolid, 1912).

23. There are four excellent recent books on medieval Burgos: Teófilo F. Ruiz, *Sociedad y poder real en Castilla* (Barcelona, 1981); Hilario Casado Alonso, *Señores, mercaderes, y campesinos: La comarca de Burgos a fines de la Edad Media* (Valladolid, 1987); Carlos Estepa, Teófilo F. Ruiz, Juan A. Bonachia, and Hilario Casado Alonso, *Burgos en la Edad Media* (Valladolid, 1984); and *La ciudad de Burgos: Actas del Congreso de Historia de Burgos* (Valladolid, 1985). A useful starting place in English for the medieval history of Burgos is the work of Teófilo F. Ruiz, "The Transformation of the Castilian Municipalities: The Case of Burgos, 1248–1350," *Past and Present* 77 (1977): 3–32. See also Manuel Basas-Fernández, *El consulado de Burgos en el siglo XVI* (Madrid, 1963).

24. José Angel García de Cortázar, *Vizcaya en el siglo XV: Aspectos sociales e económicos* (Bilbao, Spain, 1966); Antonio Ballesteros Baretta, *La marina cántabra y Juan de la Cosa* (Santander, 1954); Teófilo Guiard y Larrauri, *Historia del consulado y casa de contratación de Bilbao y del comercio de la villa* (Bilbao, Spain, 1913); Teófilo Guiard y Larrauri, *La industria naval vizcaína*, rpt. ed. (Bilbao, Spain, 1968); Luis Suárez Fernández, *Navegación y comercio en el Golfo de Vizcaya: Un estudio sobre la política marinera de la casa de Trastámara* (Madrid, 1959).

25. For the latest synthesis and the most recent bibliography, see José Angel García de Cortázar et al., *Vizcaya en la Edad Media*, 4 vols. (San Sebastián, Spain, 1985). The classic work on Bilbao is Teófilo Guiard y Larrauri, *Historia de la noble villa de Bilbao*, 4 vols. (Bilbao, Spain, 1906–1912, rpt. 1971).

26. Carla Rahn Phillips, "Spanish Merchants and the Wool Trade in the Sixteenth Century," *Sixteenth Century Journal* 14 (Fall 1983): 259–282; Carla Rahn Phillips, "The Spanish Wool Trade, 1500–1700," *Journal of Economic History* 42, 4 (December 1982): 775–795.

27. Philippe Dollinger, *The German Hansa*, translated and edited by D. S. Ault and S. H. Steinberg (Stanford, Calif., 1970); Margery Kirkbride James, *Studies in the Medieval Wine Trade* (Oxford, 1971); María del Carmen Carlé, "Mercaderes en Castilla, 1252–1512," *Cuadernos de Historia de España* 21/22 (1954): 146–328; Suárez Fernández, *Navegación y comercio*; Betsabé Caunedo del Potro, *Mercaderes castellanos en el Golfo de Vizcaya (1475–1492)* (Madrid, 1983). With the truce signed in 1443, the Germans were conceded limited trade with Castile.

28. García de Cortázar, *Vizcaya en el siglo XV,* 214–216, 222, 226; Joseph Maréchal, "La colonie espagnole de Bruges du XIVe au XVIe siècle," *Revue du Nord* 35 (January-March 1953): 5–40. For the Spaniards in Antwerp, see J. A. Goris, *Étude sur les colonies marchands méridionales (Portugais, Espagnoles, Italiens) à Anvers de 1468–1567* (Louvain, Belgium, 1925; rpt. New York, 1971).

29. Cortes of Toledo, 1436, petitions 4–5, in *Cortes de los antiguos reinos de León y de Castilla,* edited by the Real Academia de la Historia (Madrid, 1861–1903), 3:263–265.

30. Cortes of Burgos, 1453, in *Cortes de los antiguos reinos de León y de Castilla,* edited by the Real Academia de la Historia (Madrid, 1861–1903), 3:659–660.

31. Wendy R. Childs, *Anglo-Castilian Trade in the Later Middle Ages* (Manchester, Eng., 1978); Teófilo F. Ruiz, "Castilian Merchants in England, 1248–1350," in *Order and Innovation in the Middle Ages: Essays in Honor of Joseph R. Strayer,* edited by William C. Jordan, Bruce McNab, and Teófilo F. Ruiz (Princeton, N.J., 1976); M. M. Postan, *Medieval Trade and Finance* (Cambridge, Eng., 1973); Eleanora Mary Carus-Wilson, *Medieval Merchant Venturers,* 2d ed. (London, 1967).

32. Franscique Xavier Michel, *Histoire du commerce et de la navigation à Bordeaux, principalment sous l'administration anglaise* (Bordeaux, 1870), 1:145, 153; Carmelo Viñas y Mey, "De la Edad Media a la moderna: El Cantábrico y el Estrecho de Gibraltar en la historia política española," *Hispania* 1–5 (1940–1941): 1:52–70, 2:53–79, 4:64–101, 5:41–105; Michel Mollat, *Le commerce maritime normande à la fin du Moyen Age* (Paris, 1952); Michel Mollat, "Le role international des marchands espagnols dans les ports de l'Europe occidental à l'époque des Rois Catholiques," *Anuario de historia económica y social de España* 3 (1970): 41–55; M. Delafosse, "Trafic rochelais au XVe et XVIe siècles: Marchands poitevins et laines d'Espagne," *Annales, Economics, Sociétés, Civilisations* 1952: 61–64; Étienne Trocmé and Marcel Delafosse, *Le commerce rochelaise de la fin du XVe siècle au début du XVIIe* (Paris, 1952); Henri Touchard, *Le commerce maritime bréton a la fin du Moyen Age* (Paris, 1967); Philippe Wolff, *Commerces et marchands de Toulouse (vers 1350–vers 1450)* (Paris, 1954).

33. Miguel Angel Ladero Quesada, *La ciudad medieval (1248–1492),* vol. 2 of *Historia de Sevilla* (Seville, 1976); Antonio Collantes de Terán Sánchez, *Sevilla en la Baja Edad Media* (Seville, 1977); Ruth Pike, *Enterprise and Adventure: The Genoese in Seville and the Opening of the New World* (Ithaca, N.Y., 1966); F. Melis, *Mercaderes italianos en España (siglos XV—XVI)* (Seville, 1976).

34. Julio Rey Pastor and Ernesto García Camarero, *La cartografía mallorquina* (Madrid, 1960); Ruy González de Clavijo, *Narrative of the Embassy to the Court of Timour,* translated by C. R. Markham, Hakluyt Society Publications, ser. 1, 26 (London, 1859); Francesco Balducci Pegolotti, *La practica della mercatura,* edited by Allan Evans (Cambridge, Mass., 1936); Miguel Gual Camarena, ed., *El primer manual hispánico de mercadería (siglo XIV)* (Barcelona, 1981); J. R. S. Phillips, *The Medieval Expansion of Europe* (Oxford, 1988).

35. For the general context of late medieval European expansion, see Felipe Fernández-Armesto, *Before Columbus: Exploration and Colonization from the Medi-*

terranean to the Atlantic, 1229–1492 (Philadelphia, 1987); Vitorino de Magalháes Godinho, *A economia dos descobrimentos henriquinos* (Lisbon, 1962); Vitorino Magalháes Godinho, *Os descobrimentos e a economia mundial*, 4 vols. (Lisbon, 1983–1987); Charles Verlinden, *The Beginnings of Modern Colonization: Eleven Essays with an Introduction*, translated by Yvonne Freccero (Ithaca, N.Y., 1970); Pierre Chaunu, *European Overseas Expansion in the Later Middle Ages* (Amsterdam, 1979).

36. Felipe Fernández-Armesto, *The Canary Islands after the Conquest: The Making of a Colonial Society in the Early Sixteenth Century* (Oxford, 1982); John Mercer, *The Canary Islanders: Their Prehistory, Conquest, and Survival* (London, 1980); Antonio Rumeu de Armas, *España en el Africa atlántica*, 2 vols. (Madrid, 1956); Antonio Rumeu de Armas, *La conquista de Tenerife* (Santa Cruz de Tenerife, Spain, 1975); E. Aznar Vallejo, *La incorporación de las Islas Canarias en la corona de Castilla* (Seville, 1983). For recent interpretive accounts of this period of Canarian history, see Alfred W. Crosby, *Ecological Imperialism: The Biological Expansion of Europe, 900–1900* (Cambridge, Eng., 1986), 70–103; and Fernández-Armesto, *Before Columbus*, 151–217.

37. On the Canarian sugarcane industry, see Guillermo Camacho y Pérez-Galdos, "El cultivo de la caña de azúcar y la industria azucarera en Gran Canaria (1510–1535)," *Anuario de Estudios Atlánticos* 7 (1961): 1–60; Vitorino de Magalháes Godinho, "A economia das Canarias nos séculos XIV e XV," *Revista de Historia* 4 (1952): 311–320.

38. Manuela Marrero Rodríguez, *La esclavitud en Tenerife a raíz de la conquista* (La Laguna de Tenerife, Spain, 1966); Manuel Lobo Cabrera, *La esclavitud en las Canarias orientales en el siglo XVI: Negros, moros y moriscos* (Grand Canary, Spain, 1982).

39. Marrero Rodríguez, *Esclavitud en Tenerife*, 29, 34–35.

40. Fernández-Armesto, *Canary Islands*, 37 n. 19; Antonio de la Torre y de Cerro, "Los canarios de Gomera vendidos como esclavos en 1489," *Anuario de Estudios Americanos* 7 (1950): 47–72; Vicenta Cortés Alonso, "Los cautivos canarios," in *Homenaje a Elías Serra Rafols*, (La Laguna de Tenerife, Spain, 1970), 137–148.

41. Lobo Cabrera, *Esclavitud en las Canarias*, scattered references.

42. Lobo Cabrera, *Esclavitud en las Canarias*, scattered references; Marrero Rodríguez, *Esclavitud en Tenerife*; Fernández-Armesto, *Canary Islands*; Manuel Lobo Cabrera, "Esclavos indios en Canarias," *Revista de Indias* 43, 172 (1983): 515–533.

TWO

The Cutting Edge:
An Analysis of the Spanish Invasion
and Overthrow of the Inca Empire,
1532–1539

John F. Guilmartin, Jr.

The invasion of Peru in 1532 by a small band of Spaniards led by Francisco Pizarro marks a watershed in Andean history and, at the same time, the beginning of one of the most seemingly implausible episodes in the history of warfare. Between their entry into Tawantinsuyu in the spring of 1532 and their consolidation of power in the wake of Manco Inca's great rebellion in early 1539, the conquistadors, by armed force, diplomacy, and political negotiation, carved out for themselves and for their imperial master Charles I a domain of unprecedented size and richness. Their feats cast a long shadow on subsequent events; Habsburg greatness and Peruvian silver were inextricably linked in the years to come, and the overthrow of Tawantinsuyu is arguably the salient political and cultural event of modern Andean history.

Viewed from the perspective of military history, the invasion of Peru and the overthrow of Atahualpa's empire has a peculiar fascination. Spanish methods of warfare underwent a revolution during the first decades of the sixteenth century, a revolution that did much to transform Spain from a regional to a global power. The tactical innovations of Gonsalvo de Córdova, the development of the Spanish musket, and the appearance of the *tercio*, arguably the first permanent military formation in the modern sense, give evidence of the Spanish genius for war during this pivotal era. The invasion of Mexico provided the first major test of the fruits of this military revolution beyond its native habitat, but the conquest of Peru was to pose the most extreme challenge to Spanish arms, in cultural, in geographic, and in quantitative tactical terms. Nowhere else did the Spanish fighting man face such extreme tests, and nowhere else did he perform with such sustained valor, however re-pugnant in its manifestations, for the overthrow of the Aztec empire required a bare two years, while that of the Inca took almost seven.[1]

Spanish arms and methods of warfare played a pivotal role in the repulse of the Ottoman Turks from Vienna in 1529 and from Malta in 1565; they played an equally central role in the Habsburg containment of Valois ambitions, notably in the Wars of Italy (1494–1559). In the broad sweep of history, the role of Spanish arms in the overthrow of the Aztec and Inca states and the consolidation of Spanish power in the New World was no less important. For this reason, if for no other, the military aspects of the overthrow of the Aztec and Inca empires—the latter of which is our focus—deserve scholarly attention.

It is difficult to approach the military exploits of the conquistadors with objectivity. Nowhere is this more apparent than with the conquest of Peru, where the problem is amplified by the magnitude and improba-bility of their deeds. We are, after all, dealing with the overthrow of a huge, prosperous, and well-ordered empire, buttressed by religious legitimacy and successful traditions of governance, by a small band of determined individuals.

Scholars have only recently embarked on in-depth analysis of the role of military tactics and technology in the military successes of the Spanish invaders of the New World, and to date the emphasis has been on Meso-america.[2] Early attempts to explain the reality of Spanish victory sub-sumed technological advantage (tactics were hardly mentioned) within the overall heading of cultural or even racial superiority.[3] Operationally naive arguments emphasizing the psychological shock of the unknown and crediting Spanish success to the impact of gunpowder and horses were quickly rejected. Cursory analysis of the Cortés or Pizarro cam-paigns shows that the Aztec and Inca alike adapted quickly to horses and gunpowder within the limits of the means available to them; their defeat hardly can be attributed to simple inability to cope with the unknown. Monocausal cultural explanations of the Spanish military superiority have fared no better. The notion that the Spanish prevailed over in-digenous polities accustomed to ritual warfare because they fought to win might have limited applicability to the conquest of Mexico but ut-terly fails in the case of the Incas, who waged war for political domina-tion with single-minded ruthlessness.

More recent explanations have revolved around sophisticated eco-nomic, political, and cultural analysis, emphasizing the role of political fragmentation and preconquest strife among indigenous peoples and the assistance rendered the Spanish by local allies.[4] Accepting as a given the superiority of Spanish military technology, they focus on these other factors, pointing out—correctly—that Spanish military superiority took effect acting in combination with them. In the case of Peru, relevant considerations include the destructive civil war that ravaged the Inca domains in the years immediately preceding the Spanish invasion and the impact of an epidemic, probably smallpox, which swept through the indigenous populations just before the Spanish arrived.[5] Geoffrey Conrad and Arthur Demarest argue persuasively that the economic structure and religious ideology of Tawantinsuyu forced the Incas to adopt frenetic expansion to forestall social and economic collapse from within; against this backdrop, they argue, the civil war between Huascar and Atahualpa left the empire "shattered and all the Spaniards had to do was pick up the pieces."[6] This conclusion, though perhaps overstated for effect, aptly highlights the pivotal underlying political realities.

These ethnohistorical hypotheses, rich and complex in detail yet suggestively elegant in their essential logic, are infinitely more satisfying than earlier explanations. The picture that they paint, of social and political resistance and attempted accommodation followed by economic and social collapse, has great explanatory power. But while recognizing the importance of military factors to the reality of conquest, the ethnohistorians quite properly have placed their emphasis elsewhere. In consequence, their explanations are incomplete where military factors are concerned. Nathan Wachtel poses the essential problem succinctly in the form of a thoughtfully phrased question:

> How could empires as powerful as those of the Aztecs or the Incas be destroyed so rapidly by a few hundred Spaniards? Undoubtedly the invaders benefitted from superior arms: steel swords against lances of obsidian, metal armor against tunics padded with cotton, arquebuses against bows and arrows, cavalry against infantry. But this technical superiority seems to have been of limited importance: The Spanish possessed few fire-arms at the time of the conquest and these were slow to fire: their impact at the beginning was, like that of the horses, primarily psychological.[7]

My purpose here is to answer Wachtel's question with respect to the overthrow of the Inca state, approaching the problem by means of careful military analysis. In short, my objective is to supplement the ethnohistorians' analysis, adding an additional, complementary dimension to their explanations. The social and political factors that the ethnohistorians emphasize were real considerations indeed, no less militarily than in other spheres of activity. They shaped the impact and dictated the pace of the Spanish invasion, and no military analysis can ignore them.

Finally, it is important to recognize that the political settlements and so-cial, economic, and cultural accommodations that wars bring about are powerfully shaped by how they are fought; it was this set of relationships that the nineteenth-century German theoretician Carl von Clausewitz had in mind when he noted that in war the result is never final.[8] The overthrow of the Inca empire was no exception.

Nevertheless, Spanish arms and tactics exercised a preemptive influ-ence during the critical, early stages of the struggle which are the focus of our concern here. Following the overthrow of Tawantinsuyu, the Spanish, in a commanding though not dominant position, could turn in-creasingly to nonmilitary means of expanding their social and politi-cal control and securing economic advantage. In the early stages of the struggle, however, they did not have that luxury; if Peru was to be brought within the Spanish orbit, the Inca state had to be overthrown, and if that could not be achieved by force of arms, it could not be achieved at all. In short, the Inca armies had to be dealt with first. From Pizarro's entry into Tawantinsuyu in the spring of 1532 until the col-lapse of Manco Inca's final revolt in 1539, the Spanish were forced of necessity to assign first priority to strategic and tactical military concerns. Spanish arms formed the cutting edge of contact between the two civili-zations during the period in question, both metaphorically and literally.

Differences between the experience of the Peruvian conquest and European historical parallels are both important and instructive. Clause-witz's principal point of reference in his reference cited above was the wars of eighteenth- and early nineteenth-century Europe. In these wars, the very existence of the nation was rarely threatened and, of greater importance, the underlying social order was not at risk in any funda-mental sense.[9] His main point was to demonstrate the existence of inher-ent limitations to the total application of force and to show their nature. The limitations that concerned Clausewitz derived in large part from the lack of any real threat to the underlying social order; explicit in his analysis, however, and acting as his limiting case, was the notion of a total application of force applying in the absence of social and political con-straints. The overthrow of the Inca empire comes as close to this limiting case as we are likely to find in the pages of history. There was, moreover, an implicit awareness of the totality of the issues involved among par-ticipants. For that reason alone, the subject matter has a relevance which goes far beyond regional western hemispheric concerns.

The absence of any sort of social compact between Spaniard and Andean and its connection to the attendant horrors unleashed was evi-dent to contemporary observers. One conquistador wrote,

I can bear witness that this is the most dreadful and cruel war in the world. For between Christians and Moors there is some well-feeling, and it is in the interests of both sides to spare those they take alive because of their ransoms. But in this Indian war there is no such feeling on either side. They give each other the cruelest deaths they can imagine.[10]

And this description was not hyperbole. During the 1536–1537 siege of Cusco, Hernando Pizarro, noting the importance to the Inca efforts of women employed for porterage, food preparation, and so on, ordered all captured Indian women killed; he also ordered the right hands of several hundred captured male noncombatants cut off, after which they were released to spread fear and demoralization.[11] These acts were the results of carefully considered decisions and apparently had the desired effect. It should hardly surprise us that the outcome of a war so total should itself approach totality.

Military history is irrelevant unless undergirded by a sound understanding of salient social, technological, economic, cultural, and political considerations; conversely, the consequences of wars cannot be fully understood without an appreciation of how they were fought. The Spanish overthrow of the Aztec and Inca empires, where the incredible swiftness and completeness of conquest led to the establishment of a new social, political, and economic order within a single generation, provides a compelling test of this thesis. The links between the two cases are many, and each is the only true analogue to the other; any serious analysis of one must consider both, and I shall do so. The parallels are of limited value in an overall strategic sense, however, since the political texture of Mesoamerica was utterly different from that of the Andes. Moreover, Hernán Cortés's style of leadership and the political problems he faced were appreciably different from those of Francisco, Hernando, and Pedro Pizarro, Diego de Almagro, Sebastián de Benalcázar, and the rest. Technologically and tactically, however, the two cases offer useful comparisons and contrasts that enhance our understanding of the peculiar conditions of the Andean peoples, and I will use them for this purpose.

Enormous advances have been made in the theory and practice of history since William Prescott penned his classic narrative of the conquest of Peru in the mid-nineteenth century.[12] As anthropologist John V. Murra has noted, Prescott's account still reads remarkably up to date, but Murra's observation is more a plea for the integration of insights produced by anthropology, ethnology, and archaeology into mainstream historiography than a commentary on Prescott's remarkable skills as a narrative historian.[13] The same point can be made with respect to military history, which has come into its own as a subdiscipline in the century and a quarter since Prescott wrote. To rephrase a point made earlier, it is my purpose to apply the methodology of military history to the cutting edge of conquest, where Spaniard and Indian met in combat. Such an endeavor proceeds along untraveled ground, for there are few Latin American military historians, and the secondary literature is thin.

As a specialist in the military history of early modern Europe, I am acutely aware of the limitations of applying Old World precedent to the military experience of Europeans in the New World. Operational analyses grounded in European parallels, for example, are plainly inadequate to explain the outcome of combats where the Incas enjoyed seemingly overwhelming numerical advantages and lacked not at all in organization or courage, yet were utterly defeated. At the same time, most of what we know about the technological and tactical factors derives from European experience. Indeed, because of the enormous technological disparity between Spaniard and Andean, we must cast our net far wider than usual, drawing on ancient and classical examples as well as medieval and early modern. It goes without saying that any such endeavor must proceed with care, taking pains to examine the implicit and explicit assumptions behind any historical parallel.

With this caveat in mind, we will focus on contact between conquistador and Andean in combat, at the cutting edge. But there is more to it than that. Such a focus demands consideration of broader operational and strategic issues, and in considering the strategic objectives of the two sides we must take into account the Spanish and Inca—indeed, the Andean—worldviews. In evaluating the impact of weaponry we will become heavily embroiled in technological issues. No competent operational analysis slights the all-important motivational factors, and these bring us up against a host of cultural and religious considerations. Our analysis begins with the initial Spanish preparations and reconnaissances. It ends with the extinction of the last Inca successor state in 1572, though the emphasis will be on the period prior to the suppression of Manco Inca's great rebellion in 1539, for the Inca threat to Spanish rule waned markedly thereafter.

We must contend with limitations in the evidence which go beyond the problem of imbalance noted above. The Incas had no written language, and, in testimony to the shattering completeness of their defeat, no dynastic oral traditions survive.[14] Some few Indian accounts of the conquest of Mexico based on contemporary and near-contemporary sources survive; these, whatever their limitations as sources for the cultural or political historian, contain operational detail invaluable to the military historian, all the more useful for the disingenuousness with which it is reported.[15] What little survives of contemporary indigenous sources for the conquest of Peru comes to us through the "double filter" of the Spanish observer and his Andean informant, in most cases a member of the Cusco elite opposed to Atahualpa's accession.[16] There is no Peruvian parallel to Hernán Cortés's letters to King Charles I, for Francisco Pizarro was illiterate, nor is there an equivalent to Bernal Díaz del Castillo's classic account of the conquest of Mexico, written from the perspective of the rank and file. There are, however, accounts by participants, including those of Francisco Xerez and Pedro Pizarro and several letters by Hernando Pizarro, effectively his brother's second in command. On the Amerindian side we have the second-generation account of Felipe Guaman Poma de Ayala, particularly useful for its illustrations, as well as woodcuts prepared by Andean artisans within living memory of the events depicted, and the celebrated history of the mestizo El Inca Garcilaso de la Vega. These must be used with care, but they can be used, and here the military historian has an advantage, for operational military events tend to possess an unequivocality of outcome, rarely present in social and political history, which even the hopelessly biased author cannot totally ignore.

To set the stage, a cursory assessment of the magnitude of the military success of the Spanish conquerors of Peru is in order. Though population figures for preconquest South America are in dispute, the population of the Inca empire probably numbered somewhere between two and nine million people at the time of the Spanish invasion.[17] The size of the preconquest Inca military establishment is equally uncertain, but it is clear that the Inca empire could put three armies of some 30,000–40,000 more or less professional combatants each in the field at one time and that some 100,000 Inca soldiers were under arms when the conquistadors entered Inca territory in the spring of 1532.[18] When Francisco Pizarro turned inland to begin his penetration of the Inca heartland that September, he led a force of 62 mounted fighting men and 106 on foot.[19] This tiny force overwhelmed the bodyguard of the emperor Atahualpa, a force reasonably estimated at some 5,000–6,000 men, to effect the capture of the Inca emperor at Cajamarca on 16 November in the pivotal initial military encounter.[20] When Manco Inca's armies attacked Cusco in early May of 1536, his generals commanded a host variously estimated at from 100,000 to 400,000 by contemporary observers; the Spanish defenders of the city at that point numbered 190, only 80 of them mounted, yet they successfully held the city for almost a year; they did have the help of Indian allies, but these seem to have been considerably less numerous than the besiegers.[21]

Other examples could be cited, and some will be discussed below, but the basic point is clear: conventional wisdom based on unconscious extrapolations from European military experience cannot explain hard-fought victory gained in the face of such enormous numerical disparities. Instead, we must go to root causes and circumstances. We will begin with a comparative assessment of underlying strategic factors, including weaponry, followed by an evaluation of the sources of Spanish tactical superiority, and will conclude with a strategic analysis of the campaign—or, more properly, campaigns—by which the conquistadors overthrew Tawantinsuyu.

UNDERLYING STRATEGIC FACTORS

The operational ebb and flow of any conflict depends on those factors that exercise a dominant influence on success and failure in combat: weaponry, morale, leadership, logistics, and the rest. But all need not be addressed in detail in each instance, for every conflict possesses unique operational characteristics that combine to make certain factors practically irrelevant and others critically important. Those particularly relevant here include security and loyalty, command and control, logistics, geography and climate, the worldviews of the opposing sides, and weaponry.[22]

In the crucial areas of security and loyalty, neither the Spanish nor the Incas held a clear-cut advantage. The barely resolved and bitterly contested struggle between Huascar and Atahualpa posed particularly acute problems for the Incas which the Spanish were quick to exploit. But even without the turmoil of the succession, the conquistadors would have found native allies, for memories of independence were fresh in the minds of many recently conquered groups.[23] In any case, we may be confident that many *ayllus* (Andean kin groups) would have found common cause with the invaders as soon as they demonstrated effectiveness against Inca arms.[24] Conversely, those who adhered to the Inca tended to be steadfast in their loyalties, and their number increased as the nature of the invaders' objectives became apparent, making the Incas the only effective focal point of resistance. In a practical sense, the Spanish could depend on allies for logistical support, auxiliary troops, and local intelligence, but the communications of the Inca and his armies were essentially secure from Spanish penetration.

The Incas held the advantage over the invaders in two key areas:

strategic command and control and logistics. The Inca's subordinate commanders could be relied upon to carry out whatever orders he issued with efficiency and dispatch, and the Inca road net and courier system provided sure and swift communications to all corners of the realm. The extreme centralization of authority at the top was a weakness that Pizarro exploited with ruthless efficiency, but so long as the Inca was willing to take action against the Spanish, his commands were turned into action. The clearest and most dramatic demonstration of this was in the great rebellion of 1536–1537, in which Manco Inca's mobilization orders, issued while he was nominally a Spanish puppet, were carried out with remarkable efficiency. These advantages persisted through the collapse of Manco's second rebellion in early 1539, then swiftly eroded as the futility of further large-scale resistance became apparent and as the structure of the Inca state broke down under the impact of Spanish-induced social and economic change.[25]

Logistically, the Inca armies were supported by an extensive network of warehouses in which provisions, clothing, weaponry, and protective equipment were prepositioned to support campaigning armies. The value of these warehouses was magnified by the nature of Andean crops and methods of preservation; these produced an array of desiccated, high-energy food products that were light, were easily transported, and could be stored indefinitely.[26] We can only speculate about the administrative details, but it is difficult to imagine a more efficient source of ready nourishment for an army on the march than the freeze-dried tubers and animal flesh that the Inca's warehouses must have contained. The llama, the only native Andean pack animal, is relatively inefficient compared to mules or horses, and Inca armies seem to have made little use of them except as meat on the hoof. But near-total dependence on human locomotion would not have slowed the deployment of Inca armies, since draft and pack animals tended to reduce rather than increase the mobility of armies, except over relatively short distances.[27] Though we can only speculate concerning the specifics, the efficiency of the Incas' rations and the advantages of prepositioned supplies and equipment must have given them an overland strategic mobility surpassed prior to railroads only by mounted armies campaigning in areas of abundant forage and fodder. Also to the Incas' advantage was the fact that their troops were acclimated to the high altitudes at which the main campaigns of the conquest were conducted; this was both by virtue of greater lung capacity, for the Incas recruited selectively from ethnic groups that had adapted genetically to the high altitudes at which they lived, and by virtue of their knowledge of Andean conditions.

For their part, the Spaniards and their horses suffered from the rugged geography and climatic extremes; even the Inca roads, designed for the passage of humans, were hard on the horses' feet. But the conquistadors traveled light, moved swiftly, and displayed remarkable ingenuity in dealing with the unprecedented conditions that they encountered. Fodder does not seem to have been a problem—clear, if implicit, evidence not only of the richness of the country but also of intelligent planning and improvisation. The small numbers of horses involved no doubt helped, but it is clear that the Spaniards recognized their critical importance to the enterprise and took special pains to protect their health and well-being. Indicative of their concern, they procured locally made horseshoes of copper and silver,[28] and on one occasion the conquistadors set up an improvised forge at night in unfamiliar mountains to reset horseshoes thrown on the rough track, a remarkable piece of fieldcraft which seems to have been taken more or less for granted.[29] The Spanish could not have been supplied without the efforts of their native allies, but this in no way lessens the impressiveness of their logistical feats; they had to be not only logisticians but diplomats as well.

It is easy for the analysis of modern events to take worldview and religious outlook for granted or to dismiss them as deviations from the "rational" norm. This perceived rationality plainly did not apply in the sixteenth century, and there was a marked dissymmetry in the Spanish and Andean worldviews. For the Spanish, reversals and misfortunes, however serious, did not undermine their faith in God, their cause, and themselves. The sources of their perceived legitimacy were deeply rooted in the robust orthodoxy of Iberian Roman Catholicism and the searing reality of seven centuries of Reconquest. We should not make modern men of them, or even Renaissance men; no less than King Charles, after all, regarded the great storm that destroyed his fleet before Algiers in 1541 as a sign of divine displeasure (though Hernán Cortés, who was present, apparently did not). But it is clear that their fortitude had spiritual as well as physical and economic foundations, and that those foundations were extraordinarily solid.

The Incas and their Andean subjects viewed the world in very different terms. From our standpoint this is most strikingly apparent in the great importance attached to the Inca himself, for in his person and in the mummies of his ancestors resided the legitimacy of the realm. All of this must be seen in the light of the relative youth of the Inca empire. It is for this reason that Atahualpa's capture at Cajamarca and his subsequent execution and burial hamstrung the Incas so badly. Nor did the dissymmetry extend only to matters of legitimacy and sovereignty. Andean beliefs, for example, led them to suspend military activity in favor of religious celebration on nights of the new moon, a belief that the Spanish were quick to exploit.[30] This is not to imply that the Andeans were not adaptable; to the contrary, they learned quickly and well, but their worldview was constrained in a way the conquistadors' was not. This is illustrated in mundane fashion by an incident during the siege of Cusco in which the Amerindians, apparently tricked by a Spanish captive, threw captured letters into the Spanish lines as proof that they had annihilated a relief expedition, as indeed they had. From the torn-up letters, the garrison learned of Charles I's capture of Tunis from the Turks the previous year and took heart in consequence.[31]

The cutting edge of the Spanish advantage was in weaponry, and to comprehend the nature, degree, and tactical implications of that advantage, we must break things down into their essential components. A more complex and sophisticated typology would be required if we were concerned with differences in the effects of weapons on ships, structures, and fortifications, but our concern is almost entirely with the effects of weapons on men and horses, and a simplified scheme will suffice. First, weapons fall into two basic categories, offensive and defensive. The latter are quickly dealt with: steel armor, particularly steel helmets, gave the conquistadors a considerable advantage, but one that took effect offensively. The relative security that effective armor afforded enabled the Spanish to extract full benefit from their offensive capabilities. In simple terms, relative invulnerability made them more aggressive. But steel armor, though important, was not in itself decisive; if anything, steel provided more protection than was ordinarily required except for the head, and, as they had in Mexico, the Spanish supplemented and partially replaced their steel armor with lighter, warmer, and more flexible protective garments of quilted canvas and padded cloth.[32] Horses were armored only seldom, and then lightly and partially.

Offensive weapons fall into two categories, according to the means of employment: hand-held and missile.[33] In the first instance, the weapon is retained by the user, who inflicts damage by swinging or thrusting with it. In the second, damage is done by a projectile that is thrown, slung, or fired. Next, offensive weaponry can be categorized according to the means of inflicting damage. The principal offensive weapons of the sixteenth century inflicted damage by one of three means: piercing, cutting, or crushing. Fire might be considered a fourth, but incendiary weapons were cumbersome and their role minor and specialized; the use by the Inca host of heated sling stones to fire the roofs of Cusco during the rebellion of 1536–1537 is the only example worth noting.[34]

Concerned as we are with the tactical characteristics and effect on man and beast of piercing, cutting, and crushing weapons, we can quickly summarize their effects in two categories, hand-held and missile. Because piercing and cutting weapons depend on shape rather than mass for terminal effect, far less total energy is needed to do lethal damage. Piercing and cutting weapons substitute velocity for mass, and, since impact energy increases with the velocity squared, a lighter weapon has, in theory, more destructive potential for the amount of energy imparted to it.[35] In reality, this theoretical advantage is limited by two constraints. The first and most basic is that with the exception of gunpowder weapons, the maximum velocities attainable were limited by the abilities of the human body. The human arm can swing a sword or throw a dart or javelin only so fast, and while mechanical aids such as the bow, throwing stick, and sling permit much higher velocities, they can do so only with relatively light missiles. The crossbow circumvented this limitation by providing a means of storing energy, and gunpowder weapons bypassed it altogether, but the advantages of these weapons lay entirely with the Spanish.

The second constraint on the ability to increase the lethality of a piercing or cutting weapon by reducing mass and increasing velocity lies in the need to penetrate. A light, high-velocity weapon or projectile that penetrates is potentially lethal; conversely, one that fails to penetrate is ineffective regardless of the total energy imparted. Whether or not penetration occurs is a function of impact energy, the area over which it is applied, the hardness, sharpness, and toughness of point or edge, and the target's resistance to penetration. The physics are fiendishly complex in detail, but the basic relationships are readily demonstrated by observing the force needed to pierce the skin with a needle, as opposed to a thumbtack, or by drawing a razor blade and a table knife across a piece of leather with equal force.[36] It is easy for us, living in an age in which individual weapons capable of penetrating steel armor are commonplace, to lose sight of the toughness of horsehide and human skin, but for most of the millennia during which humankind has been civilized, weapons capable of reliably piercing or cutting either in combat have been a rarity.[37] It would be only a slight overstatement to say that a steel edge is required; bronze swords showed no clear advantage over axes in antiquity,[38] and the Andean civilizations did not possess effective weaponry of bronze, let alone steel.[39]

In summation, the piercing or cutting weapon does damage by means of the sharpness of its point or the keenness of its edge. The crushing weapon, by contrast, inflicts damage by sheer kinetic energy; it is hence inherently slower and more cumbersome for the amount of damage that it is capable of doing. The conquistadors, with their slender blades of good Spanish steel, thus had an immense advantage over the Andeans, for they could strike much more quickly and with far greater lethality, an advantage magnified by the Indians' lack of effective armor. The Andeans apparently had no slashing weapons at all, but depended exclusively on clubs and axes; there is no evidence to the contrary in battle narratives or surviving physical evidence to which I am privy.[40] This conclusion is supported by analysis of the near-contemporary illustrations in Guaman Poma de Ayala's *Nueva corónica y buen gobierno,* which emphasize Spanish swords, lances, and armor and depict Indian warriors armed with short spears, maces, and slings.[41] Here, the contrast with Mexico is instructive, for the Mexicans possessed an effective slashing weapon in the *macuahuitl,* a sword of dense wood shaped like an oversized cricket bat edged with razor-sharp obsidian flakes; though more cumbersome than Spanish swords, the *macuahuitl* was a powerful weapon and figures prominently in the battle narratives.[42]

Tactical analysis leaves little doubt that the most effective Andean weapon was the sling, a conclusion indirectly supported by the depiction in the *Nueva corónica* of prominent Inca commanders, notably the general Calcuchima, wielding the sling in battle.[43] Sling stones were said to be capable of shattering a horse's thigh or snapping a sword blade in two with a square hit at short range, and the Spanish feared these missiles as they feared no other indigenous weapon, no doubt in part because of their random nature.[44] But the stone shot could not penetrate human skin or horsehide; it was a crushing weapon, and its effect fell off sharply with range. Even armor of quilted cloth provided reasonable protection against it. This heavy reliance on crushing weapons explains the frequent references to wounded horses in Spanish accounts of the conquest and does much to explain Spanish superiority.

Though they would have expressed it in very different terms and knew they could not be certain until the shock of battle came, Pizarro and his men were well aware of the basic tactical considerations when they entered Inca territory. Most had had practical experience with them in Panama, Nicaragua, or the Caribbean and must have anticipated fighting under conditions similar to those they had already encountered. They were no doubt astonished by the size and organization of the Inca hosts, but insofar as weaponry was concerned the Incas, for all their administrative and political sophistication, posed a familiar problem. Like Cortés's men before them, Pizarro's conquistadors were no doubt poorly equipped by contemporary European standards.[45] But that does not mean that they were poorly equipped for the task at hand. To the contrary, while they would no doubt have welcomed additional reinforcements on occasion—prior to the distribution of plunder—they would have been hard pressed to have made better choices in outfitting, arms, and equipment.

ELEMENTS OF SPANISH TACTICAL SUPERIORITY

Because the consequences of tactical factors can be observed more or less unequivocally in the results of combat, tactical analysis tends to be more straightforward and less tentative than strategic analysis. We need not theorize on what might have been, but can concentrate on explaining what happened, beginning with the central reality of clear Spanish tactical advantage. The causes of that advantage were complex and interrelated; they took effect in synergistic fashion and cannot be isolated cleanly one from another. They can be summarized nevertheless under a limited number of headings, listed below in diminishing order of importance.

1. Spanish Steel

The single biggest tactical advantage accruing to the conquistadors was that Spanish swords, pikes, and lances could strike far more quickly and lethally than Andean copper- or stone-tipped spears, clubs, and axes. This was due partly to the swiftness of the lighter Spanish weapons and partly to the ineffectiveness of crushing weapons against armor and horsehide; acting together, these factors were decisive. While Spanish success in combat cannot be attributed to a single factor, it is clear that the other elements of Spanish superiority took effect within a tactical matrix established by the effectiveness of Spanish hand-held slashing and piercing weapons. Spanish tactics were driven by a keen awareness of the magnitude of that superiority and an eagerness to exploit it. If one factor were to be singled out, it was the utter deadliness of Spanish swordplay. Pikes do not seem to have been used much; there was little need to keep the Indians at arm's length. That Francisco Pizarro himself, in an age in which mastery of equestrian combat skills carried heavy social connotations, fought by preference on foot armed with a sword provides eloquent, if indirect, testimony to the importance that he and his men accorded swords and swordplay.[46]

2. Horses

Horses gave the Spanish crucial advantages in striking power, shock effect, and speed. The well-mounted Spaniard could strike harder and more swiftly and reach farther with his sword than could his companion on foot; he could use the speed and mobility of his mount to drive home the point of his lance, and could do so without coming within reach of his enemy's hand-held weapon. The importance of quickness in this context is reflected by the fact that the Spanish horsemen generally rode *a la jineta*—that is, in the Moorish style, with shortened stirrups for maximum lateral mobility—rather than *a la brida,* leaning back in the saddle with extended legs in the classic style of European chivalry.[47] In addition, well-trained and well-ridden cavalry horses develop shock power directly. Modern horses, at least, will not deliberately run into an ordered line of men at full tilt,[48] but the living bulk of a horse is psychologically intimidating and physically imposing to a crowd. The Andeans never learned to form in ordered masses to repel cavalry, and it would have been futile for them to do so, for their weapons were outreached by Spanish lances; that left them in loose formations that were handily scattered by a well-delivered charge. It is difficult to overstate the vulnerability of the bravest of foot soldiers under these circumstances, for well-mounted cavalry can move in among them with a quickness and power impossible to convey with words; this was true as late as the Napoleonic wars, where whole infantry battalions caught disordered by cavalry were effectively obliterated in minutes.[49]

The Spanish advantage was more in speed than power, though the two acted in concert. A *corrida de rejoneadores,* a mounted bullfight, might give some sense of what the Indians were up against. Posting outlying guards gave the Incas little protection against surprise, for Spanish horses could overrun a picket line and reach the main body ahead of the fleeing pickets, and at times in advance of the news of their coming. The conquistadors were keenly aware of the importance of horses to their success, and so long as the conquest proceeded in Peru, horses were exceedingly expensive if they were for sale at all.[50] An unequivocal measure of the importance accorded horses can be seen in the division of booty after Cajamarca: the horseman's share was, on average, twice that of his dismounted fellow.[51]

Indeed, the conquistadors seem to have regarded their horses almost as partners in the enterprise; Bernal Díaz del Castillo lists "all the mares and horses that were shipped" in Cortés's expedition by name along with the names of their owners—and of those deemed competent to ride them in battle, for the two were not always the same.[52] That the horse's owner would, at the moment of battle, relinquish his place in the saddle to one who could better fight there brings us up against a ruthless Spanish realism; social pretension counted for little against value in combat. The lack of reported debate concerning who was chosen to ride and by what process is perhaps an even more remarkable commentary; these men were rampant individualists, sticklers on points of personal pride and honor, but on this point there seems to have been no need for debate: they knew. Cortés's comments in his Third Letter to King Charles on the plight of a riderless mare wounded by the Amerindians early in the siege of Tenochtitlan provides eloquent testimony to this feeling:

> That day there were no casualties in our camp, except that when we emerged from our ambush, some of the horsemen collided and one fell from his mare, which rushed straight at the enemy, who shot at her and wounded her with arrows; whereupon, seeing how badly she was being treated, she returned to us but so badly wounded that she died that night. And although we were much grieved by this loss, for our lives were dependent on the horses, we were pleased that she had not perished at the hands of the enemy, as we thought would happen, for their joy at capturing her would have exceeded the grief caused by the death of their companions.[53]

We should not make too much of Pedro Pizarro's pungent assessment of the relative value of horse and foot in the siege of Cusco, for it relates to special circumstances, but it is worth repeating: the horsemen, he said, "did all the fighting, because the rest were non-fighters and infantrymen, and these last did but little for the Indians hold them in slight account."[54] It is surely indicative that the three illustrations in Poma de Ayala depicting actual combat between Spaniards and Andeans show only mounted Spanish combatants.[55]

3. Tactical Skill and Cohesion

The self-confident skill with which the conquistadors used the instruments at their disposal welded them together into a seamless whole, multiplying their impact. Cohesion, the social force that holds units together in combat and that makes the difference between a unit and a mob of individuals, was a Spanish strong point. Spanish fighting men were notoriously fractious in victory. The conquest of Peru offers rich examples, but under pressure they stuck together with a seemingly instinctive solidarity rarely matched in the history of war. Furthermore, their cohesion and the discipline through which it manifested itself in combat was not mechanical and unthinking; Spanish fighting men invariably showed high levels of initiative. Leadership emerged from the ranks when needed and was followed with panache. The attitude of Pizarro's force before Cajamarca, overwhelmingly outnumbered and facing the unknown no less than the Andeans, is indicative; in the words of a near-contemporary chronicler, "On that day, all were knights," and through the long watches of the night *hidalgos* took their turn standing guard.[56]

The Spanish quickness to appreciate Andean tactical vulnerabilities and the use of surprise played a decisive role. Spanish leaders were keenly aware of the multiplying effect of surprise on combat effectiveness, quickly learned how to apply it most effectively, and took pains to achieve it. Most of the Spanish captains had experience fighting Amerindians in Panama, Nicaragua, and the Caribbean, a point rightly emphasized by James Lockhart;[57] they gained more during their trek south along the Ecuadorian coast. They learned, and their knowledge served them well. On the pivotal occasion of Cajamarca, Pizarro was able to exploit the psychological shock of the unknown by capturing Atahualpa and slaughtering the bulk of his retinue.[58] Such an action was not repeated, but it did not have to be.

The Spaniards' awareness of the importance of tactical coordination in combat is evident most clearly in their treatment and handling of their limited equine resources, but extended to all areas. The Spaniards fought as integrated units, sword, pike, and shot acting in seemingly automatic concert with horse. Tactical finesse and solidity had become a Spanish hallmark in the Wars of Italy (1494–1559), a fact reflected in the retention of an uncommonly large number of sixteenth-century Spanish military terms in modern English.[59] Few of the men who fought under Francisco and Hernando Pizarro, Diego de Almagro, and Sebastián de Benalcázar in the conquest of Peru were soldiers, but militarily useful skills, values, and patterns of socialization were so deeply embedded and so widespread in early sixteenth-century Spanish society that the distinction is, from our standpoint, functionally unimportant.

This is not to imply that the Incas were tactically inept; to the contrary, the Incas showed remarkable tactical perspicacity and adapted quickly to the capabilities and limitations of Spanish arms. The battle of Vilcaconga, for example, fought in mid-November of 1533 when the Incas had virtually no experience in contesting Spanish arms in the open field, was a classic ambush in which the Incas displayed exquisite timing and a thorough understanding of Spanish vulnerabilities, exploiting every advantage at their disposal. Catching the Spanish advance guard under Hernando de Soto at dusk after a long day's march, overextended and exhausted, the Andeans attacked down a slope and by surprise, using terrain to perfection.[60] Exploiting a shrewdly chosen topographical advantage, darkness, and Spanish fatigue, they came as close to success as they ever did in a major engagement, overrunning and very nearly overwhelming the tired men and horses—Pedro Pizarro reports that the Indians got in so close that they even laid hands on the horses' tails—but de Soto and his men fought their way to the top of the slope and held out until relief arrived, killing some eight hundred Andeans and suffering five Spaniards and two horses killed and a dozen or so horses wounded.[61] It was a close call, and the Spanish suffered greater loss in men and horses in this engagement than in all the rest combined, but they prevailed by sheer hard fighting.

4. Spanish Missile Weapons

Spanish cannon, crossbows, and harquebuses were not in themselves decisive in the overthrow of the Incas. Their role was a supporting one, and here the contrast with Mexico, where cannon and harquebuses were an essential element of Spanish success, stands out clearly.[62] In Peru, by contrast, Spanish missile weapons were no more than useful auxiliaries except perhaps in the siege of Cusco, where harquebuses and crossbows must have been important, though detailed confirmation is lacking. Cannon were more of an encumbrance than a necessity.

At bottom, the power of Spanish weapons, horses, and cohesion gave the conquistadors a tactical advantage that was all but insurmountable, except under special circumstances the Spanish generally managed to avoid. The Incas wiped out several relief expeditions sent to the aid of the beleaguered garrison of Cusco by ambushing them in mountain defiles and rolling rocks and trees down from above, but this was the exception; more to the point was the ease with which the Spanish-led forces routed the immense Indian host under Quizo Yupanqui before Lima in August of 1536.[63] John Elliott is probably correct in his belief that a balanced force of as few as fifty Spaniards, horse and foot, could hold their own against a numerically superior force of Amerindians—on reasonably open and level terrain—unless overcome by exhaustion.[64]

STRATEGIC ANALYSIS

It remains to show how these technological and tactical elements were brought into play by Pizarro, his followers, and his rivals, and by the Incas—that is, to integrate them into a strategic analysis of the conquest.[65] As I have suggested above, it would be a mistake to assume that the tiny band of Spaniards that turned inland to invade the core of the Inca empire in September of 1532 did so armed with brute force and ignorance, ill-prepared for the trials that lay before them. There can be no doubt that the Spanish were surprised by the geography and climatic extremes that they encountered in penetrating Tawantinsuyu. The Andean geography has no true analogue elsewhere, and the invaders had no experience of anything remotely similar; they were amazed as well by the richness of the land, both in human resources and in portable wealth.[66] Similarly, there can be little doubt as to their astonishment and apprehension at the size of the Inca's armies. But we must remember that much of what we know about their initial reaction to the Inca's empire comes from accounts written to impress Charles I and his court with the richness of their conquests and the audacity of their deeds.

In the first instance, they had provided themselves with translators: three men taken from the complement of an Inca trading vessel seized by Bartolomé Ruiz during his reconnaissance south along the Peruvian coast in 1527, and taught Spanish in the intervening years.[67] Their services were invaluable during the initial stages of the invasion.[68] This advantage was ameliorated by the fact that they, and whatever other translators Pizarro might have obtained, apparently were not conversant with the nuances of court Quechua (Atahualpa seems to have had little difficulty in issuing orders to his officials while in captivity) nor well informed on the inner workings of the Inca state. They may well have used their position to personal advantage on occasion, but this misses the point.[69] The information they possessed was potentially of great value, and Pizarro and his associates were no fools. Their captors had every opportunity to question them at length on the nature of the Inca's domains, resources, and military assets and no doubt did so, obtaining valuable, if mundane, information.

Pizarro's decision in early 1531 to land his expedition over three hundred miles north of the previously discovered Inca town of Tumbes on the Gulf of Guayaquil also is suggestive. Little that Pizarro did lacked purpose, and the argument that he exposed his men to needless delay and torment by landing them so far north is unconvincing.[70] That there is no evidence of significant disaffection among his band during its arduous progress south along the coast is powerfully indicative, for conquistadors were not given to suffering inept or dilatory leaders gladly. Pizarro must have proceeded deliberately, basing his decisions on the systematic seeking out and exploitation of information sources of which no record survives. And this should not be surprising, for Iberians were notoriously closemouthed about intelligence, and Extremadurans—like the Pizarros—were notoriously the most closemouthed of all. The Portuguese dispatch of agents to the Indian subcontinent well in advance of Vasco da Gama's voyage is a classic example, and the Spanish were no less sensitive to the value of good intelligence . . . and the penalties of a loose mouth.[71]

A close study of early Spanish maps of the Caribbean, for example, reveals that accurate plotting of the landmass proceeded in advance of the recorded voyages of discovery.[72] In any case, the confidence evident in Pizarro's decision to move inland to confront the Inca emperor at Cajamarca suggests something more than reliance on blind luck.

In the second instance, Pizarro and his band possessed an impressive amount of practical experience relevant to the task at hand, fighting the hostile geography and indigenous peoples of the Americas. Granted, the heights of the Andes were to confront them with problems for which there was no Old World precedent, but the jungles of Panama also had posed challenges for which European experience was irrelevant.

The tactical shock of the initial military encounters was a genuine surprise to both parties, but it was a far greater one to the Incas, fighting uphill against a steep technological gradient. It is easy to underestimate the surprise of the Incas and the other Andean peoples, however, which amounted at times to utter bewilderment. The desperate, stoic courage that Inca armies displayed in battle on occasion—Vilcaconga and the battles before Quito come to mind—serves only to underline the profundity of that surprise. Advanced technology was decisive, but only under conditions that its possessors forecast with reasonable accuracy. The failure to appreciate this point reflects a traditional, excessively narrow definition of technology. The lesson is that a society or civilization can hardly anticipate and effectively deal with the impact of entire categories of technology of which it has gained knowledge only recently.

Inca institutions came under stain in the early encounters as well. The fact that the legitimacy of Inca rule was accepted by many *ayllus* only under compulsion, and the inability of Inca ideology to provide a viable alternate focus for dynastic loyalty in the wake of Atahualpa's capture combined to provide the conquistadors with a series of opportunities. Here the Spanish and Andean worldviews are thrown into stark contrast by their strategic repercussions: on the one hand, we have a befuddled Calcuchima meekly surrendering to Pizarro, presumably on orders from an Atahualpa plainly acting under compulsion; on the other, we have Diego de Almagro returning from Chile in the spring of 1537 to raise the siege of Cusco, only to claim control of the better part of Peru from the Pizarros and fight them for it, all the while negotiating with Manco Inca, and at no great loss to the Spanish cause.

Whatever their internal differences and whatever their proclivity to settle them with the sword, the Spanish owed allegiance to the same emperor and the same church on terms that all understood. Their long-term strategic objectives were the same: to carve the Inca domains, extract wealth from the Andean communities, and convert the indigenous peoples to Catholicism. It was clearly understood among the Spanish, if not among the Incas, that Almagro's negotiations with Manco Inca were purely tactical; while they may initially have caused Manco to take heart, no Spaniard seems to have felt seriously threatened by them.[73]

Inca strategic objectives from Atahualpa's death through the collapse of Manco Inca's second rebellion were to recapture their domains, to restore Inca rule, and to drive out the invaders. Following the collapse of the rebellion, they were to remain sovereign over Vilcabamba, the remote remnant of empire that they had managed to retain. Their chances of succeeding in this were, as we can appreciate and they no doubt suspected, minimal.

CONCLUSIONS

As many recent studies attest, several factors, including political discontent with Inca rule, the impact of epidemic diseases, and the assistance of Andean allies, contributed to the Spanish destruction of Tawantinsuyu. At the same time, the role of technology, tactical skill, and leadership have been less well understood. In the early stages of the struggle the superiority of Spanish arms, strategy, and tactics proved decisive. Indeed, as this study has attempted to demonstrate, a number of important conclusions can be drawn from the military encounters between the Spanish invaders and the Andean peoples in the years from 1532 to 1539.

First, the Spanish advantage in the technology of war was, in fact, a vital factor in their stunning military victories. This was so, however, not just because of the steepness of the technological gradient against which the Inca armies had to struggle. That would no doubt have been the case in the long run; as we have indicated above, the Spanish technological advantage was all but overwhelming, in both weaponry and the manner in which the weapons were employed in battle. Moreover, we are not concerned purely with differences in military capability on a one-for-one basis; rather, our focus has been on the way combatant groups maintained their cohesion under stress. Cultural and religious factors are crucial components of cohesion, and these, acting in conjunction with superior technology, proved an important Spanish advantage. But while Inca defeat was probably inevitable sooner or later, its reality was, in the event, heavily shaped by the fact that Pizarro and his men understood the nature and degree of their advantage and took steps to maximize it to a degree not commonly appreciated.

Second, the Incas responded intelligently and well to the Spanish challenge, pressing to the limit the means at their disposal. Indeed, tactically the Inca commanders were extraordinarily quick studies; they simply did not possess the means to profit from their understanding of the Spaniards' weaknesses and limitations. This was true strategically as well. Significantly, those bounds at the strategic level were set as much by ideological factors as by technology; the vulnerability of the Inca empire to the capture of Atahualpa and the instinctive Spanish appreciation of that vulnerability are the critical case in point. The strengths of the Inca system can be seen most clearly in the impressive logistical and strategic planning behind Manco Inca's great rebellion of 1536. If it could have been done with the resources available, it would have been. It is difficult to fault Manco and his subordinates in regard to staff work, courage, or leadership.

Third, the shock of military contact across so vast a cultural and technological gap was so great that significant technology transfer proved impossible before the Andeans' ultimate defeat. On occasion, individual Inca captains used captured Spanish swords and helmets to considerable effect, notably in the siege of Cusco, but that was about that.[74] Some twenty years, or two generations, were needed for the indigenous populations of the Americas to absorb effectively the military technologies that might have enabled them to survive on their own cultural terms. In 1564 Spanish authorities in Peru discovered large stores of weapons secretly manufactured and stockpiled in preparation for revolt.[75] Significantly, the stockpiled weapons included large numbers of pikes, the one weapon that might have enabled the Andeans to prevail against the Spanish horse. At about the same time, the Chilean Araucanians, arguably the most successful indigenous resistors of Spanish penetration, were learning the use of pikes, as well as how to breed horses and ride them in combat.

Here, the importance of the steepness of the technology gradient is particularly apparent; it took the Spanish only a year or so to learn the same lesson in Italy a half century earlier. Scattered by armored French mounted men-at-arms and Swiss pikemen at the Battle of Seminara in June of 1495, Gonsalvo de Córdova's men had learned to cope with the problem by the next year and proved themselves masters of pike drill— if not quite the equals of the Swiss—at Cerignola in April of 1503.[76] As an important subsidiary lesson, the Inca hosts provide the military historian with a limiting case to establish just how little ill-equipped infantry in loose formations, however well motivated and courageous, can do against even small numbers of aggressive and skillful cavalry.

Finally, having noted the way in which underlying cultural factors manifest themselves in combat, it is also important to observe that the way wars are fought frequently exercises a dominant influence over the ensuing peace. It would seem that the suddenness and totality of the Inca military defeat lessened the amount and scope of cultural transfer in other areas of human endeavor. Having learned to despise the Indians as armed foes, the conquistadors and their descendants were ill-disposed to respect them as subjects. This cultivated contempt—which, make no mistake, was partly fueled by a realistic fear of Andean courage—can be seen in Garcilasco de la Vega's condescending description of Indians fleeing in blind panic from horses in the streets in later years.[77] Might one see in the subsequent sorry tale of Spanish exploitation of indigenous labor resources in Peru a reflection of the enormous technological and tactical imbalance between Andean and conquistador in initial military contact at the cutting edge?

NOTES

1. Cortés landed at Veracruz on 22 April 1519; Tenochtitlan surrendered on 13 August 1521, just under two years and four months later.

2. Notably by Inga Clendinnen, *Ambivalent Conquests: Maya and Spaniard in Yucatan, 1517–1570* (Cambridge, Eng., 1987); Clendinnen's masterful comprehension and elucidation of guerrilla warfare conducted in an environment unfamiliar to modern scholars marks her work as seminal.

3. Early explanations often attributed the conquistadors' success to divine assistance, and in the early nineteenth century phrenology was used to explain the "inferiority" of native Peruvians. For a useful summation, see Waldemar Espinoza Soriano, *La destrucción del imperio de los incas* (Lima, 1973), 12–19.

4. See, for example, J. H. Elliott, "The Spanish Conquest and Settlement of America," *Colonial Latin America*, vol. 1 of *Cambridge History of Latin America* (Cambridge, Eng., 1984; henceforth *CHLA*), 174; Nathan Wachtel, "The Indian and the Spanish Conquest," *CHLA*, 210–211, notes that "it was the Indians themselves who provided Cortés and Pizarro with the bulk of their conquering armies, which were as large as the Aztec and Inca armies against which they fought."

5. John Hemming, *The Conquest of the Incas* (London, 1970), 28, citing, among other sources, E. Wagner Stern, *The Effect of Smallpox on the Destiny of the Amerindian* (Boston, 1945) and P. M. Ashburn, *The Ranks of Death: A Medical History of the Conquest of America* (New York, 1947).

6. Geoffrey W. Conrad and Arthur A. Demarest, *Religion and Empire: The Dynamics of Aztec and Inca Expansionism* (Cambridge, Eng., 1984), 138; the core of Conrad and Demarest's argument, summarized on page 136, is that Inca royal ancestor worship, manifested in split inheritance, left title to a growing proportion of productive agricultural resources in the hands of dead rulers and their heirs. This forced reigning Incas to seek additional lands through conquest and led to increased cultivation of marginal lands.

7. Wachtel, "The Indian and the Spanish Conquest," 210.

8. Carl von Clausewitz, *On War,* translated by Michael Howard and Peter Paret (Princeton, N.J., 1976), 80.

9. The political objectives of revolutionary France no doubt seemed extreme to most contemporary Europeans, as did the social and political forces that the French revolution unleashed and then harnessed so effectively to war. But this was true in an objective sense only against the backdrop of the Age of Reason; in the broad sweep of history they were modest.

10. Alonso Enríquez de Guzmán, *Libro de la vida y costumbres de Don Alonso Enríquez de Guzmán* (1543), translated by C. R. Markham, Hakluyt Society, 1st ser., 29 (London, 1862), 101, quoted in Hemming, *Conquest of the Incas,* 204.

11. Hemming, *Conquest of the Incas,* 204.

12. William H. Prescott, *The Conquest of Peru* (New York, 1847).

13. John V. Murra, "Andean Societies before 1532," *CHLA,* 60; see also James D. Cockcroft, "Prescott and His Sources: A Critical Appraisal," *Hispanic American Historical Review* (henceforth *HAHR*) 48, 1 (February 1968): 59–74.

14. Murra, "Andean Societies before 1532," 60.

15. *The Broken Spears: The Aztec Account of the Conquest of Mexico,* edited by Miguel Leon-Portilla, translated by Angel María Garibay K. and Lysander Kemp (Boston, 1962).

16. John V. Murra and Nathan Wachtel, introduction to *Anthropological History of Andean Polities,* edited by John V. Murra, Nathan Wachtel, and Jacques Revel (Cambridge, Eng., 1986), 2.

17. Murra, "Andean Societies before 1532," 64; for the difficulties in estimating preconquest population figures, see Noble David Cook, "Population Data for Indian Peru: Sixteenth and Seventeenth Centuries," *HAHR* 62, 1 (February 1982): 73–75. John Hemming, *Conquest of the Incas* (London, 1970), 349, 604–605, gives a useful discussion of the methodology behind various population estimates on the way to his own estimate of 6,300,000.

18. Hemming, *Conquest of the Incas,* 65, 68, credits the Inca general Calcuchima as commanding thirty-five thousand effectives in the early spring of 1533, based on the testimony of Hernando Pizarro, who saw the host and watched Calcuchima's scribes tick off the numbers on their *quipus.* Hemming credits the general Quisquis with commanding thirty thousand at the same time, and the third major Inca force in the field, under the general Ruminavi, was at least as large. Though hardly precise, these figures seem credible, and the Inca armies had, if anything, probably declined in size since the previous fall.

19. James Lockhart, *The Men of Cajamarca: A Social and Biographical Study of the First Conquerors of Peru* (Austin, Tex., 1972), xiii, 10; Hemming, *Conquest of the Incas,* 26. I agree with Lockhart, 18, that Pizarro's men were not soldiers in the modern sense of the word.

20. Hemming, *Conquest of the Incas,* 39, 555, citing a letter written by Hernando Pizarro shortly after the fact. Hemming, 630, supports Pizarro's estimate with a convincing analysis of the layout and size of the town square in which the ambush occurred. Francisco Xerez, *Verdadera relación de la conquista del Perú y Provincia del Cuzco* (Seville, 1534) in *Historiadores primitivos de Indias,* edited by Enrique de Uedia (Madrid, 1923), 2:327, credits Atahualpa with a total force of fifty thousand men during his approach to Cajamarca.

21. Hemming, *Conquest of the Incas,* 190–191, 577–578.

22. There is no set formula for comparative strategic assessment. Factors other than those I have selected might be legitimately isolated for analysis, and I would focus on other factors in addressing another problem. I have approached the problem from an operational perspective, focusing on those elements that seem to have affected the historical actors most in terms of their effect on strategic decisions. That is another way of saying that I do not believe in the inevitability of outcomes and conduct myself accordingly—as did the actors themselves, though in quite different ways. While it is easy for us to perceive with the hindsight of four and a half centuries that the long-term Inca chances for victory were virtually nil, the actors themselves did not see it that way. It would be singularly unrealistic to evaluate their actions and the situations that framed them as if they did.

23. Murra, "Andean Societies before 1532," 63: most of the empire's populace had fallen under Inca control only within the previous three or four generations.

24. See Steve J. Stern, "The Rise and Fall of Indian–White Alliances: A Regional View of 'Conquest' History," *HAHR* 61, 3 (August 1981): 461–491, for a penetrating analysis of the underlying factors. The *ayllu* was the basic social unit of Andean society. Originally it represented an endogamous lineage claiming descent from a common set of ancestors; after 1532 it formed the basic kin unit, allocating land and labor duties for the Andean communities. See Brooke Larson, *Colonialism and Agrarian Transformation in Bolivia: Cochabamba, 1550–1900* (Princeton, N.J., 1988), 333, and other scattered references.

25. Stern, "Indian–White Alliances," 472–475.

26. Murra, "Andean Societies before 1532," 64.

27. The reason for this seeming paradox is that the weight of forage consumed by pack and draft animals quickly exceeds the amount that they can carry or pull, setting an inflexible limit on the maximum distance they can proceed from sources of supply. In classical times, the limit was three or four days' march, according to Donald W. Engels, *Alexander the Great and the Logistics of the Macedonian Army* (Berkeley, Calif., 1978), 20–23. The development of the horse collar and pivoting front axle in medieval Europe improved the utility of

drayage, but the limit was relaxed, not eliminated; by the 1860s it was about one hundred miles from base, according to Martin van Creveld, *Supplying War: Logistics from Wallenstein to Patton* (Cambridge, Eng., 1977), 113.

28. Hemming, *Conquest of the Incas*, 68.

29. This was in the later stages of the Quito campaign, according to Hemming, *Conquest of the Incas*, 165, quoting Agustín de Zárate, *Historia del descubrimiento y conquista del Perú* (Antwerp, 1555).

30. Hemming, *Conquest of the Incas*, 203.

31. Ibid., 216.

32. For a useful discussion see Terence Wise, *The Conquistadores* (London, 1980), esp. 12–14; though intended primarily for hobbyists, this little book, lavishly illustrated with photographs, drawings, and color reconstructions of Spanish and indigenous combatants by artist Angus McBride, is solidly based on archaeological and textual evidence.

33. Hand-held weapons are sometimes called shock weapons, but the typology is misleading since shock effect is a psychological distinction rather than a technological one.

34. Pedro Pizarro, *Relación del descubrimiento y conquista de los reinos del Perú* (1571), translated and edited by Philip Ainsworth Means as *Relation of the Discovery and Conquest of the Kingdoms of Peru* (New York, 1921), 2:302–303.

35. The relevant formulas are $F = ma$ (force equals mass times acceleration) and $v = at$ (velocity equals acceleration times time), to obtain the velocity of the weapon or projectile, and $K_e = \frac{1}{2} mv^2$ (*kinetic energy equals one-half mass times velocity squared*), to obtain impact energy.

36. For the only rigorous, scientifically based analysis of the terminal ballistics of pre-gunpowder missile weapons of which I am aware, see Peter Jones, "The Target," appendix 3 in Robert Hardy, *Longbow: A Social and Military History* (Portsmouth, Eng., 1986), 204–208.

37. So far as we know, the problem was first solved with the development by the Sumerians of piercing axes of bronze in the third millennium B.C., as discussed by Yigael Yadin, *The Art of War in Biblical Lands in the Light of Archaeological Study* (London, 1963), 1:41–42.

38. Yadin, *Art of War in Biblical Lands*, 1:44–45, 60–61, 78–80.

39. The larger issue of whether the Andeans possessed bronze at all is, so far as I can determine, an open one. The Andeans apparently combined tin with copper to produce alloys harder than pure copper, at least on occasion; it is clear, however, that they did not possess meaningful numbers of weapons made of bronze sufficiently hard and tough to furnish a useful cutting edge, and I see no evidence that they possessed such weapons at all.

40. Hemming, *Conquest of the Incas*, 115–116, for his examination of museum examples of Inca weaponry; n. 37 above. My review of the secondary literature failed to turn up an unequivocal statement that bronze metallurgy was unknown to preconquest Andean societies; I conclude that it was on the basis of negative evidence and operational analysis. In light of the sparse utilitarian use of metals

of any kind by preconquest Andeans, the distinction between bronze and copper is an academic one in economic, political or cultural terms. Militarily, however, it is crucial: swords (and reasonably efficient spear and arrow heads) can be made of bronze, but not of copper. It speaks volumes for the undeveloped state of early American military history that the distinction has not been highlighted.

41. Felipe Guaman Poma de Ayala, *Nueva corónica y buen gobierno*, edited by John V. Murra, Rolena Adorno, and Jorge L. Urioste, 3 vols. (Madrid, 1987). Guaman Poma was separated from the conquest by at least a generation but seems to have rendered remembered details with fair accuracy.

42. Though heavier and therefore more cumbersome than a steel sword, the *macuahuitl* was capable of inflicting horrendous injuries on man or horse; it was limited by the brittleness of its obsidian blades and their ineffectiveness against steel armor. The Spanish accorded considerable respect to these weapons, which Bernal Díaz del Castillo called "fearsome broadswords," *The Discovery and Conquest of Mexico, 1517–1521*, translated by A. P. Maudslay (New York, 1956), 126. A careful reading of indigenous accounts suggests respect for the slashing efficiency of Spanish swords, an efficiency that the Aztecs could well appreciate, as shown in León–Portilla, *Broken Spears*, where the emphasis on slashing wounds inflicted by Spanish swords underlines the perceived effectiveness of such weapons; see particularly the account of the Spanish massacre of the Aztec leadership during the festival of Huitzilopochtli, 73–76. I am indebted to Philip George of Time-Life Books, a penetrating student of pre-Columbian Mexican culture and technology, for his elucidation of this point.

43. Four of the illustrations in Poma de Ayala depict Inca commanders in battle; of these, two—and the most recent two, including Calcuchima—are armed with slings. See Guaman Poma, *Nueva corónica*, 159, 163. Though we should not make too much of it, it is worth noting that the last use of the sling by a prominent leader in the European historical tradition was by David against Goliath, 1 Samuel 17. Significantly, the conflict in question was between an Iron Age culture and a Bronze Age one; see Yadin, *Art of War in Biblical Lands*, 1:32–74. See also James K. Muhly, "How Iron Technology Changed the Ancient World—and Gave The Philistines a Military Edge," *Biblical Archaeology Review* 8, 6 (November/December 1982): 40–54.

44. Hemming, *Conquest of the Incas*, 192, reaches this conclusion based on contemporary Spanish accounts.

45. Elliott, "Conquest and Settlement of America," 175.

46. Lockhart, *Men of Cajamarca*, 121–122.

47. Robert B. Cunninghame Graham, *The Horses of the Conquest*, edited by Robert M. Denhardt, (Norman, Okla., 1949), 17–20.

48. John Keegan, *The Face of Battle* (New York, 1973), 153–155.

49. This did not happen often, but that was because European infantry was the beneficiary of five centuries of experience in avoiding and repelling cavalry charges. A British brigade caught unexpectedly in flank by Polish lancers at the Battle of Albuera in the Peninsular campaign suffered casualties of 85.3 percent,

75.9 percent, and 61.6 percent, respectively, in the three battalions nearest the point of impact, according to Philip Haythornthwaite, *Weapons and Equipment of the Napoleonic Wars* (Poole, Dorset, Eng., 1979), 52. These were first-rate, bayonet-armed infantry who knew exactly what to do; the fourth battalion had time to form square and was effectively untouched. The Inca hosts at best were worse off than these men at worst.

50. El Inca Garcilaso de la Vega, *Royal Commentaries of the Incas*, translated by Harold Livermore (Austin, Tex., 1966) 1:580–581. Xerez, *Verdadera relación*, 343, has horses going for around twenty-five hundred ducats of gold (*el precio común*) during the interlude after the distribution of the treasure at Cajamarca; this was nearly a third of a horseman's share of the booty and about half of a foot combatant's. To put these figures in perspective, in 1534 the cost to the Spanish crown of a war galley, fitted with masts and sails but without artillery, was between 240 and 350 ducats, according to article 4, document 28, in vol. 1 of the Colección Sanz de Barutell (Simancas) (Museo Naval, Madrid), and the salaries of a galley captain and an ordinary soldier assigned to the galleys were 7 ducats and 1½ ducats per month, respectively; see John F. Guilmartin, Jr., *Gunpowder and Galleys: Changing Technology and Mediterranean Warfare at Sea in the Sixteenth Century* (Cambridge, Eng., 1974), 293.

51. Xerez, *Verdadera relación*, 343; a horseman's share was 8,880 gold ducats and 372 silver marks, while a foot combatant's was 4,400 ducats and 181 marks.

52. Díaz, *Discovery and Conquest of Mexico*, 38–39. Cunninghame Graham, *The Horses of the Conquest*, 63.

53. Hernán Cortés, *Hernán Cortés: Letters from Mexico*, translated by Anthony Pagden (London, 1986), 252.

54. Pizarro, *Relation of the Discovery*, 2:303.

55. Poma de Ayala, *Nueva corónica*, 2, 394, 404, 434. These depict the death of Quizo Yupanqui before Lima (pierced, perhaps metaphorically, by a Spanish lance), the relief of Cusco (in symbolic fashion, with a mounted Santiago brandishing his sword in triumph above a prostrate Indian), and a Spanish defeat in Hernández Girón's rebellion against the crown.

56. Hemming, *Conquest of the Incas*, 35–36, quoting the account attributed to Cristóbal de Mena, *La conquista del Perú, llamada la Nueva Castilla* (Seville, 1534); Pedro Pizarro reports that during the night "many of the Spaniards made water without knowing it out of sheer terror." Pizarro, *Relation of the Discovery*, 1:177–180.

57. Lockhart, *Men of Cajamarca*, 23–24. The same point applied to the rank and file to an only slightly lesser degree: 52 of the 101 men present at Cajamarca whose experience prior to 1532 is known or can be surmised had spent five years or more in the Indies.

58. For Spanish devices to amplify the shock of surprise, hanging bells on the horses and signaling the attack with trumpet blasts and the discharge of a cannon, see Pizarro, *Relation of the Discovery*, 1:183–184.

59. For example, "colonel" from *cabo de colunela* (head of the column) and

"point blank" from *punto de blanco* (pointed at the *blanco* or "white," a technical artillery term; the equivalent in modern Spanish is *quemarropa*, clothing-burning range).

60. Pedro Cieza de León, *Obras completas* (Madrid, 1984–1985), 1:304–305; originally *Parte primera de la crónica del Perú* (Seville, 1553); Pizarro, *Relation of the Discovery*, 1:236–240: "There was a sharp slope [which has an upward incline more than a league long] which it seemed to the Indians would cause the horses to be weary when they finished going up the grade, and [the Indians thought that] they would avail themselves the more than if the land had been flat, and so it almost turned out to be."

61. Cieza de León, *Obras completas*, loc. cit.; Hemming, *Conquest of the Incas*, 14.

62. Cortés's letters and Bernal Díaz del Castillo describe close coordination between horse and foot, shot and shock, from beginning to end, revealing a closely woven tactical tapestry of which harquebus shot and crossbow bolts were essential. Gunpowder weapons were particularly important in the siege of Tenochtitlan, and both cannon and small oared vessels armed with swivel guns, *bergantines*, were essential to the reduction of the city. In Peru, by contrast, missile weapons were ordinarily a luxury.

63. Hemming, *Conquest of the Incas*, 212.

64. Elliott, "Conquest and Settlement of America," 175–176.

65. Strategic analysis provides us with an invaluable analytical lens through which to view initial contact between cultures, for military strategy by its very nature seeks to bring into play every cultural, social, and economic strength and weakness that opposing societies possess. This is particularly true when the stakes are high and recognized as such, as was the case here. But strategy is exceedingly subtle and context dependent, not easily broken down into discrete components as with technology and tactics. Our analysis is therefore best done by example, using a selective operational recounting of the conquest as a framework.

66. Murra, "Andean Societies before 1532," 61–62.

67. Pizarro, *Relation of the Discovery*, 1:138–139; Hemming, *Conquest of the Incas*, 25.

68. The parallel with Doña Marina or La Malinche, Cortés's Indian mistress and confidante, is inescapable; La Malinche, however, initially spoke no Spanish, and intermediate translators were required.

69. Hemming, *Conquest of the Incas*, 82.

70. Hemming, *Conquest of the Incas*, 27, labels the decision inexplicable.

71. The epic travels of Alfonso de Pavia and Pero de Covilha, who visited India and East Africa during the 1490s, the latter ending up in Ethiopia after the death of the former, are a dramatic example, though da Gama's use of a local pilot, Ibn Madgid, to guide his expedition from the East African coast to Calicut is perhaps more characteristic; see Francisco Mello, *Viagens de Pero de Covilha* (Lisbon, 1988). I am indebted to Timothy Coates of the University of Minnesota for this citation.

72. Donald Keith, "The Molasses Reef Wreck" (Ph.D. diss., Texas A&M University, 1987); Keith, personal communication to the author.

73. It is worth noting that the Aztecs stand comparison to the Incas surprisingly well in this area. Impressed by the administrative and governmental achievements of the Incas and perhaps overly struck by the unabashedly fragmented character of the Aztec empire and the bloodthirsty nature of Aztec religion, scholars have tended to take for granted the Mexicans' remarkable resilience. The Mexicans were quick to recognize the threat posed by Montezuma's collaboration while a Spanish captive, and they took decisive action. The contrast between the relatively leisurely Spanish sojourn at Cajamarca of nearly a year and the swift and savage Aztec retaliation leading to Montezuma's death and the nearly catastrophic fighting Spanish retreat from Tenochtitlan, the Noche Triste, is instructive. The Aztecs were briefly able to battle the Spanish and smallpox at the same time; the Incas were unable to come to grips effectively with the former alone, until Manco Inca restored the uncompromised and unchallenged sovereignty of the Inca in 1536. We should not be surprised at the contrast in light of the Mexicans' higher level of technological development, notably in the possession of a glyphic writing system and markedly more advanced weaponry.

74. Pizarro, Relation of the Discovery, 2:313–315.

75. Hemming, Conquest of the Incas, 305–306.

76. Charles W. C. Oman, A History of the Art of War in the Sixteenth Century (London, 1937), 51–53.

77. Garcilaso de la Vega, Royal Commentaries of the Incas, 1:581–582.

PART TWO

European and Andean Resources in the Encounter Period

THREE

"Nos Hazen Mucha Ventaja": The Early European Perception of Andean Achievement

John V. Murra

The effort to understand the Andean achievement before the European invasion has been part of a steady inquiry that began long before 1532, the date of peninsular success—the cataclysm that destroyed the Inca state, "the world upside down," a *pachakuti,* as seen from the Andean side.

The year 1532 is a late date in Europe's penetration or even awareness of the Andes. Decades earlier, the Portuguese are alleged to have heard of a mighty empire to the west; thirty years before Pizarro, Sir Thomas More was supposed to have used descriptions of the Inca as a model for his *Utopia.*[1] In 1525 Aleixo García, a Portuguese, walked up the Andes from Brazil in the company of a raiding group of Guaraní.[2]

The penetration of the Andes from the Pacific side was long delayed and with it our awareness of Andean civilizations as including a significant maritime component. Recent archaeological research in both Ecuador and Peru attempts to redress this balance.[3] Almost twenty years before King Atahualpa was captured and executed by Francisco Pizarro, another European had contemplated a southward adventure: on 29 September 1513, Vasco Núñez de Balboa, accompanied by sixty-six soldiers and uncounted Panamanian allies, took possession of the Southern Sea in the name of Ferdinand the Catholic. A settler at the Isthmus since 1509 and in the Americas since 1500, Vasco Núñez was reported to have maintained unusual face-to-face relations with the aboriginal population.

From one of their ethnic lords Vasco Núñez learned that across the mountains there was another sea; on its shores lived peoples who wore even more gold ornaments. They were said to be traveling in boats, with oars and sails, much like the Europeans. In exchange for the gold, the sailors were said to take cotton cloth.

In later years, legend claimed that Comogre, Vasco Núñez's informant or his son, had been talking about Peru and its riches. However, if one examines the contemporary early reports in the Spanish archives, it is plain that these did not refer to the Andes but dealt with populations in the vicinity of what later became the city of Panamá. Most of the reports still stress the opportunities in the spice trade, across the Pacific, which had been stimulated by Magellan's voyage. Núñez's notarized report of his sighting in 1513 lists the names of the sixty-six men accompanying him in the "discovery" of the Pacific, among them Francisco Pizarro, one priest, one sailor, a Sicilian, and Ñuflo de Olano, "black in color."

Vasco Núñez had every intention of continuing the search for the gold and the ships reported from the Southern Sea. He was deliberately and laboriously prevented from undertaking the search. Spanish historiography is unanimous in condemning those who committed the judicial murder of Vasco Núñez.[4] His enemies, while unable to repeat his crossing of the Isthmus until 1519, prevented him from sailing the South Seas. The Catholic king's designation of Vasco Núñez as governor of the Southern Seas was for naught.

The person whose career best links the frustration of Vasco Núñez's quest with the eventually successful invasion of Peru nineteen years later was the lawyer Gaspar de Espinosa. He was a member of a notorious merchant clan—bankers in Seville and Antwerp, slave traders and politicians—whose role in early American history deserves thorough study.[5] Espinosa's skills at court and in the Caribbean were widely recognized. Although a royal decree prohibited lawyers from settling, Espinosa arrived at the Isthmus as the *alcalde mayor,* a kind of federal inspector of the first Spanish administration on the American mainland. His salary may indicate his formal position: by royal decree he earned less than either the treasurer or the bookkeeper of the settlement.

Espinosa was the functionary who devised the bureaucratic maneuvers that prevented Vasco Núñez from carrying out the exploration and settlement of the Pacific shore. It took Espinosa close to six years to bring Vasco Núñez to the scaffold after having ruined him by imposing fines for real and fabricated misdemeanors. The man who went to fetch the *adelantado* for Vasco Núñez's beheading was Francisco Pizarro. The detailed record of the trial is still unavailable, but one of its consequences was that the *alcalde mayor* inherited several small ships that Vasco Núñez had been building on the Pacific shore.⁶ The date of the murder, 1519, is also when Espinosa and his allies settled at Panamá, on the Pacific side of the isthmus. The new crowd took possession of the ocean on behalf of the crown, as if the original testimony had never been filed. Among the legal witnesses of the "discovery" was Francisco Pizarro.

Unlike Vasco Núñez, who meant to explore southward, Espinosa, Pizarro, Andagoya, and their friends diverted the confiscated ships and some built later to adventures and settlements in Honduras and Nicaragua, where they soon ran into Cortés and Alvarado's people moving south from Mexico and Guatemala.

There are still many lacunae in our knowledge of the early exploration of the Pacific: we can document archaeologically that one or more sea routes existed between what today are Ecuador and Guatemala, but the historical documentation is scarce.⁷ The early Spanish pilots who plied these seas frequently had a detailed knowledge of the coasts (see the Bartolomé Ruiz map of the gulf near the city of Panamá, dated 1526). Alvarado, in Guatemala, was informed of their movements; he also welcomed at his Guatemala court Portuguese sailors who had crossed the Pacific westward from the spice islands; in the 1520s, everyone knew of Magellan's eastward crossing from Europe.

Compared to such distances and Andean seafaring skills, the Spanish explorations south of Panamá seem modest and extremely slow. In 1522, one of Espinosa's protégés, Pascual de Andagoya, received permission to look for "the chief Birú," whose country was located somewhere near the present Panamanian-Colombian border. Birú was "rich," but again rumors pointed to greater wealth beyond, to the south. Again, there was talk of "traders" coming by sea, but contemporary details are few, even those provided by Andagoya, who wrote his detailed report in 1540, long after the riches of the central Andes had been located.⁸

When Andagoya was unable to continue his exploration, permission was granted to a partnership financed by Gaspar de Espinosa and led by Pizarro and Almagro. The text authorizing the expedition mentioned the spice trade; the leaders did not listen to Andagoya's advice to avoid the coastal winds and currents and strike out for the high seas. Pizarro's ship took years drifting down Colombia's coast. The main event of this laborious search occurred elsewhere: pilot Bartolomé Ruiz filed a report (1526?) about a seagoing raft he encountered in his explorations. He estimated the crew at twenty men; some of these he captured, some were trained as interpreters at Pizarro's court, but these were not the "tongues" used in the later invasion. The pilot estimated the craft's capacity as "twenty toneles."[9] Among the cargo Ruiz listed textiles of cotton and wool, reminding him of Moorish clothing, all richly embroidered in red, yellow, and blue, with figures of birds, fish, trees; there were some objects of gold and silver "for barter" and a steelyard. But what attracted the pilot's eye was the bulk of the cargo: "all of these they were bringing to barter for seashells which they use for red and white beads—the whole vessel seemed to be freighted with them."[10]

Ruiz's report is short, but it is one of the few eyewitness accounts available about those years. It has been the object of a detailed study by Adám Szaszdi, who thinks that Ruiz did sight the arid coast of Peru but does not think he saw Chanchán or Chincha.[11] Still, the information provided by the captives kept Pizarro persevering. We have a short letter from Pizarro, dated 2 June 1527, addressed to an incoming governor at Panamá. His description follows closely Ruiz's report:

> [T]hey live by buying and selling, with ships on the sea and also by land and they deal by weighing; . . . and all of this Your Highness will see and hear through the information provided by this Indian who is being sent. . . . [Y]ou will know all about this land from him.[12]

Eventually Pizarro did reach the dry coast of Peru, beyond the mangrove swamps to the north. His flotilla faced the Inca port of Tumbes; his crew also heard rumors of the glories of Tumipampa, a major administrative center in the highlands of Ecuador. Those who went ashore brought back more jewelry; llamas, seagoing rafts, and other exotica were collected for the trip he planned back to Spain in 1529. When he returned, it took him weeks to travel from Panamá to Tumbes, not four years. This time he was accompanied by hundreds of men and horses, royal accountants, and assayers. From here on, attention was turned inland, and that story is well known.

During the confrontation with Atahualpa's army, the Europeans noticed that there was one other personage beyond the Inca king who was carried in a litter. Many years later, Pedro Pizarro recalled that his cousin, the marqués, had inquired who that was; he was told it was the lord of Chincha, master of 100,000 rafts on the high seas.[13] Such long-distance maritime traffic deserves attention even if Ruiz's raft had not come from Chincha. And we need not take the quantitative statement as accurate—even if there were ten thousand or just one thousand oceangoing craft, it would point to a scale of operations that has remained little investigated in our inquiries.

María Rostworowski has published an account of the Chincha polity unique in our records of the Andean world.[14] While the date of the *aviso* she reproduced is uncertain, it reflects conditions early in the colonial regime: by 1560, the Chincha population had disappeared like all other coastal ethnic groups. The claim that the valley had been inhabited by thirty thousand households may well be an exaggeration, like the "100,000" rafts. Quantitative statements are particularly questionable in Andean research: the decimal Inca vocabulary reported by some observers as a feature of administrative reckoning beyond the *khipu* strings skews the information.[15]

What matters for any seagoing inquiry is that the anonymous author of the *aviso* claims that a third of the inhabitants were "fishermen," hence familiar with the Pacific coast; there were also six thousand long-distance "traders," some active by land, southward, while others, an unspecified number, used ocean-braving rafts.[16] These connected Chincha with the *Spondylus* shell-producing tropical waters of modern Ecuador, while ferrying southern ores and probably other commodities northward.

To test these suggestive but very brief accounts, the Institute of Andean Research of New York has recently initiated archaeological inquiries at Chincha, in an effort to check the claims for long-distance maritime operations. As at Huánuco, we do this in order to verify early written records against the physical presence of roads, buildings, docks, rafts, and storehouses.[17] Similarly, our colleagues at the Escuela Politécnica (ESPOL) in Guayaquil have attempted to locate the warm-water ports of call for rafts on the alleged exchange route.[18] All this research is still in process.

We get a hint of how attractive Chincha seemed even to outlanders when we hear that the port was considered as a possible capital of colonial Peru. Earlier, Chincha was one of three extraordinarily "rich" polities that the Pizarro brothers had been forced to yield to the person of Charles V, when the emperor complained that his share of the Andean loot was too small.[19] This affiliation may have been a factor in their preference for Lima as the colonial capital.[20]

The scale of social, political, and economic endeavor in the Andes at the time of the invasion has consistently been underestimated. The structural and managerial preconditions to build, maintain, and dispatch an oceangoing fleet; to assemble and feed and provide with raw materials a thousand weavers concentrated at Lake Titicaca, near Huancané; twenty years to fill more than a thousand warehouses above the provincial capital at Xauxa,[21] or to trace and construct twenty-five thousand kilometers of highway[22]—all these technological achievements presuppose a macro-organization on a scale beyond anything familiar to the inhabitants of contemporary Europe.

This comparison was readily made by the chief investor in the invasion of the Andes, lawyer Gaspar de Espinosa, who did not get to Peru till 1537 but who had his informants among the invaders from the very first day. Less than a year after the capture of Atahualpa, on 3 October 1533, he wrote to Charles V:

> These Indians of . . . Peru are the people most qualified to serve Spaniards and will do it more willingly than any seen anywhere and it will be easy to urge them to do so because they are able and they live together in their republic and also the common people are used to serve their lords and the military.[23]

One project that Espinosa and the other settlers at the Isthmus had long had in mind, and which had been authorized ten years before the invasion, was a canal that would connect the river Chagres, flowing into the Gulf of Mexico, with the Pacific Ocean. In his letters to the emperor, Espinosa had noted the difficulties of unloading the ships on the Pacific shore and the shortage of mules or slaves to carry the goods, including the royal fifth, across the Isthmus. Now he could tell the emperor that

> these Indians of the provinces of Peru are very skilled at making and opening roads and causeways and fortresses and other buildings of stone and earth and to open water canals and in this buildings it is said that they are far ahead of us.[24]

The question that Espinosa now posed to Charles V was how to justify transporting two thousand of these skilled builders from the Andes to Panamá. Since it was prohibited to enslave Americans, the legal solution lawyer Espinosa arrived at was that they could be brought if they were "rebels or deserving a death sentence . . . [they could] be deported to this jurisdiction."

Another early observer who thought that the people of the Andes "nos hazen mucha ventaja" was Pedro Cieza de León, who is generally considered the most reflective of the early observers of the Andean achievement. He tried to explain the relevance of public works to Charles V:

> [I]t seems to me that if the emperor would want [to build] another road like the one that runs from Quito to Cuzco or leaves Cuzco to go to Chile, it is certain that despite all his powers he would not be powerful [enough], nor is there human strength to undertake it were it not for the great order that the Inca commanded.[25]

Among the European observers of early interaction, I want to single out one man whose contribution seems notable, yet remains neglected.

He came to the Andes around 1540, about the same time as the lawyer Polo de Ondegardo, and conducted a lifelong debate with that attorney of the crown. He also helped Cieza de León in many acknowledged and subliminal ways. Having served on the three-man commission that revised and lowered the *tasa* owed by all Andean ethnic groups to their new masters (1549–1552), he was one of those who understood the complexity and efficiency of Andean institutions. As time went by, he thought they could be the basis of a new policy for governing the Andes.

Domingo de Santo Tomás was a Dominican friar. He is familiar to many as the author of an early, possibly the first, grammar and dictionary of an Andean language. He is known to have been a close collaborator of Bartolomé de Las Casas and was probably the author of much that was circulated in Spain under the bishop of Chiapas's signature. We do have a preliminary biography of the Dominican and two later master's theses, but a serious study utilizing his order's archives is still pending.[26]

Here I want to stress his major life's effort: to convince the Council of the Indies and Phillip II to abolish the *encomienda*. This was a European institution, an "entrusting" of a group of local inhabitants to a deserving soldier. In exchange for undertaking to Christianize the Andean population, the beneficiary received a royal grant of a number of villages for one or more "lives."

These grants ignored the existing political and economic boundaries and broke up functioning networks of economic, social, and religious ties. They encouraged small-scale, parochial interests and challenged Andean efficiency. They were a major cause of a new poverty.

Fray Domingo was not alone in holding this position at court; friars and administrators returning from New Spain and from the Andes urged the crown to abolish the *encomienda*. Fray Domingo went beyond that: he argued that after the *encomienda* was abolished, the Andes as a whole should be returned to their *señores naturales*, natural lords.

If the crown wanted to arrest depopulation and increase its revenues, this could be achieved only if the country was ruled by those who in 1560 were still close enough to Andean economic and political models. The crown would benefit from such indirect rule since the ethnic lords would not charge for their services; under prevailing conditions, the crown knew that much of the royal fifth and other revenues stuck to the fingers of peninsular officials. Fray Domingo was ready for a new Andean "order"; confident that the lords were still fit for self-government, he suggested that the immigration of Europeans be discouraged, if not stopped.

To achieve this aim Fray Domingo returned to the peninsula, where he remained for several years, until 1560. He renewed his contacts with fellow Dominicans at Seville, but most of the time he accompanied the court on its rounds through the realm. While awaiting the pleasure of the king and the Council of the Indies, he worked on his grammar and dictionary with the help of Don Mateo Yupanqui, an Inca informant who had traveled with him from home.

The late 1550s, after the death of the emperor, were a time when the debate about the perpetuity of *encomiendas* was in full swing; endless inquiries were made of learned prelates and also of men with American experience. Establishment figures, Trentine by vow or inclination, testified on behalf of continuity and perpetuity. As we know, they won.

Fray Domingo de Santo Tomás did not oppose such continuity from merely humanitarian considerations: his position was that the Andean lords were ready for self-government. They might have required assistance on matters of faith, but otherwise they were ready to govern and assure the crown's interests; he knew that in many ways the peoples of the Andes were "far ahead of us."

I think I recognize Fray Domingo's pen in the drafting of an inquiry dated 23 July 1559 and signed by the king at Ghent. The witnesses, both Americans and Europeans resident in the Andes, were to be asked:

First of all what were the tributes which the Indians had paid their sovereign ruler and to his governors and to the lords whose personal vassals they were. . . .

Fourth: you will also inquire if the tributes paid were based on the lands they worked and cultivated or on the wealth they possessed or if it attached to their persons or by headcount. . . .

Ninth: you will inquire if in olden times there were corporal services and in what form so that if these had prevailed, one would understand in all fairness what they could and should pay.[27]

The references to the Cusco kings as "sovereigns" and those to the local, ethnic leaders as "lords," *señores,* reflect an approach to Andean political organization which is only one of my reasons for the attribution to the Dominican. He understood that the revenues of these *señores* were based on the "corporal" prestations owed by their subjects and were not taxes or tribute turned over in kind.

Although it was meant to be applied throughout the empire, I know of only two occasions when this extraordinary questionnaire was filled out in the Indies:

First, by lawyer Polo de Ondegardo, who did not use it as it was meant for field inquiries but answered from his ample experience as *corregidor* of Cusco, *justicia mayor* at Potosí, quartermaster of the royal army at Xauxa, *encomendero* in Cochabamba, and settler at La Plata. In his answers, Polo complained about having to answer the questionnaire in Lima, without access to his papers, filed at home, in what today is Bolivia. However, his answers, filling under one hundred short pages, are the best and the most unselfconscious example of his work. The questionnaire was so sensitive and familiar with Andean realities that it evoked from this crown official one of our two or three best sources on Andean structures.[28]

Second, by a newcomer, Iñigo Ortiz de Zúñiga, who was sent by the viceroy to conduct an inspection of the Huánuco region. He was supposed to survey two *encomiendas* in the Huallaga valley and record the answers, house by house.[29] However, in this case, the aims of the Ghent questionnaire were short-circuited, since Ortiz was issued a second, more traditional instrument, shaped in Lima, which he used in preference to the royal inquiry.

Meanwhile, at court, endless petitions arrived from Peru, sent by settlers who threatened that the country would be "lost" if the *encomiendas* were terminated. Still, Fray Domingo thought he had a chance: in his absence, his Dominican and Franciscan allies had collected hundreds of powers of attorney from Andean traditional rulers. Some of these have survived in the Archives of the Indies.[30] Among the signers were some of the lords of the Wanka, particularly the Cusichaq lineage at Xauxa, the very same who twenty-seven years earlier had opened the country to the Europeans, moved by hatred for the Inca.

All signers asserted that they had accepted Christian doctrine and were ready now to pay His Majesty a *servicio* amounting to more than he received from all his representatives and collectors of the royal fifth—all this without deductions for services rendered. In exchange they wanted to retrieve their ancient (if pre-Inca) rights and privileges as "natural rulers."

At about this time, the new viceroy, the Conde de Nieva, prepared to sail for his appointment. He was accompanied by several *comisarios*, assigned by the crown to inquire into what to do once and for all about *encomienda* grants. They were ordered to allow free rein to Fray Domingo, who also sailed at about this time, to consult Andean opinion by summoning regional "conferences" of local lords. He was to elicit their opinions on perpetuity on the one hand and on the *servicio* they had previously endorsed on the other.

Several such meetings actually did take place at Arequipa, Hua-manga, Cusco, and possibly elsewhere, but the only one reasonably well documented is the one held at Mama,[31] a natural ecologic frontier, out-side and above Lima. Such places of convergence, known as *tinku* in the Andes, were important loci for asserting differences while working out agreements. Fray Domingo was accompanied by several members of his order and also by Fray Francisco de Morales, a Franciscan.[32]

While addressing those present, Fray Domingo had to face Polo de Ondegardo, assigned to argue the contrary position, in favor of per-petuity. The two men knew each other well from the 1540s; we still do not know how they handled the debate, which was renewed at each con-clave. At one point, the Dominican complained that he had no notary to certify certain testimony, and Polo loaned him his own.

Among those present at Mama we find again the lord of Xauxa. At Mama, however, he was protesting that past services to the Christians were poorly rewarded; if his people were to be granted in *encomienda*, Cusichaq considered that he was their "natural" *encomendero*.[33] Among others present were lords from as far north as Huaraz, Conchucos, and Huánuco, and from Nasca and Acari on the southern coast. Ethnic groups that had been enemies since pre-Inca times, like those of Canta and Yauyos, were both present. Fray Domingo stated under oath that he knew personally every one of the said lords and many of their subor-dinates. They claimed:

> We have gathered at this settlement of Mama to . . . entreat Your Majesty . . . that he give an order we be placed in personal dependency on the royal crown . . . and that we be granted jurisdiction to elect among us mayors, judges and *regidores*, and other officials.[34]

After some debate, those present approved the *servicio* to be offered His Majesty, to match and outbid by 100,000 *castellanos* whatever the *en-comenderos* were ready to pay. Nor did the lords limit themselves to a claim that they replace peninsular officialdom. They pretended that they "wanted to keep our good customs and laws that once existed and still do among us, appropriate for our government and justice and other things we used to have when we were infidels."[35]

Since "it would be difficult to gather again," the lords renewed their earlier powers of attorney by granting them to "several persons we trust." Among them were the archbishop of Lima, another Dominican, and the "illustrious and very reverend *señor don* Bartolomé de Las Casas . . . a resident of Spain." They also asked "that we should get back all the lands, fields, and other inheritances and possessions, real and other estates that the Spaniards have taken and usurped against our will and against justice."[36]

The next gathering after Mama was to be at Huamanga, in the highlands east of the Lima episcopate. No details of that congregation are available so far, but the threat felt by the settlers is reflected in Polo's preemptive actions. As the meeting of Huamanga lords became imminent, Polo proclaimed an *ordenanza de minas,* regulating the participation of the region's ethnic groups at the newly located silver mines.[37] There was to be no coercion; all work was to be by volunteers; protection was offered against abuses with which Polo was only too familiar from his work as *justicia mayor* at Potosí in 1549. We still do not have access to the resolutions approved by the lords of Huamanga; there is no reason to assume that they were different from those agreed to at Mama.

The mines, however, are likely to have made a difference. In his study of what he calls *el partido de los yndios* (the pro-Indian "party"), Carlos Sempat Assadourian suggests that on the issue of mining Domingo de Santo Tomás was less assertive. We know that the Huamanga authorities petitioned him on "the notable harm they endured" when their subjects were forced into the mines, and the matter must have been on the agenda of the gathering, as was Polo's *ordenanza.* We have a letter written by the friar in April of that year to the clerks minding Philip's revenues in which he claims that

> they will go [into the mines] given the ordinances of lawyer Polo sent to your highness which now are reasonable but for the pay which is too low. Do proclaim the instructions noted here [by Polo]; that way my conscience will be relieved.[38]

Even less is known about the gatherings at Arequipa, Cusco, and elsewhere. It became obvious very soon that nothing substantial would emerge from these meetings. The king had already decided to keep the *encomienda* when he sent the viceroy and his *comisarios* to inquire into the issue. A consolation token was offered to Fray Domingo: he was granted a bishop's see that he had turned down while still at Valladolid. Eventually he did accept what amounted to retirement, at the very margins of the viceroyalty, as bishop of Charcas. He did take part in the Second Council of the Peruvian church, where pro-Andean voices were still heard; parish priests were expected to know an Andean language for preaching and hearing confessions. Since we still have not located the records of the proceedings, we do not know what the bishop's role may have been. A glimpse into his commitments was his argument from his see claiming that an Indian's sons owed no tribute, no matter how old, if still unmarried. Such a rule had prevailed in Inca times. To bring this up in the 1560s seemed preposterous to the officials he addressed.

Shortly before his death, in 1570, Fray Domingo earned the condemnation of the canons at his own cathedral: they accused him of hiding his many misdeeds behind the *librillo*, a pamphlet, which is what they called his two volumes on Quechua grammar. After some twenty more livid pages, the king was finally informed that the bishop had no right to call himself Navarrete, the family name he had added to his ecclesiastic signature when sent to Charcas. According to the good canons, Fray Domingo's father was one Molina, of Moguer, who had been a *sastre remendero,* a patching tailor, and also a Jew; his mother, a baptized Moor. Fray Domingo's real biography has not attracted the interest of historians.

By the late 1560s, Fray Domingo and his allies were fighting a rearguard battle. There was no longer any talk of returning the country to its natural rulers; there may be vehemence in the language of some friars, like Francisco de Morales,[39] but the battle had been lost.

The early observers, those who witnessed the Andean world as a functioning system, speak frequently of the "order" that had prevailed. The waning of this perception began while some of its protagonists were still alive, during the 1560s. Guillermo Lohmann has pointed to that decade as the era that is best documented because so many notions about the Andes were being debated: the old lords who had functioned as adults before 1532 were dying out; massive depopulation, a factor in the Andes as elsewhere in the Americas, could not be ignored; mines and where to get mine workers were now the issue, not *encomiendas*; thousands of mestizos and *mulatos* were coming of age at a time when no provision had been made about their fate.[40] All this encouraged writing.

For our purposes, the earlier decades are more relevant.[41] And yet it is remarkable how few sources dated before 1560 we have located or even looked for during the last few decades. What sources on the early interaction do we have beyond what William Prescott had in the 1840s, Heinrich Cunow in 1896, Louis Baudin in 1936, John H. Rowe in 1946, and R. Tom Zuidema in 1964?[42]

These early sources do exist, though they may not be filed in the obvious repositories. Recently I worked in peninsular archives on behalf of the Institute of Andean Research and its study of the seagoing kingdom of Chincha. While the traffic in *Spondylus* shells did not attract the attention of the European scribes, information about Chincha did surface when I stressed the fact that the people of that valley had been the

emperor's own. But in the case of Chincha there was no post-1560 population to describe.[45]

While awaiting the location of what Raúl Porras once called the "lost,
alleged and forgotten" sources, let me close with a further evocation of
Polo, a writer from whom I still expect revelations. He lived long enough
to witness the utter devastation of the Andean "order" by Viceroy Francisco de Toledo. The first ruler to climb up to the altiplano, Toledo
decided that this Andean "order" had to go. In a long letter to His
Majesty, he explained how most of the old-timers among the European
inspectors he had hired to conduct a census of the viceroyalty had
resisted his policy of relocating every ethnic group away from its multi-
tiered dispersed territory. An early partisan of what in recent history
have become known as "strategic hamlets," Toledo had hoped that the
inspectors would help him redraw Andean geography.

Polo, who had been sent by Toledo to Cusco for a second tour as
corregidor, was the most articulate in expressing his reservations. In a
long memorandum, called "Of the reasons for the serious harm that en-
sues if one does not respect the Indians' own order," Polo argued that
the only way to get anything done in the Andes was to understand what
Cieza had talked about a quarter of a century earlier.[43] As he put it,
"Even to convert them to Christianity, the road is a known one; you need
to know their own beliefs and customs in order to eliminate them."[44]

It is true that compared to his answers to the king's questionnaire a
decade earlier, Polo is cautious and makes concessions to prevailing
clichés. Still, even in 1571 his words are a source in which the Andean
"order" is still perceptible. Polo died in 1575.

Another to resist Toledo's campaign to liquidate the Andean social
system was a sitting judge on the Royal Court of Charcas, Dr. Barros.
At risk to his own life, he consistently challenged the policy of strategic
villages, the *reducciones.* He also attacked the death sentence imposed in
his own court on the surviving scion of the Inca royal family, Tupac
Amaru I. Judge Barros argued that the charges against the monoglot
young prince had been based on a perjured translation, ordered by the
viceroy. When the judge succeeded in getting the interpreter, one
Ximénez, to confess to perjury, the viceroy had the "tongue" burned on
a charge of sodomy.

In 1582, with Toledo safely returned to an ignominious reception at
court as a regicide,[45] the lords of Charcas petitioned the crown: "We are
the counts and the marquesses of this realm," they claimed.[46] Each listed
his genealogy, reaching to before the Inca conquest. But only fifty years

after Gaspar de Espinosa's successful enterprise, all they asked for was privileges at the mines of Potosí and knighthoods in Spain.

NOTES

1. Arthur E. Morgan, *Nowhere Was Somewhere: How History Makes Utopias and How Utopias Make History* (Chapel Hill, N.C., 1986).

2. Charles E. Nowell, "Aleixo García and the White King," *Hispanic American Historical Review* 26 (November 1946): 450–466.

3. Olaf Holm, "El tatuaje entre los aborígenes prepizarrianos en la costa ecuatoriana," *Cuadernos de Historia y Arqueología* (Guayaquil) 3, 7/8 (1953): 56–92. Miguel Rivera Dorado, "Hipótesis sobre relaciones entre Meso-América y el área andino septentrional," *Revista Española de Antropología Americana* 7, 2 (1972): 19–31. In 1971, Carlos Zevallos Menéndez organized a conference at Salinas, Ecuador, to discuss this topic.

4. See Gonzalo Fernández de Oviedo, *Historia general y natural de las Indias*, edited by Juan Pérez de Tudela Bueso, vol. 3, bk. 29 (Madrid, 1959). Oviedo was an eyewitness of the events and personalities described.

5. See Guillermo Lohmann Villena, *Les Espinosa: Une famille d'hommes d'affaires en Espagne et aux Indes* (Paris, 1968).

6. While many of Espinosa's letters to the crown are available, he apparently did not refer to the trial. By 1519, Ferdinand was already dead, and young Charles V had more immediate worries: the rebellion of the *comuneros*, for example, had just begun.

7. J. Jijón y Camaño, "Una gran marea cultural en el noroeste de Sudamérica," *Journal de la Société des Américanistes* 22 (1930): 107–197; Holm, "El tatuaje"; María Rostworowski, "Mercaderes del valle de Chincha," *Revista Española de Antropología Americana* 5 (1970): 135–178; José Alcina Franch et al., "Navegación precolombina: Evidencias e hipótesis," *Revista Española de Antropología Americana* 17 (1987): 35–73.

8. Hermann Trimborn, *Pascual de Andagoya* (Hamburg, 1954).

9. Ruiz's own ship was estimated at forty *toneles*.

10. A copy made at court for Charles V's brother was located in the archives at Vienna. See Adám Szaszdi, "¿Fue Francisco de Xérez el autor de la relación Sámano?," *Anuario de Estudios Americanos* 33 (1976): 453–554; and also "Dos fuentes para la historia de la empresa de Pizarro," *Historiografía y Bibliografía Americanistas* 25 (1981): 89–146.

11. Raúl Porras Barrenechea, *Cartas del Perú* (Lima, 1959), 5–6.

12. Ibid.

13. Pedro Pizarro, *Relación del descubrimiento y conquista* . . . (Madrid, [1571] 1965).

14. Rostworowski, "Mercaderes del valle de Chincha," 135–178.

15. See Gordon J. Hadden's essay comparing the decimal vocabulary with

actual demographic data in Iñigo Ortiz de Zúñiga, *Visita de la provincia de León de Huánuco*, vol. 1 (Huánuco, [1567] 1967). For a different assessment see Catherine J. Julien, "Inca Decimal Administration in the Lake Titicaca Region," in George A. Collier et al., *The Inca and Aztec States 1400–1800* (New York, 1982), 119–151.

16. For the debate on the presence of "trade" in the Andes see John V. Murra, *The Economic Organization of the Inka State* (Greenwich, Conn., [1955] 1980), 139–152. Also, Olivia Harris, Brooke Larson, and Enrique Tandeter, *La participación indígena en los mercados surandinos* (La Paz, 1987).

17. John V. Murra, "An Archaeological Re-study of an Andean Ethnohistorical Account," *American Antiquity* 28 (1962): 1–4; Craig Morris and D. E. Thompson, *Huánuco Pampa, an Inca City and Its Hinterland* (London, 1985).

18. Jorge Marcos, "Cruising to Acapulco and Back with the Thorny Oyster Set," *Journal of the Steward Anthropological Society* 9, 1/2 (1978): 99–132.

19. Silvio Zavala, *El servicio personal de los indios en el Perú* (Mexico City, 1978). "Los yndios señalados a Su Majestad son los mejores," claim the brothers Pizarro.

20. John V. Murra, "Los olleros del Inka: hacia una historia y arqueología del Qollasuyu," in *Historia, problema, y promesa: Homenaje a Jorge Basadre*, edited by Francisco Miró Quesada C., Franklin Pease G. Y., and David Sobrevilla A. (Lima, 1978): 415–423.

21. T. d'Altroy, "The Xauxa Region of Perú under the Incas" (Ph.D. diss., University of California, Los Angeles, 1981). The emperor's personal attorney in Peru, Juan Polo, fed some two thousand men in the royal army from what he found in the Xauxa warehouses in 1547.

22. John Hyslop, *The Inca Road System* (New York, 1984).

23. "Estos yndios destas prouincias del Perú es la gente mas aparejada para servir españoles y que con mejor voluntad lo haran de quantos se an visto y avra poco trabajo en apremiarlos para ello ansy porque son acostumbrados a servir . . . a los señores e gente de guerra." Porras Barrenechea, *Cartas del Perú*, 73.

24. "Los yndios de las provincias del peru es gente muy diestra en hacer e abrir caminos y calçadas e fortalezas y otros edificios de piedra y tapieria e de sacar agua e acequia tanto que visto los edificios diezen que nos hazen mucha ventaja. . . ." Porras Barrenechea, *Cartas del Perú*, 72–73.

25. "Me parece que si el Emperador quisiese mandar otro camino real como el que va del Quito a Cuzco o sale del Cuzco para ir a Chile ciertamente que con todo su poder para ello no fuese poderoso ni fuerza de hombre le pudiese hazer si no fuese con la orden tan grande que para ello los incas mandaron que hubiese . . . ," in Pedro Cieza de León, *El señorío de los incas*, (Lima, [1553] 1967), 45 (bk. 2, chap. 15).

26. *Grammática o arte de la lengua de los indios de los reynos del Perú y Lexicón o vocabulario de la lengua general del Perú* (Lima, [1560] 1951). Both were originally published at Valladolid in 1560. José María Vargas, *Fray Domingo de Santo Tomás, defensor y apóstol de los indios* (Quito, 1937); Patricia J. Bard, "Domingo de Santo

Tomás, a Spanish Friar in the Sixteenth Century" (M.A. thesis, Columbia University, 1971); Leoncio López Ocón, "Fray Domingo de Santo Tomás" (M.A. thesis, Facultad Latinoamericana de Ciencias Sociales, Quito, 1987).

27. "Primeramente se ha de averiguar que son los tributos que los yndios pagaban al señor soberano y a sus gobernadores y a los señores cuyos vassallos particulares eran." Ortiz de Zúñiga, *Visita de la provincia,* 17.

28. Juan Polo de Ondegardo, "Informe al licenciado Briviesca de Munatones . . . ," *Revista Histórica* 13 (1939): 125–196.

29. Ortiz de Zúñiga, *Visita de la provincia*: see questionnaire on pages 16 to 19 with questions asked on pages 12 to 16.

30. Archivo General de Indias, Contaduría, 1825 (hereafter cited as AGI).

31. AGI, Lima, 121.

32. Carlos Sempat Assadourian, "Las rentas reales, el buen gobierno, y la hacienda de Dios: El parecer de 1568 de Fray Francisco Morales, sobre la reformación de la Indias temporal y espiritual," *Histórica* 9 (1986), 75–130.

33. When his suit at the royal Audiencia in Lima was turned back, Cusichaq filed an appeal in Spain, sending his own Spanish-speaking son to press the claim before the king.

34. "Nos abemos juntado en este asiento de Mama para . . . suplicar a su Majestad . . . que nos manda poner e ponga en su cabeza e corono real . . . e que nos den la dicha juridicion para que entre nosotros se elixan alcaldes juezes e regidores e otros oficiales. . . ."

35. "Que nos guarden nuestras buenas costumbres e leyes que entre nosotros a abido y ay justas para nuestro gouierno e justicia y otras cosas que soliamos tener en tiempo de nuestra ynfidelidad. . . ."

36. "Que nos sean bueltas y rrestituidas todas las tierras chacaras y otras heredades e posesiones rayzes y otros bienes muebles que contra nuestra boluntad e contra justicia nos tienen tomadas e husurpadas los españoles. . . ."

37. Steve J. Stern, *Peru's Indian Peoples and the Challenge of Spanish Conquest: Huamanga to 1640* (Madison, Wisc., 1982), 47–48 nn. 79–80.

38. "An de yr de su voluntad y creo yran si con las ordenanças que el licenciado Polo ha ymbiado a vuestra alteza que al presente son razonable aceto en la paga que es pequeña. Se provee lo que aqui apunto y con esto descargo mi conciencia." Assadourian, "Las rentas reales."

39. See Assadourian, "Las rentas reales," n. 31.

40. Guillermo Lohmann Villena, "Unas notas acerca de curiosos paralelismos y correspondencias entre cuatro documentos históricos sobre la época incaica," *Fénix: Revista de la Biblioteca Nacional* 16 (1966): 174–197.

41. John V. Murra. "Current Research and Prospects in Andean Ethnohistory," *Latin American Research Review* 5, 1 (1970): 3–36.

42. William H. Prescott, *History of the Conquest of Peru* (New York, 1846); Heinrich Cunow, *La organización social del imperio de los Incas: Investigación sobre el comunismo agrario en el antiguo Peru* (Lima, [1896] 1929); Louis Baudin, *L'empire socialiste de les Inkas* (Paris, 1928); John H. Rowe, "Inca Culture at the Time of

the Spanish Conquest," *Handbook of South American Indians* (1946), 2:183–330; R. Tom Zuidema, *The Ceque System of Cuzco: The Social Organization of the Capital of the Inca* (Leiden, 1964).

43. Juan Polo de Ondegardo, "Relación de los fundamentos acerca del notable daño que resulta de no guardar a los indios sus fueros," in *Colección de documentos inéditos relativos al descubrimiento, conquista, y organización de las antiguas posesiones españoles de América y Oceania,* 1st ser., (Madrid, 1872), 3:5–177.

44. "Avnque para hacerlos christianos esta savido el camyno . . . cs ncsccsario sauer sus opiniones y costumbres para quitarselas." Polo (1571), "Relación de los fundamentos," 81–82.

45. Felipe Guaman Poma de Ayala, *El primer nueva corónica y buen gobierno,* edited by John V. Murra and Rolena Adorno, Quechua translations by Jorge L. Urioste (Mexico City, [1615] 1980), 460–461.

46. Waldemar Espinoza Soriano, "El memorial de Charcas: 1582," *Cantuta: Revista de la Universidad de Educación* 3 (1969): 117–152.

FOUR

Trunk Lines and Feeder Lines: The Spanish Reaction to American Resources

James Lockhart

It may seem strange to speak of sixteenth-century Spanish American behavior in the language of nineteenth- and twentieth-century railroads. But despite the anachronism, the terms have the right flavor of economically rational action working itself out in a context of markets, populations, raw and manufactured materials, and geographical realities. In a way it must be accounted a shame that Latin American history got its start with the extravagant language and often chimerical notions of the Italian Columbus. Actually, a strong realism and an active search for and exploitation of every economic possibility were the norm for the Spaniards, and no less the Portuguese, though the latter were mainly employed elsewhere for most of the sixteenth century.

The Spaniards were far more pragmatic and quick to adjust to the new situation than were Columbus and the Italians in general, who remained centered in the Mediterranean and Europe—a rational strategy, in fact, given their location, strengths, and possibilities. The Genoese (the main Italian representatives in matters concerning America) were wedded to a set of procedures that had proved markedly successful from the eastern Mediterranean to West Africa and that they were not prepared to change. In fact, as they saw what was involved in America, they increasingly pulled back to financing and indirect participation (it would be too much to say that the Spaniards pushed them out).[1] Much of the pragmatism and flexibility of the Spaniards had to do with the fact that, relatively speaking, from a very early time large numbers of them came, forming a whole sector irrevocably committed to the new situation, devising its own solutions on the spot, beginning to build up its own traditions and techniques even if these were originally but variants of European models.

Our topic being resources, let us stop for a moment to consider what resources are. In a given time and place various raw materials, natural species, human populations, and climatic conditions either exist or do not in an unconditional way, but often that is not the decisive factor. First, these things have to be recognized to exist. Then, they must pass through technological, cultural, and economic filters before they can be considered meaningful resources for a given society at a given time. It would be interesting to discuss the resource orientation of the indigenous societies, but from the point of view of colonization, the society that comes directly into question is the European, specifically the Spanish, and most especially that segment of the Spanish population that was already in the Indies. Though differential immigration directly from Spain to various specific American regions was a crucial factor in the overall ensemble, it was determined not so much through weighing and sifting by Spaniards at home as through the differential success of the settlers, who called to their relatives and neighbors to join them only where they had had good luck and could use colleagues.

What resources mattered, then, depended in the first instance on who the immigrants were and what their goals and needs were. Almost from the beginning the immigrants were a broad selection of ordinary Spaniards from many occupations, ranks, and regions, increasingly including Spanish women as well. Their ultimate goal, in many cases, was sooner or later to return wealthy to Spain. In fact, rarely did return prove possible, and the alternate goal was to live in the New World fully in the style of a high-ranking Spaniard.[2] In either case, the Spaniards of the Indies somehow had to gain leverage on the European economy, sending to Europe items that could be converted into large amounts of currency—to be spent directly in Spain, if they were able to return, or to permit the importation of European products that would make a Spanish life-style possible, if they had to remain in the Indies. Let us not blame them for not producing everything they needed in the New World itself. The ever-increasing but still limited number of local Spaniards included only an insignificant fraction of the persons with relevant skills; the materials available were not identical, and the still nascent local market could not support the requisite specialization even when the skills and materials were available. The indigenous population was numerous, but it did not require large amounts of European-style goods and in any case could not have paid for them in ways that would have rewarded the settlers meaningfully.

To home in on what drove the conquerors and immigrants (for the two groups are one) and what they were looking for, we need to look at what did *not* drive them. Popular stereotypes on exotic topics are not only as pernicious as weeds but also as hardy, and must be combated anew each season. The Spaniards were not driven by a lighthearted or reckless sense of adventure, leading them to ignore the solid benefits of a given situation and strike out for wider spaces and fresh challenges. Those who were established stayed where they were; those who went on were the newly arrived and unestablished, who had no choice. Even in recent and reputable work, the term "adventurers" is at times applied to the group of men who went with Francisco Pizarro to conquer Peru, but some time back I did a book that proved that they were no such thing.[3]

Because of the later prominence of these individuals, their lives can be traced, and I was ultimately able to track down the fates of the great majority. Those who were senior and best connected received the greatest monetary rewards and promptly went home to create establishments. Most of the rest, junior or less well connected, stayed in Peru and did the same there, receiving the best *encomiendas** and becoming the leading citizens of the major Peruvian cities. Few indeed went anywhere else in the Indies. But a few did. Surely among these would be some adventurers. In fact, however, certain major leaders who were serious rivals of the Pizarros (Hernando de Soto, Sebastián de Benalcázar) were pushed off to find their own areas to dominate, where they would be no threat to Pizarro hegemony. Practically all others who left central Peru for Chile or other destinations in the Indies were regional compatriots and close allies of the Pizarros' greatest enemies, and they knew full well that they would not receive good treatment, perhaps not even be tolerated, in Peru itself. We do find one person from Pizarro's homeland, with an impressive family name, Ulloa, who nevertheless went to Chile with Almagro. Here then, we might say, must be at least one adventurer among 168 pragmatists. But looking at the list of the division of gold and silver among the conquerors, we find that the wretched Ulloa re-

---

*An *encomienda* was a grant issued to a Spaniard by the governor of a given region, giving that Spaniard the right to receive labor, tribute, or both from the Indians of a particular sociopolitical unit, channeled through their already existing authorities and based on whatever type of duties the local indigenous people had performed in preconquest times. Only early conquerors and very high-ranking later arrivals were eligible to receive such grants. During the conquest generation, the *encomienda* was the primary basis of larger estates among Spaniards in the Indies. In central areas, the institution was greatly weakened in subsequent generations, but it pointed forward to later estate types.

ceived hardly a token share, by far the smallest among the whole group. He lacked enough money to go home to Spain, he was clearly out of favor with the Pizarros, and he did well to take his chances in Chile.

Nor were the Spaniards avid explorers intent on advancing world geographical knowledge and mapping. The best pilots among them were usually Italians, other Mediterraneans, Portuguese, or at least Basques and mariners, and if there was anything Spaniards held in lower esteem than a foreigner it was a sailor. Let me tell, not for the first time, the story of my encounter with the editors of *World Book Encyclopedia* over Vasco Núñez de Balboa. The encyclopedia had Balboa down as an explorer pure and simple, who allegedly sat at his doorstep as a child peering into the distance and dreaming of new discoveries in far lands. In the new article I wrote for them I called Balboa a conqueror rather than an explorer; this brought on stout resistance, and finally I had to compromise on "conqueror and explorer." No one ever deserved the epithet explorer less. Balboa probably never gave a thought to distant lands until internal family politics demanded that he seek his fortune away from home. On the Caribbean coast of Tierra Firme he was long concerned with assigning *encomiendas* to his men and using the Indians to mine gold. The indigenous people virtually tugged at the hems of his clothing, telling him that not far away was another vast ocean, on whose shores pearls were to be found, but as long as the Caribbean coast economy held up, he shrugged them off. When the population and the gold fields declined, he finally, in effect, asked the Indians, "Where's this ocean you've been talking about?" They thereupon led him and a group of Spaniards a short distance along a trail well known to them, until approaching a large hill, they said that the great sea of the other side could be seen from the top of it. Then, in a staged performance, the bulk of the group was held back while Balboa went up to look first, followed by others in the order of seniority, each recorded in turn by a notary. Never, then, was there a more unlikely explorer.[4] But Soto on the Florida expedition of 1541–1542 and Gonzalo Pizarro on the Amazonian expedition were no different; any new geographical knowledge was the lightly regarded by-product of a pragmatic effort to find a good way to make a living, tantamount under the conditions to finding a combination of precious metal deposits and sedentary Indians.

Nor were the Spaniards excessively swayed by myths, whether medieval, ancient, or newly coined. Yes, the Amazons, El Dorado, the Land of Cinnamon, the Land of Seven Cities, and the Fountain of Youth do turn up. But we must keep things in proportion. Such legends were used to help justify to neophytes ultimately unsuccessful ventures off the

main track *after* nearby major areas of interest had already been conquered and opened up—ventures of whose hopelessness those most in
the know were already convinced, being not a whit deterred from the
activities they had already undertaken in proven areas. They sometimes
helped finance these "romantic" *entradas* precisely in the hope that the
ignorant, newly arrived malcontents going on them would never come
back. The romanticism grew in retrospect. The very late writer Bernal
Díaz del Castillo says for the public that in the conquest of Mexico he
was once reminded of the stories of Amadís of Gaul, the hero of chival-
ric novels,[5] but one can read the contemporary reports of conquerors
and early governors, or the private letters of early settlers, and find
nothing of the sort. It was above all the Europeans back home, and
among them above all non-Spaniards, who projected a whole series of
stereotypes of the unknown and exotic onto America; those directly involved were far more realistic, though they too could speak the language
of legend and turn it to their advantage.

It is hardly necessary to say that the Spaniards were not distracted
from resource exploitation by any military orientation. The conquerors
were not professional or permanent soldiers by any means, and even
in the heat of conquest they were business-minded and concerned primarily with resources in the sense already explained. Nor was there
any appreciable element of ideological or religious protest among them.
A manifestation such as the half-demented Lope de Aguirre (on an
Amazonian expedition of 1560) insulting the crown was the greatest rarity, something to be expected at most in an ultimately marginal situation,
very late and very far from the centers.[6] The settler "rebellions" that
took place in Peru were fights between interest groups (based mainly on
Spanish regional affiliation and time of arrival in the new country) over
the allocation of resources, all parties staying within the same framework
of justification and basic allegiance. Except for some rather deeply sub-
merged members of Jewish and Moorish minorities, I think the settlers
were nearly 100 percent loyal Spaniards and orthodox Christians. As a
result, there was no inclination to accept, in the name of a cause,
hardships and changes in material culture and general way of life, as
might have been the case in some of the English colonies. In the Spanish
Indies everyone wanted the same thing, and the settlers were distributed
strictly according to who arrived first, who had the right skills and connections, and how much opportunity there was in a given place.

But if nearly all were true believers, was religious fervor a factor
seriously affecting the utilization of resources? Surely not. Though the
conquerors in their reports to the crown sometimes emphasized the

great service they were performing in providing so many new candidates for Christianity, in the private letters that survive from them and other settlers concern about the conversion of the Indians is conspicuously absent.[7] The settlers seem to have thought of their Christianity as they thought of their Spanishness, as a facet of their obviously superior culture, not something easily imparted to anyone else or which they even expected to impart, nor something that was in the forefront of their minds. In their correspondence the divinity is invoked on every page, but almost always, even in the letters of clerics, it is in the hope that he will provide a safe journey, good health, many children, or a profitable business venture, meanwhile fending off calamities. A student of mine working with this literature once said that the Spaniards' concept of God seemed to be equivalent to good and bad luck. The religious beliefs of the majority, then, however pervasive, in no way impeded or even affected their economic activity.

When it comes to the clerics, especially in their corporate manifestation, things may seem different, but effects on the direction of the economy are hard to detect. The organized church presence was a function of the general Spanish presence. Bishoprics and provinces of the orders were established first and in greatest strength in precisely those areas where the lay Spaniards had already gone in greatest numbers for broadly economic reasons.[8] The organizations fed off and were fit into that economy. Clerics often served as *encomienda* administrators and took part in much other business, including mining, as entrepreneurs and lenders. Donations from wealthy laymen, directly out of the local economy, were an important factor in the establishment of church organizations, often in conjunction with already existing or newly arranged kinship ties between clerics and local lay Spaniards.

We must, of course, consider the noisy campaigns carried on mainly by clerics to reorganize or weaken the *encomienda* and other labor devices, with great possible repercussions on the mining industry and its support system. These were to an extent internal church disputes. Those who arrived earlier cooperated and received benefits; those who arrived later received little and wanted to bring about changes for their own benefit, not unlike the lay Spaniards who arrived too late to receive *encomiendas*. And in fact, it was only where the existence of many lay Spaniards wanting access to resources created competition and pressures that changes urged on humanitarian-religious grounds by the more radical of the churchmen took effect. Indian slavery and the *encomienda* as the main vehicle of temporary labor procurement were gradually replaced in the course of the sixteenth century in central

Mexico and many parts of Peru, where they were no longer adapted to the existing economic and demographic conditions. Despite the campaigns, however, these institutions held on for generations in a multitude of peripheral regions, where they still represented an efficient way for sparse local Spanish populations to utilize resources. Doctrinal considerations on the part of the clergy were one element entering into political, social, and economic struggles concerning Spanish utilization of resources, but in truth, one can predict the outcomes just as well without even taking doctrinal positions into the calculations.

Nor did any severe anticommercial spirit or overemphasis on nobility keep the Spaniards from seeing and using the resources available to them. By the time they came to the Indies, the Spaniards had learned all the commercial lessons the Genoese had to teach them, and indeed I think they had understood and practiced most of this lore for a long time. Not only were there numerous professional merchants in the Indies representing transatlantic combines based in Spain, and other merchants starting out on their own, but also commercialism had permeated the entire conqueror and settler population. Ordinary Spaniards knew all about credit operations, whether lending, borrowing, or buying on credit; they constantly made various kinds of partnerships among themselves, whether for conquest, mining, or other ventures.

The Spanish urge for prominence definitely included a strong striving for nobility or *hidalguía,* and in both hemispheres we find what by the standards of some other European countries could be considered an inordinate number of people claiming to be and being accepted as nobles (*hidalgos*). But this was not incompatible with a thoroughgoing exploitation of local resources; indeed, standard expectations concerning *hidalgo* status fomented certain kinds of development. Whatever else we have been told at various times, the *hidalgo* was above all one who was wealthy in a very permanent and stable way. The *hidalgo* was expected to be the head of an estate and an establishment. At the core of this establishment was the family or lineage, but that was no impediment to business. The family was precisely the best way of doing business then known, and the professional merchants themselves made it one of their primary organizing devices. It provided relatively trustworthy subordinates, even at a distance, and a natural chain of command. Since the Spanish family with its illegitimate members and poor relatives existed at several levels at once, there was a role for everyone and someone for all the roles, including managers, collectors, labor bosses, messenger boys, and other underlings. The family's often extensive ties with other ranking families were extremely important for business purposes, not least in acquiring credit. The establishment included also servants and slaves, with emphasis on their permanent membership in the entourage. In the Indies, not only Africans but also, and especially, indigenous people were quickly pressed into this role, serving as intermediaries who were in intimate contact with every aspect of the local scene, giving the Spanish presence a dimension and ubiquitousness it would otherwise not have had. It is said that it was a permanent Indian employee of a Spaniard, a *yanacona*, who discovered the silver deposits of Potosí.[9]

In both Spain and America the strategy of the estate was to maintain permanence, security, integration, and perhaps a degree of dominance by involving itself in every locally profitable branch of endeavor currently in existence. In Spain agriculture and stockraising were very important in estate activities, because they were equally important in the economy, but ventures did not stop there, extending to urban real estate, investment in craft and mercantile enterprises, and ownership of government annuities. Holding vast amounts of land was not per se the emphasis; often stock and grazing rights were more important than land. It was simply a function of what yielded the best long-term revenue. In the New World, then, there was far less greed for land, as long as the local Hispanic market was severely restricted. Enough land was taken over to supply the Spaniards of the cities and mines with Spanish foods, but that required only a tiny percent of available usable land and yielded only a relatively modest profit, so land and farming/ranching did not yet dominate Spanish estates of the conquest period. The emphasis was where it might well be, on mines, either owning them and running them or backing them indirectly. But whereas merchants specialized in dealings permitting liquidity because they had to return the profits to the head of the firm in Seville, and persons of low rank, with few possibilities, were forced into specializing in transport, a truck garden, or a craft, estate owners at the higher rank invariably diversified, scouring the local situation for every potentially profitable opportunity.

I have previously used the example of the southern Peruvian *encomendero* Gerónimo de Villegas, who in addition to supplying the mines of Potosí worked others in the area of his *encomienda* grant, raised stock there for the Arequipa market, sold whatever he could directly to his Indians, speculated in urban real estate, maintained a company for ocean fishing and supply between his *encomienda* and Arequipa, and took part in the import-export trade, partly through his merchant-*mayordomo*.[10] Villegas was unusual only in having left such a full record of his activities. Efraín Trelles has since shown that the Spaniard who both preceded and followed Villegas as holder of the *encomienda* did exactly the same things.[11]

Not all regions were as well endowed as southern Peru, however, and in these situations—the majority—the diversification emphasis in Spanish estate formation really came into its own, leading to a very broad and systematic search for every conceivable way of making money directly or indirectly. This took place within the already explained framework of looking for either an export product or something to sell to those who were already profiting from export products, but even so the surveys were broad, and indigenous products were not overlooked, nor even indigenous consumers, wherever they participated enough in the export economy to be able to pay cash. Murdo MacLeod has portrayed the process for Guatemala and the surrounding region, which after the exhaustion of precious metals and slave export involved balsam, wax, incense, canafistula, sarsparilla and other unlikely medicines, herbs, and resins, before cacao, at first primarily for central Mexican Indian consumers, became the solution—for a while.[12] As MacLeod sees it, the search went on, in the same terms, from the first moment the Spaniards arrived, with no change of mentalities or methods from conqueror to settler. Similar tales could be told of Ecuador and northern Peru.

Iberian family/estate structure, always the same at the core, could be readily adapted to a thousand purposes, depending on the local conditions; it appears in enterprises as exotic as growing coca, selling *chuñu* (Andean dried potatoes), and diving for pearls. The classic adaptation of the conquest period, however, was one in which the estate expanded to include vast numbers of unskilled temporary laborers—unskilled, that is, in the specific techniques of the enterprise, though skilled in their own often parallel enterprises, accustomed to the tasks of sedentary life, and available through existing mechanisms of indigenous government. A limited number of Spaniards of high or highish rank, with a full grasp of the whole enterprise and its social-economic political context, owned and directed it; an almost equally limited number of lower ranking Spaniards, non-Spanish Europeans, Africans, and permanently employed Indians beginning to feel the impact of Spanish culture had useful but partial expertise, serving as technicians, foremen, and cadre; and a mass of indigenous workers performed basic labor under close supervision on a temporary basis, not becoming a permanent part of the structure.

Population loss, changes in local markets, and growing technical demands gradually changed the proportions, but meanwhile organizations of this type gave impressive results, especially in mining for precious metals and in city construction. The system worked best when the tasks at the base were straightforward, uniform, and intensive rather than spread over the whole year, so that skill, responsibility, and permanence could be concentrated at the upper levels, in the still restricted sector of Hispanic and Hispanized people. If the operation was profitable enough (usually tantamount to being close to the export sector) and concentrated enough, the structure could do without the numerous lower levels altogether. Where it had the hardest time adapting, even when considerable wealth was involved, was a situation in which profit was not intensive per unit, yet great skill, spread over significant portions of the year, was required by large numbers of people at the base of the process. Things were all the more difficult when the special technology involved was indigenous. In Mexico, cochineal production and *chinampa* agriculture (mud farming at the edge of a lake) are good examples of profitable activities highly resistant to Spanish estate organization.[13] For the Andes, scholarship has not yet delivered specific relevant studies. Spaniards entered directly into coca production, while the raising of highland crops and animals remained primarily in the hands of Andeans. Coca was the most profitable, but the highland food and animal complex also had economic potential, and it may be that the nature and locus of the related activities represented a considerable barrier to Spanish enterprise.

Spanish values, habits, and concepts, then, not only were generally compatible with a rational exploitation of the resources of the New World but also specifically led in that direction and contained organizational devices highly appropriate for the purpose. I wish to expatiate a bit more, however, on two false notions that show special tenacity in the public mind: that the Spaniards had some special obsession with precious metals, a "lust for gold," and that they had an unhealthy preoccupation with goods of specifically Spanish or European origin.

Now as to gold, in the first place, the Spaniards were soon to give overwhelming emphasis to silver, because there was infinitely more of it. But even in the initial stages in many areas, when reliance indeed was on gold, there was no obsession with it in the sense of wanting to keep it, rub it, gaze at it; rather it was treated as money and an export product. The initial impetus toward it was neither a medieval admiration of the metal nor a reconquest concern for "booty," but the fact that of all the things the indigenous population of the Antilles and Tierra Firme knew and valued, this was the only one to the purpose. If any further conceptual framework was needed, it was provided by the analogy with Africa, which Columbus with his African experience, not to speak of any other Italians or Portuguese present, immediately brought to bear. The export products that the West African coast had supplied to the Portuguese were gold, slaves, and exotic items such as tropical woods and ivory. The Spaniards gave them all a try, but the woods of the Caribbean islands were mainly not suitable, and the Indians died from lack of immunities to European disease before they could be transported back to Spain for sale as slaves (one important reason that it was possible within a generation or two to abolish Indian slavery in central areas of the Indies). Gold was a big success, and it required relatively little capital investment and a relatively small amount of expertise. Even Peru and Mexico were to rely ephemerally on gold until their silver mines could be developed.

But it *was* an industrial enterprise. In Africa the Portuguese merely traded with the local population for the metal; the Africans carried on quite intensive production themselves. In the Caribbean and other American placer-mining areas, current indigenous production was slight, and the Spaniards were able to occupy the entire area, came in greater numbers, and had a greater need than did the Portuguese in Africa. The Spanish were in effect forced into direct involvement with production; but they were up to the challenge. The yield paid their debts, rewarded them, and attracted many new immigrants from Spain before exhaustion of the deposits. The Spaniards must have done a reasonable job of exploitation, since the fields they abandoned were rarely to be worked again in later centuries.

And if gold mining was already production rather than pure extraction, silver mining was a full-scale industry. It was highly technical, it required a great deal of machinery together with sophisticated experimentation and adaptation, and it involved a complex sequence of separate processes. It was large-scale and long-lasting at the same site. It called for extensive systematic prospecting and expert assaying; most of the Mexican industry was located far away from the centers of indigenous population at sites not previously worked or even known. Even in Peru the greatest site had not been worked by the Incas. Silver mining demanded great amounts of capital investment far in advance of a return, and the investment was forthcoming, since there was the legitimate expectation of a vast profit. Improvements needed could be projects as huge as the *socavones,* or adit tunnels cut into hillsides to intersect with vertical shafts, and they could affect the whole landscape: consider the dams, reservoirs, and aqueducts that made it possible for Potosí to use water power in its stamp mills.[14] The final product, nearly as negotiable as money, deserves a better name than "raw material," and silver was indeed being minted in both Mexico and Peru long before the end of the sixteenth century.

We might ask if sugar was not a realistic alternative or complement. Although a different order of activity—that is, one neither using an indigenous raw material nor practiced among the indigenous people— sugar production was an important part of the Portuguese West African complex that served as the immediate precedent for the exploitation of the Indies; indeed, it was on its way to becoming the most important part. Subsequent centuries have shown that the Antilles are a quite decent place to grow sugar, and the seaside location was also favorable. Cane fields and sugar mills did make their appearance in the Caribbean phase, often with the help and participation of the Genoese, long the main spreaders of the sugar industry.[15] But as an export enterprise sugar did not flourish; sugar production in the Spanish Indies was to be primarily for internal markets generated by silver, as with the sugar grown on the northern coast of Peru.

I attribute this result above all to the prior existence of a viable Portuguese industry on the islands off Africa, already adequately supplying the then small demand for sugar in Europe.[16] The Portuguese had a lead in techniques, plant, market contacts, and all the rest. At the time, the Portuguese were also closer to the market (after the creation of the Brazilian industry in the late sixteenth century, this would no longer be true). In the Caribbean, the reputation of the Indies was just getting established, sufficient lines of credit were not available, and a low-investment business like gold was much more attractive than a notably high-investment enterprise like sugar. Later, capital was in some sense available, but it was already being poured with excellent results into the silver industry; furthermore, in sugar one faced a formidable established competitor, in silver none at all. Location alone precluded the export of sugar from Peru in the sixteenth century, and the inland producing areas of Mexico were in the same situation. Thus, the Spaniards within hardly two generations after their first glimpse of the New World had discovered the dimensions of its primary, indeed essentially only great export resource for sixteenth-century Europe and created a complex major industry that successfully exploited it.

Turning to the question of the preference of Spaniards in the Indies for European imports, I reiterate that the accumulation of experience all over Europe, the availability of long-used and tried materials, together with the size of the European market and the great pool of people with expertise, inevitably meant that European-style goods produced in Europe would be more varied and of higher quality than those local Spaniards tried to produce for themselves. In many cases it would simply prove impossible to produce close equivalents. Some crucial raw materials were entirely lacking, such as iron, not then known to exist in the hemisphere. Local Spaniards did what they could, manufacturing many items from imported or used iron rather than importing finished products, as well as tailoring imported fine cloths locally. We must remember how different the situation was than in many struggling settlements Europeans would later establish in other parts of the world; the Spaniards of the central regions of the Indies, because of their spectacularly successful export industry, had the purchasing power to import relatively large amounts of high-quality European goods. Few settlers elsewhere were to have such possibilities.

Some goods, too perishable or too bulky, proved impractical to import. In such cases the Spanish reaction was to produce the item in the Indies rather than resort to using the closest indigenous equivalent. Eating maize and wearing indigenous clothing were at most emergency measures. Foods were the main item affected, and the production of European meat, grains, vegetables, and fruits became an essential branch of the economy—not for export of course, which would have been even more impossible than import, but to supply local Spaniards who could pay with export profits. A cultural criterion is clearly at work here rather than what one could call a purely economic one, yet cultural criteria determine value and price in all economies, including ours, especially when it comes to food and dress. The Indians too were slow to change in these respects.[17] The resource in these cases is an environment where the European plant or animal variety can successfully reproduce, and the Spaniards with a great deal of active searching and experimentation found such environments somewhere in the general vicinity of both the great central areas. The products aroused no complaint in the consumers. Buildings could not be imported either, nor on the west coast ships, so local production soon began to flourish in both these major branches of the economy.

When something could be imported but was too expensive for most of the settlers or for everyday use by the wealthy, the solution was to import as much as could be afforded and seek to produce local surrogates for the rest of the need. This led by the second generation to textile works called *obrajes*, mainly using locally produced European wool, supplying the lower end of the Indies market. The same thing happened with wine; in due course Arequipa and Chile were producing wines that could not compete directly with the Spanish originals but found sales nevertheless. One could discuss whether to call a wine a product, a value, a habit, or a need, but by all the evidence of history it takes time to develop a distinguished wine and a palate for it, and I think both the Castilians' preference for their own sherries and their valiant efforts to duplicate them meet general world standards very well. Above I said that the holders of great estates could be counted on to involve themselves to some extent in everything remotely profitable in a given region, so they are indeed found participating in the import-substitution business, but the latter was the special province of those of lesser standing, with less capital, education, and connections, or those located in out-of-the-way areas, who were not well placed to take a direct part in the import-export economy and thus sought to profit from it indirectly.

Spanish society in the Indies was import-export oriented at the very base and in every aspect. The silver industry was the ultimate source of the economic well-being of most Spaniards in the Indies, whose distribution across two continents makes sense only in terms of location with respect to silver deposits. Production for local consumption ultimately depended on what was too expensive or too bulky to import from Europe. One can only smile at the naïveté of those who debate over whether to put the entry of Latin America into the world import-export market in the late nineteenth century or in the twentieth century.

It may be that what we sometimes call "values" are ordered in the same sense as logical or linguistic processes, that without one being exactly more important than the other, some apply earlier, some later. For the development of the Indies the value that came first was to establish one's family permanently in the most solid way possible in the normal Spanish fashion, if possible in one's hometown in Spain, if not in a major center of the Indies. To do so required money, and that required finding and exploiting the assets with leverage on Europe of which we have already spoken. As Peter Bakewell has pointed out, this drive goes far to explain the incredibly rapid Spanish expansion over so much of two continents.[18] I would go even further than Bakewell does when he speaks of the Spaniards' occupation of "their portion" of the New World. The Spaniards in fact quickly surveyed the entire hemisphere for areas with the requisite qualities and more or less consciously left to whoever wanted them those parts found lacking—that is, without any apparent major export product or facilities for supplying an export-producing region.

Spaniards went to wealthy areas and avoided poor ones, which was possible and natural because immigration was primarily spontaneous, by family and region of origin. The government had little to do with the content and direction of the flow. If we want to see what happened when the state did occasionally intervene, we can look at the attempt inspired by Fray Bartolomé de Las Casas to get Spaniards to be small farmers in the hopeless fringe area of Venezuela, which not only was not well located with respect to markets (in sixteenth-century terms) but also had a mobile and hostile Indian population, so that the spontaneous stream of Spanish immigration largely bypassed the region. Few recruits signed up; of those who did, most deserted in Santo Domingo on being apprised of some of the realities of the Indies, and the rest left after finding out for themselves the unviability of the enterprise.[19]

Some of the putative ingrained values conflicting with resource exploitation really did not exist (love of adventure and exploration); others surely did in small measure or large, but they literally did not affect the basic process. Following the nexus of personal/familial ambition and money, the Spaniards went to certain places, not to others, and carried out certain economic activities, not others; additional factors came into operation only in that context, in those places and concerning that activity. Whatever importance one may give to controversies over religious indoctrination, the *encomienda,* or mining labor, they are all in this sense secondary, as they show by invariably lagging chronologically in any given area. And they are only partial expressions, one group taking a position against something in self-interest, another supporting it for the same reason. Thus *encomenderos* can appear anticommercial despite their own extensive commercial activity because they as the principal consumers often tried to set low prices for the merchants and artisans who supplied them.

A crucial resource not yet taken into account here is the indigenous population, a large topic in itself and one on which I have spent most of my waking hours for many years. We have already seen that Indians could not be exported to Europe as slaves in the manner of Africans, at root because of their low survival rate. Although they were a primary determinant of what the Spaniards could and could not do and a very important factor in attracting or deterring immigration and in determining the Spanish settlement pattern, in the Spanish resource perspective they were secondary. Hardly any of their products were exportable, and even in the case of the one that was, precious metals, their procedures unchanged would not sustain an adequate level of production. This was true even in Upper Peru, where Indians contributed mightily to mining techniques in the early period. If we had only the Peruvian example, we might tend to believe that the silver industry could not have operated without Indian inputs of technology and manpower. The Mexican example, on the other hand, inclines one to think that the Spaniards could and would have mined silver using only themselves, their own methods, and imported laborers, as the Portuguese did in the Brazilian sugar industry.

As it happened, the silver deposits were located in the general vicinity of the densest, most highly organized, and most sedentary Indian populations, which thereby came to be an integral part of the general complex in both cases. Though Mexican mine workers of the sixteenth century left their homes, their towns, and many of their organizational devices and techniques behind, it was still central Mexican Indians who provided the base of the mining labor force. Peruvian Indians did the same without abandoning their homes or political units permanently (some, it is true, became full-time miners). In both cases, the area of sedentary indigenous settlement provided an environment in which to establish a series of Hispanic cities as the permanent base of the bulk of the Spaniards who in one way or another lived from the silver industry.

The various cultivated plants developed over the centuries by the indigenous societies were an enormous potential resource. Many varieties had unique properties, and the agriculture of Mexico and Peru has been judged among the most productive in the world. From the point of view of affecting colonization, however, indigenous crops became important only to the extent that there was a market for them in Europe, or as a second best a market among local Spaniards, or failing that, enough Indians participating in the silver economy and wanting the product that they became a viable market in that particular case. Actually, the process usually started with the last possibility and gradually led, if at all, to the others. Since preconquest times both the Andes and Mexico had known, in addition to their staples, certain crops and goods that were in special demand because they were not available in all regions or took particular skills to produce; complex systems of regional exchange had evolved. Although some products, such as warrior outfits and jaguar skins, quickly faded out after the conquest, others, such as cacao, *pulque,* and cotton cloth in Mexico, and coca and textiles in the Andes, remained important in indigenous life. Indigenous people who worked for Spaniards, whether in the mines or elsewhere, or sold things to them, thereby acquiring money, spent it above all on such items. As more and more indigenous people came into direct contact with the Spanish economy, money began to circulate generally in indigenous society (we find cash sale in local indigenous markets of Mexico before

1550),[20] so that even Indians not directly touched by the Spanish economy could pay cash for certain things.

Spaniards were quick to see the possibilities. The Indians of central Mexico were the principal market for the cotton *mantas* sent from Yucatan and the cacao sent from Guatemala, produced in the traditional fashion and acquired through tribute, so that it was the central Mexican Indians who were sustaining the *encomenderos* of those marginal regions, as well as some lower-ranking Spaniards from central Mexico who became traders in the items. The greatest bonanza of this type, though, was in Peru. There, because of the relative proximity of the silver deposits to the bulk of the indigenous population, combined with the concentrated nature of the deposits, very large numbers of Indians moved in and out of a single site and had access to meaningful amounts of silver, creating a powerful secondary market not only for indigenous prestige items (coca and textiles) but also for ordinary provisions including dried potatoes and other Andean foods. As in Mexico, *encomenderos* and lowly traders both entered the trade, but with more spectacular results, including the creation of some true fortunes. Consequently, there was an earlier attempt on the part of the Spaniards to intervene in production, especially with coca, where Spanish enterprises arose, owned by *encomenderos* and others, combining indigenous technical lore with European organizational principles.[21] Although Spanish enterprises generally aimed at Spaniards as consumers, this was only because they had more money, and when Indians had sufficient specie, the process was the same even though the Spaniards might have no direct interest at all in the product, as was the case with coca through the whole colonial period.

When, however, local Spaniards took to using a given indigenous product, Spanish economic interest in it rose accordingly. The Spaniards never did warm to maize or potatoes, unless highly doctored in specialty dishes, but at some unidentified point they became convinced, the Mexican Spaniards first, of the virtues of cacao. The result was the development of Spanish-style cacao-producing estates, first in Venezuela and ultimately in Guayaquil, producing for the Spanish-Mexican market.

With that foothold, cacao then later won over the European market, becoming a viable primary export product. But for better or for worse, Europe long remained oblivious of or resistant to the merits of New World crops. It was not yet the time when the tomato would revolutionize Italian cooking, the potato would become a staple food in Poland and Ireland, and maize would feed the world's livestock. Perhaps the Spaniards of the Indies were remiss in not campaigning more actively, distributing brochures and free samples all over Europe. But such was not the way of the age, and in any case, the American Spaniards lacked motivation. These great contributions were to be donations, from which the Indians would profit not a whit, because they were untransportable or lacked the specific value to repay transport, and in any case they could be grown in Europe. If anything of this nature was to be sold to Europe, it not only must be wanted there but also must have high specific value and not be produceable there. In the sixteenth century only cochineal, a quasi-agricultural product and useful textile dye, came close to filling the bill, but the truly great interest in textile dyes was to come in later centuries, and the process was so labor-intensive and environment-specific that it resisted Spanish estate organization; production remained mainly in the hands of Indians, and Spaniards acquired the dye through sale or demanding it as tribute.[22]

We now come at last to the phenomena mentioned in my title. As the result of spontaneous immigration for economic reasons, the primacy of silver, and the very strong secondary pull of the sedentary indigenous Indian groups, those regions that combined silver and sedentary Indians quickly became what I have elsewhere called simply the central areas of Spanish occupation, with all else constituting a fringe.[23] When we look closely, however, we see a division even within the central areas themselves. The great majority of the Spaniards in the Indies were distributed along two lines—one for each central area—leading from an Atlantic port to the silver deposits, what I call the trunk lines. Spaniards living anywhere else were there more or less by mistake and from lack of choice, having wrongly thought that other regions would prove as advantageous and then being left stranded, or arriving late, without connections or skills, and being pushed off to the edges.[24]

The trunk lines did not, however, follow the straightest possible route to the mines, but took into consideration the good lands of sedentary indigenous settlement, in or near which was found a capital city acting as the hub of the route and of the whole Spanish presence. The silver deposits did not themselves become the capitals despite having relative permanence because they were in inhospitable locations and at the end of the line, whereas a central, amenable location was what was required as a headquarters on many counts—for conquerors, *encomenderos,* and entrepreneurs who wanted to establish permanent family estates; for merchants who needed to be in touch with their superiors and sources of supply in Spain; for the providers of services, from craftsmen to lawyers, who needed to be concentrated where they would be available to the whole system. Once the Spanish population and especially the wealthiest portion of it was concentrating in the two capitals, the main market for goods and services was there, even though it was ultimately sustained by the silver mines. Governmental and church organizations naturally followed suit in the location of their headquarters, for reasons too numerous to detail here; let it be clear that they were attracted to the trunk-line centers after the latter had already taken shape, not the other way around. The conquerors and other immigrants for their own reasons had already made Lima and Mexico City their principal seats before the arrival of *audiencias,* viceroys, and archbishops.

Indeed, these trunk-line complexes, responding spontaneously to social and economic imperatives, were the framework and partial determinant of everything else the Spaniards did; when the first universities, printing presses, or theaters appear, we know exactly where to expect them. It has been shown that the earliest cathedrals completed are regularly along the trunk line.[25] The effect of liquid wealth flowing back and forth along an extended line was to draw organizations of all kinds more tightly together across great distances than would happen in other regions. I have elsewhere referred to this phenomenon as "major consolidation."[26] Communications were better, hierarchies of all kinds, commercial or institutional, stiffened, always being concentrated in the capital, and family connections too were stronger and intermarriages more frequent across distance, everyone aiming for a foothold in the capital.[27] The great wealth flowing along the trunk line, created by silver production, Europe's interest in the silver, and the local Spanish population's need for the things of Europe, was thus a powerful force for concentration, consolidation, and unification. When wealth and production were less, concentration was less, as with the gold fields of New Granada, where the complex never developed a single overwhelmingly predominant route or central city.

Those who ended up off the trunk line, since they were not members of an explorers' club or worshipers of the simple life, did their best to participate in trunk-line activity and the flow of silver there by selling whatever they could to the people on the main line and using the profits to buy European goods, sometimes directly from Spain, sometimes from firms based on the trunk line. In Mexico the line ran through Veracruz, Puebla, and Mexico City and on to the mines of the north, of which there were several districts, with Zacatecas long leading. The already mentioned orientation of Yucatan and Guatemala toward central Mexico through the sale of indigenous goods gave rise to typical feeder lines.[28] Yucatan and Guatemala, though well populated at contact, with highly organized, easily utilized indigenous societies, attracted only a modest

flow of Spanish immigration in view of their disadvantageous location
with respect to the silver line, but they did have the advantage that because of geographical differences their areas had products in demand
by the indigenous poopulation of the trunk-line area.

Oaxaca, on the other hand, was a fertile, temperate region similar to
Puebla or the Valley of Mexico and hence had nothing to sell to either
the Spaniards or the Indians there. From a very humble start, Puebla,
straddling the trunk line halfway between the port and the capital, became a metropolis at times almost rivaling Mexico City, whereas Oaxaca,
far off the line, stagnated until enlarged European demand created
a cochineal boom in the eighteenth century. From the point of view
of Spanish colonization, immigration and economic development in
Oaxaca were long minimal. From the indigenous point of view, lands,
autonomy, structures, and patterns of all kinds were preserved much
longer there than in central Mexico, and so it went in general everywhere off the trunk line. William Taylor has shown us many dimensions
of the greater and earlier impact of Spanish life on the indigenous population in central Mexico as compared to Oaxaca, the whole difference
being ultimately attributable to the trunk line.[29] The trunk-line effect developed also in new areas, where Spaniards and sedentary Indians were
moving into previously thinly settled spots and starting fresh. By the
seventeenth and eighteenth centuries in northwestern Mexico, where by
then a branch of the trunk line went to the mines of Durango and Parral,
parishes were more populous and more closely spaced, and personal
mobility greater, on the line than off it.[30]

The Peruvian trunk line was somewhat more abstract than the Mexican. Its "Atlantic port" was a combination of Cartagena and Panamá,
neither anywhere near Peru or even, in the latter case, facing the Atlantic, and its capital was Lima, not in the center of the sedentary lands
where we might expect it to be, but the Peruvian system did have a more
satisfactory terminus than the Mexican, ending resoundingly and unambiguously at Potosí. Andean geography, both the high altitude of the
interior and the difficulty of land travel there, induced the Spaniards to
abandon their original inclination to put their capital in Cusco or Xauxa;
they established themselves on the coast instead. Thus the trunk line was
to bypass a great portion of the central Andean indigenous population,
most of which was to be in a situation more like that of Oaxaca and
Guatemala than like that of the Valley of Mexico and the Puebla region.

A serious but not uncommon misconception about the Peruvian system is that the main route from Lima to Potosí went inland straight
through Cusco. Actually, from the first the main route went south from

Lima by sea, then inland through Arequipa and La Paz; later, a good portion of the traffic was diverted even farther south by sea before going across land to Potosí. Huancavelica as the producer of mercury (needed in silver mining) was practically an adjunct of the silver industry and the trunk line, but generally speaking the Peruvian inland, including Cusco, resorted to typical feeder-line activity. As mentioned before, the rewards of such activity under the southern Peruvian circumstances could be large, but effects of this trade could not transform the basic situation. If the trunk line had really gone directly through Cusco, that city's development would have moved a great deal further in the direction of Puebla's than it did. Quito, not only off the trunk line but indeed far removed from both capital and mines, lived an existence closely comparable to that of the far south of the Mexican sphere.

The facts of Peruvian geography had large implications for surrounding regions. Not enough areas close to Potosí were propitious for cattle and temperate products, so the opportunity existed for a relatively intensive development of otherwise unremarkable Tucumán to the southeast. Lima lacked an adequate agricultural hinterland, so that eventually Chile, far away but reachable by sea, took up the slack in wheat production.[31] We see here that though indigenous products are perhaps typically the basis of feeder-line activity, such is not necessarily the case. Both Peruvian and Mexican systems, then, eventually included feeder lines extending long distances across both land and sea, carrying both Spanish-style and indigenous products, making possible Spanish colonization of a type that could have been sustained in the peripheral regions in no other way.

Turning now briefly to the historiography of these matters, I will concentrate on the sixteenth century, not only because it is on that period that the weight of the attention falls in the present volume but also because it is the epoch of the greatest historiographical need. We know enough by now to realize that there is a continuous social and economic history leading from the first moments of the arrival of Spaniards among Indians unbroken into the following centuries: in estate history, mining, commerce, crafts, everything. Those first moments and decades cannot be said to have determined what happened later, but they shaped and gave precedent for later developments and in that sense have and always will have a kind of primacy. Moreover, it is already clear that the deeds of the conquest period, on both Spanish and indigenous sides, were carried out in the same spirit as the more obviously routine activities of later generations.[32] Yet adequate, realistic studies concentrate overwhelmingly on later times. When some years ago Ida Altman and

I were putting together an anthology of original pieces on the provinces of Mexico in the postconquest centuries, we discovered that we had not a single contribution on the conquest period.[33] Despite some background discussions, none of the studies contained serious primary work concerning any time before about 1570 or 1580. The picture for Peru is similar, with some exceptions.

The historiographical break is not so much between the sixteenth and seventeenth centuries as between the conquest period going up to perhaps 1560, 1570, or 1580, depending on the place, and the mature period beginning thereafter. Peter Bakewell and Steven Stern, for example, have made large contributions to the socioeconomic history of early Spanish America, writing books going from the beginning into the seventeenth century, but those books begin to become noticeably more thick, original, and close to the data around the time of which I speak.[34]

Never was Charles Gibson, whom I greatly admire, so wrong as in his belief that the history of the conquest period was practically exhausted. The historical literature on the topic is mainly written some generations ago—or in that manner—consisting of conquest narrative and history of church and governmental activity. To one side is a body of writing mainly by anthropologists and mainly on preconquest indigenous antiquities; this genre has been meaningfully renovated in recent years with new approaches and sources but has tended to retain its preconquest emphasis.[35] Not only is the more Spanish-oriented part of the existing historical literature (Prescott, Ricard, Aiton, etc.) naive and unanalytical and in need of redoing on that score, but also it leaves nearly the whole social and economic dimension out of consideration. There are some works of an aggregate statistical nature: Pierre Chaunu on shipping and Peter Boyd-Bowman on emigration from Spain (note that statistical demography of Indians becomes something approaching an exact science only for the time after the conquest period). Trends in absolute amounts are an important part of the whole picture, but not only are these figures highly fragmentary but they also do not touch on and do not replace an understanding of structures, organizations, operating concepts, practices, and lives. Consider the heroic but hardly successful attempt of Lyle McAlister to write the social and economic history of the immigrants on the basis of Boyd-Bowman alone.[36]

The corpus of work in the Spanish American field which takes the whole range of activity of the conquest period as its scope and studies it as it actually was is very small. There is Enrique Otte with his many articles on commercial activity in the early Caribbean, and especially his book showing even the ephemeral and apparently exotic pearl industry of Cubagua to be a perfect illustration of all the patterns I have been discussing.[37] There is José Miranda on the economic activity of *encomenderos* in early Mexico on the basis of notarial records.[38] There is the work of Mario Góngora on early Panama and his book studying the landholdings and enterprises of *encomenderos* and others in Chile, especially important for showing the gradual rise of later estate forms out of patterns of the conquest period.[39] I have worked, a while back now, on the society and economy set up by the Spaniards in Peru in the first thirty years after their arrival.[40] One should not forget Richard Greenleaf's work related to the early Mexican Inquisition, which though it seems so different from the rest manages, by using specific litigation, to get at the level of actual individuals and the political, social, and economic factors affecting inquisitorial action.[41]

To this by now basic corpus there have been some recent additions. The still unpublished doctoral dissertation of Robert Himmerich y Valencia on the *encomenderos* of New Spain to the 1550s is a prime example.[42] Another is an important recent book by Keith Davies on the history of estates in the Arequipa region to 1650.[43] Davies gives the conquest period the full treatment, showing a detailed knowledge of the membership of all the local *encomendero* families and then following them over three or four succeeding generations as, with additions and losses, they and their heirs, relatives, and associates became the owners of Arequipa's wine-producing estates, and as the area adapted to its distance from Potosí and its lack of indigenous products for sale, on the order of Cusco's example. The relative position and outlook of the Arequipa families remained constant throughout. They were always seeking alliances with families of Lima, though by no means always successful in obtaining them. By following the entire group and its holdings over a length of time, Davies is able to make sense of developments whose significance eluded previous investigators.

One way to handle land-tenure stability has been to count the number of properties against the number of sales, which, however, often gives an illusory impression of instability and lack of orientation on the part of the owners. Davies keeps track of a family's entire holdings and the relative position of the family members. He can thus see, for example, that some sales represent not a loss to the family but a minor heir's reconsolidation of an estate by selling his part of the inheritance back to the principal heir. Families and branches of families definitely had their ups and downs, but they were managing a whole set of diversified interests as part of an overall family strategy; their rationale becomes clearer, and the degree of continuity between the conquest period and later is seen to be very high indeed. Davies has given us a valuable case study of an area located near the trunk line but without other apparent economic assets until local Spaniards developed an industry appropriate to the situation.

Efraín Trelles has worked on the same area, confining himself to the life, holdings, and economic activity of one important *encomendero* of Arequipa in the conquest period, but following that individual and all aspects of his estate through every imaginable kind of record, leading to an extremely solid exemplification of all the main trends and a greater integration of the characteristics and interests of the indigenous groups in the *encomienda* than had been possible previously.[44]

In much of what I said above it is clear how basic transportation was to the whole question of consolidation and resources. If a product would pay the transportation costs to Spain from the Indies, or to the trunk line from the fringes, then that product became a resource, and colonization gained momentum. Yet ironically, at least on the surface, transportation was neither prestigious nor especially profitable. On land, muleteers and carters were illiterate commoners with little capital or connections, ranking about as low as a Spaniard could, and on the sea the mariners were considered to be of a yet baser sort, as the Spaniards said (*de baja suerte*); even masters and pilots had much the same social profile and enjoyed little esteem among landsmen. Ships were less valuable than their cargo, and merchants avoided full ownership of them. There has also been little study of the transportation business on land or sea. Some older studies touching on carting, roads, and the like rely on such sources as official reports, ordinances, and traveler's accounts.[45] Only research at the level of specific individuals and enterprises, based on working records in which those individuals and entities appear, holds out much hope of integrating transport into the larger picture. In Peru, Luis Miguel Glave is far advanced toward a book in this vein on roads, *tambos* or inns, and *trajines* or transport convoys in the central Andes up to the seventeenth century, digging deeply into muleteers' contracts, litigation by Indian groups involved with *tambos,* and other documents at the local level. The gradual transformation of the Inca system, with many continuities, and the active participation of the indigenous people for their own purposes are among the trends clearly emerging. The transportation business and petty feeder-line trade, ranking low in the Spanish scheme, represented an early opportunity for indigenous participation in the Spanish economy in independent roles, and hence also a historiographical opportunity, if one is willing to go into difficult and miscellaneous local sources.

The ready positive reaction of the sedentary peoples to opportunities existing for European-style economic activity has now been noticed in many contexts (not least Potosí and the Huancavelica mercury mines).[46] But we have not yet demythologized Indian economic activity to the extent that we have Spanish. Every Indian adaptation to the Spanish economy tends to be seen as some sort of miracle. I am convinced that it is rather the result of deep and wide similarities already existing between two types of sedentary societies, the European and the indigenous. In central Mexico, Indian-language documents show that the indigenous people of that area knew about the trading and sale of land among individuals, the concept of hiring labor, currencies, specialized production for interregional trade, and many other patterns that, with minimal change, could function within the Spanish system (although the differences that existed would also persist indefinitely).[47] As with the Spaniards, the biggest gap, and the hardest to fill, remains the conquest period itself, before the Indians had learned to write their language in the Roman alphabet. I might add that it now begins to appear that Peru was not as devoid of indigenous-language documentation as has been thought, and the approach through this avenue may be viable there as well.[48] We must not, of course, take it for granted that the Andean situation will match the central Mexican in every respect; recent work by Susan Ramírez on early wills issued by Indians in northern Peru shows them apparently not treating their lands as inheritable individual property.[49]

The first or contact generation is without doubt the most difficult in many ways, starting with the simple greater difficulty of reading the writing the further back one goes, and the much greater volume and systematic nature of the sources in the second half of the sixteenth century. There has also been the deterrent represented by the older literature itself; scholars entering the field have often felt on the one hand that everything was already done, while on the other hand they have accepted the predominant tone of the writing as the tone of the actuality and avoided what appeared to be a swashbuckling, sensationalist, over-ideological topic. (This in fact is the sentiment that David Brading expressed to me when I first met him, as justification for concentrating on the late eighteenth century.)

Nevertheless, much can be done with known sources, and the discovery of new ones has not yet halted. Indeed, in the cyclical evolution of historical research I think I can detect a renewed interest among some current students in the very early period. And in any case, a trickle of progressive new work devoted to early Peru especially has never halted.

Although the early time can hardly claim an absolute priority, it is a period of extraordinary interest about which, despite the appearances, far too little is yet known, and it should be built into research involving any part of the sixteenth or early seventeenth centuries. Statistics on absolute quantities (prices, tonnage, number of sales, size of production, and acreage) will be to the good, but what the documentation lends itself to, and what is even more needed, is the kind of study that looks at a whole situation in terms of specific individuals, families, entities, procedures, and concepts embedded in the currently used vocabulary. Broadness at the local level is crucial because of the overall situation; it is efficient because even if one is doing a narrower topic one must look at all the local records anyway.

It is also advisable that the loci of studies be chosen and viewed within a wider context. We need close surveys of some centers off the trunk line, together with their trunk-line ties. We need studies running along the trunk line, catching, for example, commercial firms in both Lima and Potosí, both Mexico City and Zacatecas, rather than concentrating almost exclusively on one regional center as has become the general practice (and one with many advantages, to be sure). We need more studies carefully following families, town, or enterprises forward from the first generation, in the manner of Davies. The works of Himmerich, Trelles, and Glave are also useful models. Since Spain is so important as a source of immigration, a headquarters of Indies commercial firms, a market, a precedent, and in other ways, we need studies that will treat both sides of the Atlantic as a unit, following families or firms in both spheres. This is a difficult but not impossible undertaking. Ida Altman has just published a substantial book on Extremadura and America in the sixteenth century.[50] One of several significant results is documentation of the extent to which the economic attitudes and procedures of the Spaniards in the Indies replicated those at home. It remains true that the social-economic history of early Spanish America is more advanced, comprehensive, and sophisticated than that of early modern Spain; this difference has diminished considerably in recent years, but it must be erased if we are ever to acquire the right long-range perspective on the phenomena.

Since what constitutes a resource is so largely determined in Europe, and not just in Spain, studies connecting broader European prices, techniques, and demands with the phenomena of the Indies would be highly desirable, though I do not know how feasible. Problems of feasibility adhere also to studies concentrating narrowly on specific resources. There is no doubt that highly technical physical and chemical properties of specific items were crucial to the overall operation of the economy, and that historians are not doing justice to these facets of the historical process. Yet despite occasional windfalls, information on anything of this nature is, generally speaking, spread thinly across the sources and does not reward the intensive searcher for a single technical aspect alone. Moreover, without acquiring a host of archival and linguistic skills, as well as a broad grasp of the overall context in specific times and places, one will not be able to recognize such data as there really are in the records, much less interpret them correctly. Better to let historians pursue their broad studies, interested in everything, and bring any technical tidbits to technicians when they happen to come upon them. It is true that through certain kinds of research a historian sometimes gradually gains a practical grasp of a good deal of arcane and technical material, as can be seen, for example, with the historians of mining. We should make the most of such opportunities. And at times those with a narrow technical interest have the vision and ability to ground technical research in the broader context. Thus a recent work by Michael Murphy on irrigation in the Mexican Bajío[51] goes far beyond waterworks proper to carry out a thorough, many-dimensional investigation of estates in specific localities, thereby reaching a series of valuable conclusions with far-reaching implications. Murphy's example is worth emulating for other regions and other technical topics, agricultural and nonagricultural.

Here I will stop, knowing that scholars will in any case follow their own preferences, but I do hope that they will do so in the expectation of finding patterned and—in its own context—rational economic activity on the part of both Spaniards and Indians in the sixteenth-century Indies.

NOTES

1. Compare Charles Verlinden, "Italian Influences in Iberian Colonization," in *From Reconquest to Empire: The Iberian Background to Latin American History,* edited by H. B. Johnson, (New York, 1970), 55–67; Ruth Pike, *Enterprise and Adventure: The Genoese in Seville and the Opening of the New World* (Ithaca, N.Y., 1966).

2. See James Lockhart and Enrique Otte, eds., *Letters and People of the Spanish Indies, Sixteenth Century* (Cambridge, Eng., 1976); James Lockhart, *The Men of Cajamarca: A Social and Biographical Study of the First Conquerors of Peru* (Austin, Tex., 1972); idem, "Letters and People to Spain," in *First Images of America,* edited by Fredi Chiapelli (Berkeley, Calif., 1976), 783–796.

3. I refer to Lockhart, *Men of Cajamarca.*

4. See Carl Ortwin Sauer, *The Early Spanish Main* (Berkeley, Calif., 1966), chap. 11, especially 233.

5. Bernal Díaz del Castillo, *Verdadera historia de la conquista de la Nueva España,* Biblioteca de Autores Españoles 26 (Madrid, 1947), 82.

6. Compare James Lockhart, *Spanish Peru, 1532–1560* (Madison, Wisc., 1968).

7. See Lockhart and Otte, *Letters and People.*

8. See A. C. Van Oss, "Comparing Colonial Bishoprics in Spanish South America," *Boletín de Estudios Latinoamericanos y del Caribe* 24 (June 1978): 27–65.

9. Lockhart, *Spanish Peru,* 20.

10. Ibid., 27–33.

11. Efraín Trelles Aréstegui, *Lucas Martínez Vegaso: Funcionamiento de una encomienda peruana inicial* (Lima, 1982).

12. Murdo J. MacLeod, *Spanish Central America: A Socioeconomic History, 1520–1720* (Berkeley, Calif., 1973).

13. See Brian R. Hamnett, *Politics and Trade in Southern Mexico, 1750–1821* (Cambridge, Eng., 1971); and Charles Gibson, *The Aztecs Under Spanish Rule: A History of the Indians of the Valley of Mexico, 1519–1810* (Stanford, Calif., 1964).

14. See Peter J. Bakewell, "Mining in Colonial Spanish America," in *The Cambridge History of Latin America,* edited by Leslie Bethell (Cambridge, Eng., 1984), 2:105–151.

15. See Enrique Otte, "Das genuesische Unternehmertum und Amerika unter den Katholischen Konigen," *Jahrbuch für Geschichte von Staat, Wirtschaft, und Gesellschaft Lateinamerikas* 2 (1965): 30–74; and Pike, *Enterprise and Adventure.*

16. Compare Stuart B. Schwartz, *Sugar Plantations in the Formation of Brazilian Society: Bahia, 1550–1835* (Cambridge, Eng., 1985), 3–27.

17. Compare John C. Super, *Food, Conquest, and Colonization in Sixteenth-Century Spanish America* (Albuquerque, N.M., 1988).

18. Bakewell, "Mining in Colonial Spanish America," 108.

19. See Lewis Hanke, *The Spanish Struggle for Justice in the Conquest of America* (Philadelphia, 1949); Enrique Otte, *Las perlas del Caribe: Nueva Cádiz de Cubaqua* (Caracas, 1977).

20. Arthur J. O. Anderson, Frances Berdan, and James Lockhart, *Beyond the Codices* (Berkeley, Calif., 1976), document 34.

21. Lockhart, *Spanish Peru,* 25–26.

22. For some aspects of the industry, see Hamnett, *Politics and Trade.*

23. The concepts and their application are explained in some detail in James Lockhart, "Social Organization and Social Change," in *The Cambridge History of Latin America,* edited by Leslie Bethell (Cambridge, Eng., 1984), 2:265–319, and used as basic principles in James Lockhart and Stuart B. Schwartz, *Early Latin America: A History of Colonial Spanish America and Brazil* (Cambridge, Eng., 1983).

24. I first used the term in the introduction to Ida Altman and James Lockhart, eds., *Provinces of Early Mexico: Variants of Spanish American Regional Evolution*

(Los Angeles, 1976), 5, 7. In Lockhart and Schwartz, *Early Latin America,* the concept is central and copiously illustrated, but the term is not much used.

25. Van Oss, "Comparing Bishoprics."

26. Lockhart, "Social Organization and Social Change," 311.

27. See Fred Bronner, "Peruvian Encomenderos in 1630: Elite Circulation and Consolidation," *Hispanic American Historical Review* 57 (November 1977): 633–659; and also Keith A. Davies, *Landowners in Colonial Peru* (Austin, Tex., 1984), for illustrations of this phenomenon.

28. I recognize that here the analogy is not complete. A feeder line in the usual sense would send traffic into the entire larger system, whereas in this case goods and people coming on the secondary routes typically go no farther than the nearest center of consumption, usually mining districts, the two capitals, or other major urban centers located on the trunk line.

29. William B. Taylor, *Drinking, Homicide, and Rebellion in Colonial Mexican Villages* (Stanford, Calif., 1979); and idem, *Landlord and Peasant in Colonial Oaxaca* (Stanford, Calif., 1972).

30. Michael Swann, *Tierra Adentro: Settlement and Society in Colonial Durango* (Boulder, Colo., 1982).

31. Jean Borde and Mario Góngora, *Evolución de la propiedad rural en el Valle del Puanque* (Santiago de Chile, 1956).

32. For the illustration of this point in the area of estate organization, see James Lockhart, "Encomienda and Hacienda: The Evolution of the Great Estate in the Spanish Indies," *Hispanic American Historical Review* 49 (August 1969): 411–429.

33. Altman and Lockhart, *Provinces of Early Mexico.*

34. I refer to Steve J. Stern, *Peru's Indian Peoples and the Challenge of Spanish Conquest: Huamanga to 1640* (Madison, Wisc., 1982); Peter J. Bakewell, *Miners of the Red Mountain: Potosí, 1545–1650* (Albuquerque, N.M., 1984).

35. Leaders in the renovation, to mention only two, have been John V. Murra for the Andes and Pedro Carrasco for Mesoamerica.

36. I refer, of course, to William Prescott's histories of the conquests of Mexico and Peru, Arthur Aiton's biography of Viceroy Don Antonio de Mendoza, and Robert Ricard's work on mendicant activity in Mexico. The older literature devotes far more attention to Mexico than to Peru. See Lyle N. McAlister, *Spain and Portugal in the New World, 1492–1700* (Minneapolis, 1984), 108–118.

37. Otte's *Las perlas del Caribe*; his "Träger und Formen der wirtschaftlichen Erschliessung Lateinamerikas im 16 Jahrhundert," *Jahrbuch für Geschichte von Staat, Wirtschaft, und Gesellschaft Lateinamerikas* 4 (1967): 226–266; and Lockhart and Otte, *Letters and People,* contain bibliographical references that will lead the reader to his extensive article production.

38. José Miranda, *La función económica del encomendero en los orígenes del régimen colonial: Nueva España (1525–1531)* (Mexico City, 1965).

39. Mario Góngora, *Encomenderos y estancieros: Estudios acerca de la constitución social aristocrática del Chile después de la Conquista, 1580–1660* (Santiago de Chile,

1971); idem, *Los grupos conquistadores in Tierra Firme (1509–1530)* (Santiago del Chile, 1962).

40. Lockhart, *Spanish Peru,* and *Men of Cajamarca.*

41. Richard E. Greenleaf, *The Mexican Inquisition of the Sixteenth Century* (Albuquerque, N.M., 1969), and other works.

42. Robert Himmerich y Valencia, "The *Encomenderos* of New Spain" (Ph.D. diss., University of California at Los Angeles, 1983). The work is expected to appear as a book with the University of Texas Press. In view of the nature of the present volume, I have abbreviated my historiographical discussion in the text proper, but it seems appropriate to describe Himmerich's study at some length in this note because it would be highly desirable to have a similar work for early Peru.

One thing that one could reasonably expect to have been done long since by way of filling a great gap is a Mexican equivalent of my work on Peru—that is, a general survey of conquest society in Mexico. This Himmerich set out to do, but came up against the fact that because of some seventeenth-century fires in Mexico City, mundane documentation of the first generation is, contrary to expectations, actually scarcer in Mexico than in Peru. Instead, Himmerich concentrated on the *encomienda,* giving as complete as possible an account of all *encomenderos* and *encomiendas* for what amounts to a generation and a half. The first thing to emerge was the quick consolidation of the core of the *encomendero* group (despite their loud complaints that they were losing everything). Some families that were high-ranking from the beginning kept, extended, and diversified their holdings, dominating local political office in Mexico City and beginning to intermarry, often giving local alliances precedence over possible matches with regional compatriots in Spanish terms. All Mexico was treated as one unit. Important people got *encomiendas* near Mexico City, others elsewhere. Especially noteworthy was the pattern of multiple *encomienda* holding. The great of the land usually had more than one grant, one in the vicinity of Mexico City, or sometimes Puebla, where they would make their establishments, and others in the outlying provinces, which stewards would manage for them. These new insights are a valuable extension of our understanding of the operation of the trunk line and major consolidation near the time of their origin.

It should be mentioned in this connection that Ida Altman has written a substantial, invaluable article on Mexican conquest society on the basis of published notarial records. Though it is known to some scholars in the field, it has never been published, but it is now forthcoming in the *Hispanic American Historical Review.*

43. Davies, *Landowners in Colonial Peru.*

44. Trelles, *Lucas Martínez Vegaso.*

45. The anthropologist Ross Hassig has published a book on transportation and other matters of economic relevance in central Mexico before and after the conquest. For the preconquest, sources hardly exist, so the treatment is skeletal, hypothetical, and definitional, though often very enlightening; for the postcon-

quest there are so many sources that Hassig has used only one manageable portion, restrictive legislation on transport. The book should certainly be read, but it contributes relatively little to the matters of interest here beyond showing how frequently the Spaniards built on Indian patterns or used them to achieve transitions. Despite the laudable inclusion of pre- and postconquest periods in a single framework and the establishment of many continuities across the break, Hassig remains more interested in and knowledgeable about the preconquest side. He is unaware of the trunk line or of the social and economic ranking of the transportation industry.

46. Bakewell, *Miners of the Red Mountain*; Stern, *Peru's Indian Peoples.*

47. My research on these matters is related to a book at which I have been working for quite a while on indigenous central Mexican society and culture in the centuries after the conquest on the basis of indigenous-language sources. For a description of the project, now nearing completion, see James Lockhart, *Charles Gibson and the Ethnohistory of Postconquest Central Mexico* (La Trobe Institute of Latin American Studies Occasional Papers 9, 1988), n. 27. The book is forthcoming with Stanford University Press under the title *The Nahuas After the Conquest.* For some already published work in this vein relevant to indigenous economic practices, see S. L. Cline, *Colonial Culhuacan, 1580–1600* (Albuquerque, N.M., 1986).

48. George Urioste has in his possession copies of some most interesting mundane documents in Quechua from the central Andes in the seventeenth century, documents closely parallel in several ways to what has been found in Nahuatl and implying that record keeping in Quechua by indigenous people may have been widespread.

49. Susan E. Ramírez, "Indian and Spanish Conceptions of Land Tenure in Peru," paper given at the American Historical Association meeting, Cincinnati, Ohio, 1988. As interesting as Ramírez's conclusions are, we must keep in mind that this type of research is barely beginning in the Andean field, and that relevant documents in indigenous languages are so far lacking. Through the language barrier, I think it is difficult to be sure that reference to a *chácara* necessarily involves only the improvements and crop, not also the land (the Nahuas of central Mexico used the word for "field," *milli*, to mean the land as well). Moreover, most of the cases come from coastal areas where water, not land itself, was the main source of value. It is to be hoped that parallel research can be done on Andean highland areas.

50. Ida Altman, *Emigrants and Society: Extremadura and Spanish America in the Sixteenth Century* (Berkeley, Calif., 1989). For a summary of some central points within a broad context, see Ida Altman, "Emigrants and Society: An Approach to the Background of Colonial Spanish America," *Comparative Studies in Society and History* 30 (1988): 170–190. Since the main thrust of emigration from the Cáceres-Trujillo region—Altman's Spanish reference point—was toward Peru, the book contains much material of specific interest to Peruvianists.

51. Michael E. Murphy, *Irrigation in the Bajío Region of Central Mexico* (Boulder, Colo., 1986).

FIVE

Spaniards, Andeans, and the Early Colonial State in Peru

Kenneth J. Andrien

On January 18, 1546, the first Viceroy of Peru, Blasco Núñez Vela, led his small, ill-equipped army of under four hundred to the plain of Añaquito, just north of the Andean provincial city of Quito. At Añaquito, the viceroy faced a battle-hardened force of seven hundred under the command of Gonzalo Pizarro, the youngest member of that famous conquistador family.[1] Two years earlier, Núñez Vela had arrived in Peru determined to establish firm control over the unruly Pizarro clan and their fellow conquistadors. Among his royal instructions were the infamous New Laws, which threatened to end the conquistadors' un-regulated exploitation of the Andean population.[2] The younger Pizarro arrayed his superior force in a strong defensive position on the crest of the highlands rising from the plain, confident of victory and secure in his right to oppose royal interference in the lands that his family and followers had won by force of arms. The outcome of the battle promised to settle the future of royal authority in the Andes.

The struggle on the plains of Añaquito was not long in duration. The viceroy's hastily assembled force was poorly trained, exhausted from its recent marches in the north, and badly outnumbered. Núñez Vela himself fought bravely, but late in the day he fell mortally wounded on the battlefield. As he lay dying, one of Pizarro's lieutenants found the ill-fated viceroy, ordered him decapitated, and had his head hoisted on a pike. When the victorious forces tired of this gruesome display, the soldiers put a string through the deceased official's lips and carried his severed head throughout the army's march southward to Lima.[3] Their trophy served as a grim reminder of the fall of royal fortunes in the Andes.

THE YEARS OF TURMOIL AND CRISIS

Despite their decisive victory at Añaquito, the fractious conquistadors proved incapable of maintaining peace and order in the former Inca empire (Tawantinsuyu).[4] The crown dispatched a new army under Governor Pedro de la Gasca, who defeated Gonzalo Pizarro at the battle of Jaquijahuana in 1548 and later ordered his execution. After another short-lived rebellion erupted in 1553, an uneasy peace prevailed as the royalist forces moved slowly to consolidate their hold over the Andes.[5]

The slow rise of royal authority mirrored the gradual decline in the power of the original conquistadors in the old Inca heartland, radiating from Cusco and extending throughout the central Andes.[6] The original invaders from Castile numbered under two hundred, and despite their courage and audacity, they managed to overthrow the Inca only by forging alliances with dissident Andean groups, such as the Wanka and Cañari peoples. The Europeans wisely used these alliances after the fall of Cusco in 1533 to consolidate their tenuous position in the Andes. Francisco Pizarro and his followers began this process by dividing the Andean villages loyal to the Inca into grants of *encomienda*, which allowed them to demand taxes and labor from their charges, in return for military protection and religious instruction. The invaders relied on the Andean ethnic leaders (*kurakakuna*) to remit their communities' tax and labor quotas, as they had done during the rule of the Inca. By 1542 these lucrative arrangements had netted the 467 *encomenderos* in Peru over 1,200,000 pesos annually in rents and labor.[7] This system of political and economic control in the Andes began to break down slowly, however, even before the clash at Añaquito.

The first *encomenderos* proved more adept at war than at establishing a just and decent government in the Andes. As the Amerindian population declined from the ravages of European epidemic diseases and the flow of Spanish immigrants increased, the balance of power shifted in favor of the Europeans. Many *encomenderos* used this leverage to seize lands belonging to the Andean villagers and increase their demands for taxes and labor from communities now decimated by the epidemics. Even their former Amerindian allies grew disillusioned with these invaders, who seemed to bring only disease and devastation to the Andes. Within a generation, the productive capabilities of the Andean ethnic communities strained to support the escalating demands of their European overlords. Although many *kurakakuna* joined with the *encomenderos* in exploiting the villages, many others began to resist these heavy impositions. As the abuses of the *encomenderos* multiplied and the devastating diseases continued, many Andeans became bitter and disillusioned.

In addition to the abuses of *encomenderos,* the European invasion brought a number of changes to the Andes, which undermined the Amerindian communities and in turn weakened the *encomienda.* Before the arrival of Pizarro and his army, the Andean communities had developed a complex network of trade and production, spanning multiple ecological zones up and down the mountainsides. Given the geographical and climatic constraints to trade and cultivation in the Andes, ethnic communities often dispatched colonists to settle, grow crops, and supply goods to their home villages. The Andes became a vertical landscape, with neighboring groups at higher and lower elevations exchanging goods to expand their access to commodities not available in their own native climatic zones.[8] The fall of Tawantinsuyu, the demographic declines resulting from European diseases, and the depredations of the civil wars all disrupted these fragile vertical patterns of cultivation and trade, which in turn eroded the productive capacity of the Andean communities. The *encomienda* system only worsened these difficulties as grants divided ethnic communities and further broke down the vertical economies. Such problems intensified as the tax and labor burdens of the *encomenderos* came to weigh heavily on the diminished human and economic resources of the indigenous villages. The response of some Andeans was resistance and rebellion, while many others simply fled to seek work on Spanish estates or at the mines. Nevertheless, these wrenching changes weakened the very Andean communities that formed the basis for the political and economic power of the *encomenderos.*

Competition from other Spanish economic ventures also weakened the *encomienda.* Those settlers who came from Europe after 1532 usually found it impossible to secure an *encomienda.* Instead, they turned to other profit-making ventures in mining, agriculture, and trade. Moving to strategic cities like Lima, Huamanga, and Potosí, these latecomers resented the *encomenderos'* control over the labor and surplus production of the Andean peoples. The problems only intensified as merchants or miners in important cities, like the remote mining center of Potosí, found it difficult to attract mine laborers and keep their urban marketplaces supplied with food at reasonable prices.[9] They blamed the *encomenderos* for blocking the participation of their Andean charges in the emerging market economy, which inhibited the economic development of the realm. In fact, this competition over the land, material wealth, and labor of the Andean communities fueled the civil wars that plagued the first generation of Spanish rule.[10]

Despite the gradual weakening of the *encomienda* and the traditional Andean communities, the machinery of the colonial state remained feeble in the first generation after the European invasion, even in the former Inca heartland. Although the crown gave broad powers to its viceroys, the fate of Blasco Núñez Vela demonstrated graphically the gap between the law and its observance. The crown dispatched the first justices of the high court, or *audiencia*, in Lima with Núñez Vela in 1542 and granted them wide-ranging judicial and legislative powers under the viceroy's supervision. The royal government also founded subordinate tribunals in Charcas in Bolivia by 1563 and Santiago in Chile by 1565. The crown appointed only trained lawyers to staff these early tribunals, but each court had only four or five justices, whose control seldom reached beyond the cities. To curb the powers of the *encomenderos* in the countryside, by the 1560s Núñez Vela's successors began extending a network of royal treasury offices (*cajas reales*) to collect royal duties and provincial magistrates (*corregidores de indios*) to control the Andean villages. Within a few years, however, the viceregal government had either yielded to pressure from the *encomenderos* to withdraw the provincial officials or allowed the conquistador families to gain control over these key positions. In fact, the only presence of the royal government in most rural districts was the occasional visit from a member of the town council (*cabildo*), representing the nearest Spanish settlement.[11]

By the 1560s the weakness of both the *encomienda* and the colonial state contributed to a deepening political and economic crisis, which threatened to end Spanish rule in the Andes. The early colonial order, based on the extraction of surplus wealth and labor from the indigenous communities by the *encomenderos,* was in danger of collapsing. The disillusioned Andean communities faced greater hardships, and while many turned to flight, others took up arms in open revolt. In Huamanga a millenarian religious revival called Taki Unquy demanded the rejection of European customs and a united effort to expel the outlanders by 1564. The Wankas of Xauxa, staunch former allies of the Pizarro expedition, even established a shop to produce metal pikes for a planned insurrection. And the Inca pretender, Titu Cusi, still raided Spanish settlements from his frontier stronghold at Vilcabamba. Adding to these potential dangers, the silver-mining industry faced production declines, as labor shortages and lower-grade ores dramatically curtailed the profits of miners and merchants throughout the Andes. In short, the pillaging conquest economy established after 1532 had reached its limit, and only a drastic political and economic overhaul of the colonial system could revitalize Spanish rule in the Andes.[12]

FRANCISCO DE TOLEDO AND THE REFORM PERIOD
The new viceroy dispatched by King Philip II in 1569 to deal with the emerging crisis in the Andes was Don Francisco de Toledo, the fifty-

three-year-old younger brother of the powerful Conde de Oropesa. Toledo was an experienced royal servant but also a grim and unyielding autocrat, determined to suppress the fractious *encomenderos* and build a strong and effective colonial state. His twelve-year rule in the Andes marked a historical watershed, as this able official used the reinvigorated state apparatus to direct the socioeconomic development of the Viceroyalty of Peru.[13] Although Toledo legislated on most aspects of Spanish-Andean relations, the primary focus of his reforms was the attempt to resolve three key problems: (1) congregating the indigenous peoples into large strategic towns, (2) imposing a regularized system of taxation, and (3) establishing a regimen of forced labor to support the silver mines of Peru and Alto Perú (Bolivia).

After an extensive inspection tour (*visita general*) of the realm, Toledo put his administrative plans in motion by ordering all the Andean communities resettled into large Spanish-style towns, called *reducciones*. He then organized the *reducciones* into 614 administrative districts, or *repartimientos,* each headed by a *kuraka* and an appointed town council of Andean elders. These *repartimientos* in turn were grouped into eighty larger provinces and placed under the control of a Spanish *corregidor de indios.* These magistrates controlled local justice, commercial relations between Spaniards and Andeans, and the collection of the head tax (tribute) levied against the Amerindians.[14] In short, the *corregidores* served as local political and economic agents of the state who effectively took control of the countryside away from the independent-minded *encomenderos.*

Toledo's forced resettlement plans were a massive undertaking, perhaps affecting over 1,500,000 Andeans. Although historians have not examined the regional impact of the program in detail, for areas like Yauyos, this involved congregating people from over two hundred separate villages into only thirty-nine new settlements.[15] With this forced relocation into the *reducciones,* Toledo could more easily impose effective labor, tax, and religious controls over the increasingly restive Andean population.

Francisco de Toledo next focused on organizing the extraction of economic resources from the Andes and channeling them to the royal treasury. He first established consistent fixed tax rates (*tasas*), based on the material wealth of each region and its population. All adult males between the ages of eighteen and fifty paid this tribute, but the individual contributions varied according to the social status of the taxpayer. *Kurakakuna* were exempt, but members of the community clan structure (*tributarios* or *originarios*) paid the largest sums, while those outside the *ayllu* or kin structure (*yanakuna*) and recent migrants (*forasteros*) paid lesser amounts.[16] When an average is calculated, each Andean tributary contributed between five and six pesos each year, which was considerably higher than the amounts collected in Mexico.[17]

Toledo also established clear procedures for the collection and disbursement of tribute revenues. His legislation provided that the *corregidor* announce the tax assessments one month before the collection days: St. John's day (in June) and Christmas. The magistrate determined the amounts from official tax lists and census data, compiled from the local parish registers. If any population changes had occurred since the last collection, the *kurakakuna* could demand a new census and tax assessment (*retasa*). To simplify the collection procedures, Toledo also ordered that all tribute be collected in specie. When this was impossible, the viceroy entrusted the *corregidor* with setting the value of any taxes collected in kind, according to the current market prices. The village *kurakakuna* actually collected the assessments and sent the proceeds to the chief town in the *repartimiento,* where the *corregidor* and his lieutenants registered the amounts. The *corregidor* then used the funds to pay his own salary, that of the parish priests, and any other administrative expenses. He sent the remainder to the local treasury office and the *encomendero.*[18] To guarantee honesty, the crown had the parish priest supervise the process. Moreover, the *corregidor* had to post a bond (*fianza*), to secure against tribute debts and undergo a judicial review (*residencia*), upon leaving office.[19]

Another pressing problem facing Toledo involved fostering higher production at the silver mines, particularly the rich mining complex at Potosí. When the viceroy entered Potosí in December of 1572, the formerly exuberant boom town had fallen on hard times. The richest and most accessible deposits were becoming exhausted, and periodic labor shortages further inhibited production. The new amalgamation process, using mercury to separate the ore from the rock, promised to rejuvenate the town, but employing it involved large investments by miners to build refining mills and drainage adits. Unless the viceroy could ensure adequate supplies of mercury and cheap labor, the miners refused to risk such large capital outlays.[20]

Despite some moral misgivings, Francisco de Toledo dealt with the labor problem at Potosí by organizing a massive system of forced labor between 1573 and 1580, which he called the *mit'a,* after the Inca system of state service. The viceroy designated sixteen highland provinces, stretching some six hundred miles from Cusco through much of southern Peru and Bolivia, to provide laborers for Potosí. One seventh of the tributary population of these provinces served at the mineheads once every seven years—some fourteen thousand men annually. Toledo even specified the wages, working hours, and jobs of the labor force (*mitayus*). The *corregidores* and the local *kurakakuna* had to ensure that the Andean communities met these specified quotas. Along with the voluntary wage laborers (*mingas*) who migrated to Potosí, this infamous draft supplied the workers to run the mines and keep silver flowing to fill the royal coffers of Spain.[21]

Toledo kept supplies of mercury available by subsidizing production at the quicksilver mines in Huancavelica, near Huamanga. The crown declared all subsoil deposits of mercury a royal monopoly in 1582, and only leased the right to extract the mineral to the local mining guild. In return, the state would fix the price of mercury, pay a yearly subsidy to the guild, and provide an adequate supply of cheap *mit'a* labor from the region between Huamanga and Xauxa. The viceroy also entrusted the *corregidores* and the local *kurakakuna* with providing the necessary *mitayus*.[22] Despite periodic adjustments, this system furnished a steady supply of mercury to the silver mines until late in the seventeenth century.

The reforms of Don Francisco de Toledo attempted to do more than wrest control of the Andes from the *encomenderos* and end the socio-economic crisis of the 1560s. The viceroy also wished to use the state to plan and manage the emerging colonial economy in the Andes. This ambitious design involved more than merely governing. Through his labor and tax policies, Toledo hoped to redirect the flow of labor and goods from the Andean villages to the European communities and thence to Spain. In fact, one historian has noted that the formal colonial institutions established by Viceroy Toledo attempted to create "both the market demand and the supply of goods and labor," so that "without that political system, the fragile dynamism of the economy of colonial Peru floundered and disintegrated."[23] In short, Francisco de Toledo attempted to use this new institutional framework of the state to control the emerging colonial market economy. If successful, his policies would have allowed royal officials to siphon the resources of the Andes to meet the needs of Spain and her European markets.

CORRUPTION AND THE ROOTS OF POLITICAL DECAY

Viceroy Francisco de Toledo's ambitious attempt to create a strong unified state, capable of directing the socioeconomic progress of the Andes for the good of Spain, was doomed from the outset. His entire program revolved around retaining the already wavering Andean system of production and controlling its surplus labor and wealth. To achieve this end, the state had to operate at a level of honesty and efficiency unprecedented in the early modern era. Within a few years after their implementation, the Toledan reforms began to fail, as the corruption and inefficiency of colonial officials undermined the smooth operation of government. Regional European elites abetted this process by forging economic and social ties with these dishonest officials to block or alter objectionable crown policies. In addition, the decline of the Andean population and their resistance to crown policies further subverted the Toledan system. Taken together, these factors promoted a host of socioeconomic changes unforeseen by the viceroy and his advisers.

The first of Toledo's programs to falter was the system of *reducciones*. The Andean peoples bitterly resented leaving their ancestral homes, which had holy and spiritual places (*waqakuna*) important to indigenous religions. The resettlement program also wreaked havoc with the traditional Andean vertical system of landholding and settlement and further disrupted established patterns of production and exchange. Pulling different communities into larger towns separated ethnic confederations or even split *ayllu*. This in turn weakened the reciprocal ties of allegiance between the *kurakakuna* and their people.[24] Many villages also resented having the *corregidor* dictate landholding patterns, tax and labor burdens, and governmental relations inside the *reducciones*. Gathering the Andeans into larger communities made them even more subject to European diseases, which killed thousands and further undercut the social fabric. Finally, many Amerindians watched with anguish as Spaniards manipulated the law to acquire the best of their former lands to establish ranches and farms. In short, the whole pattern of resettlement restricted traditional forms of Andean liberty and led to greater potential for exploitation. Native Andean lords even offered authorities 800,000 pesos to abandon the *reducciones*, but Toledo refused.[25]

A key factor behind the deteriorating quality of life on the *reducciones* and the decline of Toledo's reform program was the corruption of many *corregidores de indios*. These crown officials commonly falsified their census and tax rolls to undercount the number of tributaries in the towns, in order to embezzle money taken from those not legally listed on the tax ledgers. Another related ploy involved forcing the Andeans to pay taxes for those who had died or left the *reducciones*, as well as the aged and others legally exempt from taxes. In these cases the tax rates applied to the *repartimiento* apparently reflected the illicit whims of the *corregidores*, rather than any legal rates set by Viceroy Toledo. Some contem-

poraries even asserted that unscrupulous magistrates assessed abnor-
mally low values to tribute collected in kind, which cheated both the taxpayers and the crown, but allowed the *corregidor* to make a tidy profit
when he sold these goods at the real market price. The *corregidores* also
withheld tribute monies belonging to the crown in order to finance their
own local business ventures. Some magistrates allegedly used unpaid
Andean laborers to advance their personal enterprises. In 1580, for
example, a crown inspection of the *corregimiento* of Cañete south of Lima
revealed that the *corregidor* used unpaid Amerindian laborers from the
town of Carabayllo to plant and harvest his wheat fields in the province.
This last abuse of the law occurred under the very eyes of viceregal
authorities in Lima during the final years of Francisco de Toledo's
viceregency.[26]

Such reports of corruption leveled against the *corregidores* can be veri-
fied by comparing the Amerindian population counts and tribute returns from the local viceregal treasury offices. Since tribute was a head
tax, levied against each Andean male between the ages of eighteen and
fifty, the biannual tax remissions should have reflected changes in the
Amerindian population over time. In fact, the crown even issued edicts
in 1546, 1551, and 1558 demanding that *corregidores* adjust tribute rates
to compensate for any changes in the taxpaying population.[27]

The most accurate and complete data on population and tax returns
exist for the Lima treasury district, which exercised jurisdiction over the
rich provinces of the central coast and highlands of what is current-day
Peru (see map 1). Given the presence of the viceregal court in Lima, this
district also should have been the most closely supervised and efficiently
administered region in the realm. If the *corregidores* broke the law in the
Lima district, they undoubtedly did so in the more remote regions of
the interior.[28]

The population figures for the Lima district, compiled from the
studies of the historical demographer N. David Cook, were plotted on
graph 1 and indicate that the Amerindian tributary population in the
Lima district dropped from 30,394 in 1580 to 14,690 in 1630—a decline
of over 50 percent.[29] The influence of epidemic disease and the flight
or outmigration of Andeans from the *reducciones* were obviously widespread in the region during this formative period.

Despite the continuous decline in the district's Amerindian tributary
population, the remissions of tribute money, plotted in graph 2, do not
reflect this demographic disaster at all. If the Toledan system had
functioned effectively, the steady decline in the taxpaying population
should have led to new census counts, lower tribute rates, and steadily

Map 1. Geographical Jurisdiction of the Lima Treasury District

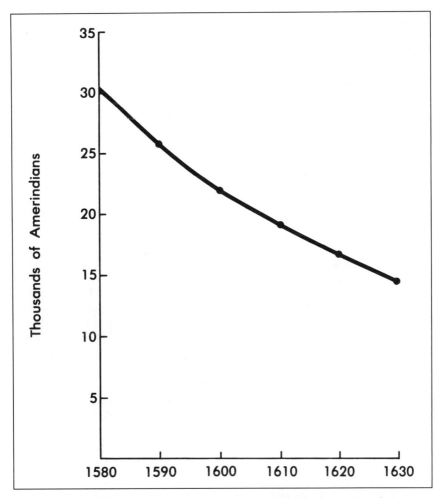

Graph 1. Amerindian Population of the Lima District, 1580–1630

diminishing tribute returns from the *corregidores* to the treasury office. Instead, the amounts recorded in the Lima office varied from peaks in 1591, 1593, 1595, and 1627 to periods of decline in 1590, 1597, and the period from 1608 to 1617 (see graph 2). These fluctuations, which ranged from 3,522 pesos in 1590 to 51,542 pesos only five years later, demonstrate that the *corregidores* sent money to Lima irregularly.[30] These remissions were also largely unaffected by changes in the number of Andean taxpayers. In fact, tax revenues began to fluctuate

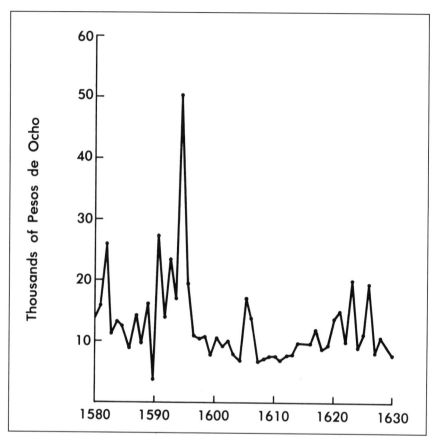

Graph 2. Tribute Receipts of the Lima Treasury Office, 1580–1630

virtually independently of the number of taxpayers from the 1590s, only ten years after the imposition of the Toledan reforms. The viceroy's attempts to force the *corregidores'* adherence to the laws obviously failed, even in Lima, the most closely supervised treasury district in the viceroyalty.

Abundant evidence from royal inspections indicates that the corruption of the *corregidores* and the loss of tax revenues were even more widespread in the interior provinces. According to one member of the viceregal audit tribunal (*tribunal de cuentas*), by 1630 the tribute debts of the *corregidores* since Toledo's time had reached 1,654,057 pesos. The rich highland provinces of La Paz (180,786 pesos), Cusco (399,588 pesos), and Potosí (1,005,282 pesos) recorded the largest debts.[31] These problems only worsened with time. An inspection of the *corregimientos* conducted in 1663, for example, found further evidence of 2,449,286 pesos in debts that had accumulated since 1600.[32] This process of institutional decline took place gradually, but by the mid-seventeenth century the system of administrative procedures and tax rates imposed by Francsico de Toledo were clearly in shambles.

Problems with the *mit'a* system and the need for deeper, costlier mining operations also undermined Toledo's plans to rejuvenate the mining economy. Although the *mit'a* initially led to a mining renaissance in Potosí and Huancavelica, by 1600 production declines became a pressing concern at both sites. At Potosí, the infusion of *mit'a* laborers and the use of amalgamation allowed the miners to draw ore from the slag heaps left by nearly thirty years of mining. These tailings were easy to collect, and the use of mercury allowed the miners (*azogueros*) to extract the silver left from less efficient refining methods. As the slag piles diminished and the miners had to return to digging deeper subterranean shafts, production costs rose and yields declined. The gradual decline of the Andean population in the highlands also curtailed the number of cheap *mit'a* laborers available for the mines, which only exacerbated these technical problems. Flooding in the mineshafts and gradual declines in ore quality further contributed to rising costs and falling profits.[33] Similar conditions prevailed at Huancavelica, which also experienced sharp declines in productivity.[34]

Working conditions at the mines deteriorated rapidly for *mit'a* laborers as the financial woes of the miners increased. Mining foremen assigned *mitayus* to the most dangerous and taxing jobs. The better, more highly skilled, and lucrative jobs went to Amerindians or mestizo (mixed Spanish and Andean ancestry) wage laborers, called *mingas*.[35] Most *mit'a* workers served as ore diggers, who often worked, ate, and slept in the mineshafts for an entire week. Other *mitayus* had to haul heavy loads of ore up long rope ladders, in tunnels lit only by the candles they carried. *Mit'a* laborers were also beaten, whipped, and forced to work long hours to meet the illegal quotas set by miners.[36] Conditions at Huancavelica were complicated further by the presence of toxic mercury dust. Sickness and death were omnipresent, and the corrupt *corregidores* installed by Toledo to prevent abuses proved useless at enforcing the law. By the end of the sixteenth century, the mistreatment of the *mitayus* and the devastating effects of epidemic diseases made the *mit'a* quotas from the *reducciones* hard to fill. The *mit'a,* in its original form, simply ceased to exist; in its place was an abusive and corrupt system that weighed heavily on the Andean communities.

Andean resistance to the *mit'akuna* of Potosí and Huancavelica also undermined the labor system put in place by Francisco de Toledo. Some Amerindians fled their villages to avoid the draft, while others petitioned the courts to eliminate abuses or escape service altogether.[37] Others even utilized a legal loophole, which allowed any Andean to buy his way out of the *mit'a* by paying the wage of one *minga* laborer. By 1606 the head of the Audiencia of Charcas, Maldonado de Torres, noted that the miners customarily received 20 percent of their *mit'a* service from such *indios de faltriquera* (literally, pocket or purse Indians) who paid cash to avoid serving. Only thirty years later whole villages escaped the mines in this way, and as much as half of the *mit'a* labor was met by such cash payments.

The miners also encouraged this deception, which provided them with needed cash at a time when the silver lodes began to decline. The law required the miners to use these deliveries in silver for hiring substitute workers, but by the mid-seventeenth century, they seldom did so. The cash subsidies to the miners even contributed to further production declines, as the *azogueros* left their less productive mines unworked and lived off the cash payments provided by the *indios de faltriquera*.[38] These abuses required the collusion of the local *corregidores*, who most often proved willing accomplices in this deception. Viceroy Toledo would have raged at such a flagrant distortion of his carefully planned system of labor subsidies to the all-important silver mines.

SPANIARDS, ANDEANS, AND THE DECLINE
OF THE TOLEDAN STATE

Local partisan interests, both Spanish and Andean, played a major role in undermining the ambitious reform policies of Francisco de Toledo. While Toledo attempted to have the state direct the economy through his tax, labor, and settlement programs, regional Spanish and Amerindian groups often conspired to control local economic surpluses, instead of dutifully directing them to the colonial treasuries in Lima and Madrid. Spanish estate owners, for example, benefited as Andeans left the *reducciones* to work on their farms, while *kurakakuna* gained as their kinsmen avoided the *mit'a* and tended community flocks, worked their lands, and produced commodities for local needs. Ambitious European elites, in particular, benefited from forging alliances with dishonest local officials or even Andean groups to modify or block any objectionable royal policies. This process began even before Toledo left Peru, but it continued to gain momentum over time. The exact configuration of

such local factional groups constantly shifted, depending on the resources at stake, but such collusion eroded the ability of the colonial state
to plan and direct the course of socioeconomic change in the Andes.

The ties forged between partisan groups and the local *corregidores de
indios* played a key role undermining the Toledan state. From the outset,
local interests gained important leverage over these strategic posts. In
Cañete, for example, the powerful *encomendero,* Nicolás de Rivera, had
his eldest son named the first *corregidor* of the district, and his family
managed to control the office and other neighboring *corregimientos* for
several generations.[39] Some viceroys even contributed to this problem by
selling the positions outright, which gave wealthy local elites a perfect
opportunity to direct the assignment of *mit'a* laborers or tax collections
throughout the rural zones.[40] Even efforts to tighten controls over the
office, such as the security bond or *fianza,* could reinforce alliances with
regional magnates. The purpose of the bond was to discourage tribute
debts, but since few magistrates could meet the obligation with their own
savings, most found prominent local citizens to post the bond. After all,
the powers of the *corregidor* over local commerce, labor, and taxes made
him a powerful potential ally for Spanish merchants, landowners, or
miners. Even the judicial review (*residencia*) process, when the *corregidores*
left office, seldom altered their ties to local elites. Partisan prejudices,
unreliable witnesses, and uncooperative local officials all hindered the
judicial process, but the most glaring weakness involved the crown's insistence on having the successor of the *corregidor* conduct the inquiry.
Most often the *corregidor*-designate had a stake in covering up illicit
business practices, graft, or abuses, which he hoped to continue after
taking office. As a result, local needs too often overwhelmed the institutional controls established by Francisco de Toledo.

Another factor undermining the Toledan system was the tendency of
Andeans to resist the abuses of the *corregidores* by fleeing their *reducciones.* Once away, the former tributaries could claim *forastero* status,
which gave them a lower tax rate and exemption from the feared *mit'a.*
Others simply sought protection from local miners or estate owners,
working as wage laborers. As Viceroy Luis de Velasco wrote in 1604:

> In order to escape from the work and vexations they suffer in the *reduc-
> ciones,* they leave and flee and hide on haciendas, in mountainous or brush
> areas, and ravines, which has resulted in the desolation of the *reducciones.*[41]

This decline of the *reducciones* caused much alarm in Lima, as the increasing numbers of *forasteros* made it impossible to monitor and control
the *mit'a* and tribute systems. In 1616 and 1628 the crown even tried to

round up the *forasteros* and send them home, but to no avail. The problem was particularly severe in the provinces subject to the Potosí *mit'a*, where royal inspectors estimated that disease and flight accounted for the loss of over 3,100 tributaries by 1633.[42] As a result, flight from the *reducciones* continued apace.

The gradual integration of the Spanish and Andean economies by the early seventeenth century also played a key role in disrupting the political and economic goals initiated by Francisco de Toledo a generation before. This process was abetted, ironically, by the very tax and labor policies established by Toledo himself. Forcing Andeans to substitute money payments for tribute in kind, for example, encouraged them to sell their goods and labor to Europeans, in order to get the cash needed for their tax assessments. Likewise, the *mit'a* obligations imposed by the state forced the laborers to migrate to Spanish mining centers, textile mills, or public works projects. This too led the Andeans to participate as consumers and producers in the colonial market economy. By 1616 the Bishop of Huamanga wrote that many Amerindian migrants had fled the poverty and oppression on their *reducciones*, in order to work in local mines or on Spanish-owned estates. Other Andeans migrated to Spanish cities, practiced a trade, and took on many of the attitudes and behaviors of the Europeans. According to the census of Lima in 1614, the Andean quarter (*cercado*) in the city had nearly two thousand Hispanized Amerindian residents.[43] These trends made it impossible to maintain the fiction that Andeans remained isolated and protected on their Toledan *reducciones*.

This greater circulation of goods and people in the emerging colonial market economy was also encouraged by Spanish entrepreneurs, eager to profit from the labor, land, and other economic resources of the Andeans, particularly the increasing numbers of *forasteros*. In the provinces of Huacho and Végueta near Lima, for example, Spanish landowners benefited from the labor of migrant Andean males, who traveled from the highlands to supply the seasonal demand for labor on the local wheat estates.[44] As greater numbers of Andeans left the *reducciones* and entered the market economy, the taxation and labor systems established by Toledo decayed progressively.

Francisco de Toledo's ambitious designs to create a state-controlled colonial economy in the Andes had eroded further by the mid-seventeenth century. Apart from the decline of the tax, labor, and settlement policies of the state, mineral wealth in the Andes proved a wasting asset. As the productivity of the silver lodes in Potosí and elsewhere began to decline by 1650, so too did mining taxes. Along with the recession in the transatlantic trade with Spain, these falling tax receipts threatened to undermine the fiscal strength of the colonial state by the second half of the seventeenth century. In fact, by the 1680s state revenues fell to barely two million pesos, the lowest levels since Francisco de Toledo left the Andes in 1581 (see graph 3). Officials in Lima and Madrid tried to rejuvenate the colonial state and expand the tax base of the realm, but the same sorts of corruption and inefficiency that undermined Toledo's reforms also stifled these later fiscal initiatives. In short, the monumental efforts of Francisco de Toledo to create a unified, fiscally solvent, and efficient colonial state, capable of directing the socioeconomic development of the Andes, was in utter ruins by 1700.[45]

CONCLUSIONS

The resurgence of central authority under viceroy Francisco de Toledo proved a passing phenomenon in the Andes. When Toledo came to Peru in 1569, King Philip II entrusted him with ruling a kingdom torn by civil war and mired in a deepening economic crisis. Given the threat of a renewed outburst of civil strife and the danger of an Amerindian uprising, led by the Inca Tupac Amaru in Vilcabamba or a number of other dissident Andean chieftains, the colonial bureaucracy and the Spanish colonists were bound to be receptive to the reformer's plans to unify the kingdom under a strong central government. In 1569 a powerful state apparatus seemed the only way to avoid economic chaos and political tumult. Like a true representative of the crown, Francisco de Toledo took advantage of his temporary political leverage to begin solidifying state power, controlling the socioeconomic relations between Spaniards and Andeans, and channeling the flow of economic wealth to Spain.

Toledo's attempts to plan and direct the dynamism of the emerging colonial economy to meet the Spanish and international demands for silver, however, proved overly ambitious. As a result, the key royal officials at the local level, the *corregidores de indios,* abused their powers and made strategic alliances with a series of local, regional, and supraregional networks of Spanish and Andean elites to undermine objectionable royal policies. In addition, as the exploitation of the *corregidores* and their allies worsened, many Andeans fled the alien world of the *reducciones* to seek work in Spanish towns, mines, and estates. The numbers making this transition began as a trickle but swelled steadily during the seventeenth century, further complicating the task of those colonial authorities in Lima and Madrid seeking to monitor and control the

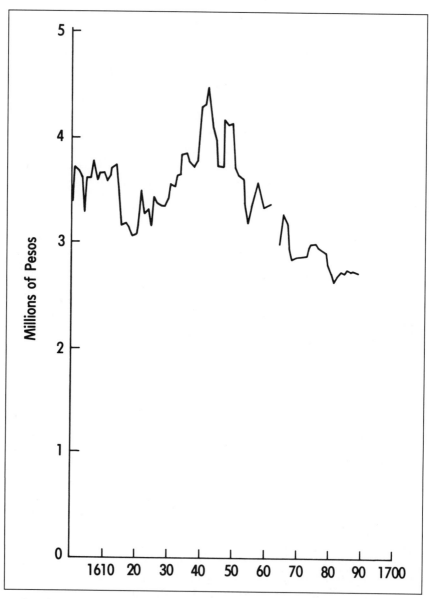

Graph 3. Three-Year Moving Average of Total Treasury Receipts for the
Lima Treasury Office, 1600–1700

Andeans.[46] In fact, by 1660 these factors contributed to the decline in tax revenues flowing into the viceregal coffers, which dramatically undercut royal authority in the Andes.

In the early days of the colony, the independent *encomenderos* under Gonzalo Pizarro thwarted the royal prerogative on the battlefield of Añaquito. By the middle of the seventeenth century, Pizarro's successors among the colonial elite had achieved a more permanent victory over state power through other indirect and devious means—corruption, inefficiency, and cooptation. This was a gradual process that began during Toledo's viceregency and gained momentum throughout the seventeenth century. As the state's power declined, Spanish efforts to acquire land and mines, engage in trade, and alter the human and ecological landscape of the Andes proceeded apace. For the Andean peoples, however, the decline of state power brought both pitfalls and opportunities. The emerging market economy did provide opportunities to acquire wealth for some, and noxious institutions like the dreaded *mit'a* were undermined. But so were the minimal paternalistic state controls established by Francisco de Toledo, which helped marginally to protect the Andeans from the unfettered exploitation of the European settlers.

HISTORIOGRAPHY

Although Francisco de Toledo failed to create an all-powerful colonial state in the Andes, the influence of crown policy remained pervasive in many areas. Despite its shortcomings, the colonial government did oversee the forced resettlement of the Andeans in the *reducciones,* it developed a massive system of forced labor, and it extracted millions of pesos in tribute from the Amerindian villages. Despite the large number of works dealing with colonial Peru published in the last fifteen years, most recent studies have downplayed the importance of political structures. Many younger scholars have associated studying the colonial state with older "legal" or "institutional" works and have focused instead on the socioeconomic interaction between Europeans and Andeans on the regional level. The dividing lines between the political, social, and economic forces shaping the Andean landscape are not so easily delineated, however, particularly in the sixteenth and seventeenth centuries.[47] As a result, many scholars are coming to realize that studying the colonial state and its impact on the "encounter" between Spaniards and Andeans affords many fruitful opportunities for research.

Scholars know far too little about the formation of the colonial state in the Andes. Although some newer studies have examined the careers of key crown officials, there remains no systematic analysis of the first generation of royal officers to compare with James Lockhart's study of the conquistadors and his broad survey of colonial society.[48] Apart from a few recent works, even the location, structure, functioning, and profitability of the *encomiendas* are unknown, while the relations of the *encomenderos* with their Andean charges or government officials in Peru have also received little detailed attention.[49] Building on the pioneering institutional studies of Guillermo Lohmann Villena, some historians have examined the *corregidor de indios,* but most of these works focus on the later colonial period.[50] Even Francisco de Toledo, the principal architect of the colonial state in the Andes, has not been the subject of a modern biography.[51]

Although many historians have shunned institutional history, Jeffrey Cole's recent study of the Potosí *mit'a* has demonstrated the continuing importance of such work.[52] Additional regional examinations of the *mit'a,* the tribute system, and Amerindian town councils could provide important information on local Andean social hierarchies and their interaction with Hispanic society. The administration of the Toledan *reducciones* also awaits systematic study.[53] Recent work has shown how regional Andean communities manipulated Spanish judicial institutions to resist European exploitation, but scholars must examine this question more thoroughly.[54] In addition, ethnohistorians still know too little about the continuities and discontinuities between Spanish and Incaic political and social institutions.

Detailed examinations of the colonial state as an instrument of social change are more numerous, but much productive work remains. Karen Spalding and María Rostworowski de Diez Canseco have done fundamental studies on the changing role of the *kuraka,* and a number of scholars continue working to extend the range of these earlier studies.[55] Although the colonial church was integrally tied to the state in Peru, the relations among the religious orders, secular clergy, and the Andean peoples have received surprisingly little attention by historians in recent years.[56] Likewise, apart from a few groundbreaking studies, government attempts to regulate the relations among the Europeans, Amerindians, mixed bloods, and blacks have not yet received adequate attention.[57] Finally, no social historian has yet undertaken a systematic study of patterns of violence, drinking, and rebellion; even the famous Inca rebellions of Manco Capac, Titu Cusi, and Tupac Amaru II, based at Vilcabamba, have received no monographic coverage by modern scholars.[58]

Most studies in the 1980s dealt with the state and socioeconomic change in the Andes. Following the seminal demographic study of N. David Cook—which charts the rapid demographic decline of the indigenous population in the first century after the European invasion— a number of scholars have documented the regional demographic, social, and economic changes in this formative period. Some have examined the interplay between the global forces of mercantile capitalism and the local struggles among Andeans, Spaniards, and the colonial state.[59] Others have dealt with the impact of change in key economic sectors like mining and agriculture.[60] Another important area of investigation has concerned the interaction between the state and public finances, American markets, and socioeconomic change.[61] Following the pathbreaking work of Cook and Nicolás Sánchez Albornoz, a growing number of scholars have also begun to study important demographic trends, especially migration and disease, as an index of socioeconomic change in the Andean communities.[62] Each of these newer studies has employed, to some degree, the methodological tools of the ethnohistorian and combined them with methods borrowed from the new social history and economic history.

Despite the emergence of a rich and distinctive scholarly literature dealing in part with the colonial state and the socioeconomic formation of the Andes after 1532, much important work remains. Too few of the recent studies deal with the period before Toledo's viceregency, and many important opportunities for research remain for the later period as well. A wide range of archival sources, usually generated by the colonial bureaucracy, are available in Andean and Spanish repositories. Viceregal treasury accounts, government correspondence, workbooks, trade records, policy proposals, judicial documents, and reports from royal inspection tours all provide information on the evolution of the colonial state in the Andes. These records are often dispersed, written in turgid prose, and present difficult paleographical problems, but they hold vast rewards for the diligent and imaginative scholar.

NOTES

1. His elder brother Francisco de Pizarro, the Marqués de la Conquista, had been murdered in Lima by members of the Almagro clan, a rival conquistador faction, in 1541. Another elder brother, Hernando, languished in prison in Spain from 1538, while his other older sibling, Juan, had died during Manco Inca's siege of Cusco in 1536.

2. Among the most controversial provisions of the New Laws of 1542 were the following: (1) an end to Amerindian slavery, (2) that no Amerindian be sent

without just cause to labor in the mines, (3) the establishment of a just and honest system of tax rates for all Amerindians, (4) that all *encomienda* grants held by public officials and the clergy revert to the crown, and (5) that all *encomienda* grants pass to the crown upon the death of the current holder. Agustín de Zárate, *The Discovery and Conquest of Peru*, translated by J. M. Cohen (Baltimore, 1968), 236. A good Spanish-language edition of this account may be found in *Biblioteca de Autores Españoles*, 26 (Madrid, 1947), 459–574.

3. Lewis Hanke, *The Spanish Struggle for Justice in the Conquest of America* (Philadelphia, 1949), 96. According to William H. Prescott, Gonzalo Pizarro gave Núñez Vela an honorable burial. William H. Prescott, *History of the Conquest of Peru* (Philadelphia, 1871), 2:312–314.

4. The Incas called their realm Tawantinsuyu, or the empire of four parts, which referred to the administrative division of the domain into four provinces. For a more detailed summary of the Inca system of administration, see Nathan Wachtel, *The Vision of the Vanquished: The Spanish Conquest of Peru through Indian Eyes, 1530–1570* (New York, 1977), 61–81.

5. Despite its age, a lively account of the Spanish invasion and its aftermath may be found in Prescott, *History of the Conquest*. A newer one-volume study is John Hemming, *The Conquest of the Incas* (New York, 1970). For accounts emphasizing the Andean perspective, see Wachtel, *Vision of the Vanquished*; Waldemar Espinoza Soriano, *La destrucción del imperio de los incas* (Lima, 1973); and Edmundo Guillén Guillén, *Visión peruana de la conquista* (Lima, 1978).

6. This highland zone from Cusco and stretching through Peru to Bolivia in the west and Ecuador in the north was the principal center of Tawantinsuyu. It was also the homeland of the largest sedentary Amerindian population in South America. It formed the nucleus of the Spanish Viceroyalty of Peru in the sixteenth century and is the primary focus of this chapter on the colonial state. Political and socioeconomic patterns varied greatly in the more peripheral regions, such as Chile or Argentina. For a good overview of this matter see James Lockhart and Stuart B. Schwartz, *Early Latin America* (Cambridge, Eng., 1983), 31–59.

7. Hemming, *Conquest of the Incas*, 386.

8. Seminal works on patterns of vertical cultivation and trade are John V. Murra, *The Economic Organization of the Inca State* (Greenwich, Conn., 1955, rev. 1980), and "El control vertical de pisos ecológicos en la economía de las sociedades andinas," in *Formaciones económicas y políticas del mundo andino* (Lima, 1975), 59–115. A concise summary of this position may be found in Wachtel, *Vision of the Vanquished*, 61–81.

9. These issues are covered in Peter J. Bakewell, *Miners of the Red Mountain: Indian Labor in Potosí, 1545–1650* (Albuquerque, N.M., 1984), 61–80; and Jeffrey A. Cole, *The Potosí Mita, 1573–1700: Compulsory Indian Labor in the Andes* (Stanford, Calif., 1985), 1–23.

10. *Encomiendas* frequently changed hands as factional leaders redistributed the spoils of victory following each battle, to reward their friends and punish

their enemies. The most drastic example of this process occurred after the suppression of Gonzalo Pizarro's rebellion in 1548. Hemming, *Conquest of the Incas*, 353–357.

11. Ibid., 381–383; and Guillermo Lohmann Villena, *El corregidor de indios en el Perú, bajo los Austrias* (Madrid, 1957), 30–33.

12. For three studies that cover the crisis of the 1560s, see Steve J. Stern, *Peru's Indian Peoples and the Challenge of Spanish Conquest: Huamanga to 1640* (Madison, Wisc., 1982), 44–50; Karen Spalding, *Huarochirí: An Andean Society Under Inca and Spanish Rule* (Stanford, Calif., 1984), 134–167; and Brooke Larson, *Colonialism and Agrarian Transformation in Bolivia: Cochabamba, 1550–1900* (Princeton, N.J., 1988), 51–54.

13. The only biographies of Francisco de Toledo are the following older studies: Roberto Levillier, *Don Francisco de Toledo, supremo organizador del Perú: Su vida, su obra*, 3 vols. (Madrid, 1935–1942); and Arthur F. Zimmerman, *Francisco de Toledo, fifth Viceroy of Peru, 1569–1581* (Caldwell, Ida., 1938).

14. Francisco López de Caravantes, "El govierno, administración, y valor del patrimonio real y sus gastos y lo que da libre y se remite a su magestad cada año," pt. 4 of "Noticia general de las provincias del Perú, Tierrafirme, y Chile," vol. 3, 30 April 1632, Manuscritos 1634, folio 182, Biblioteca del Palacio Real, Madrid; Ronald Escobedo, *El tributo indígena en el Perú (siglos XVI-XVII)* (Pamplona, Spain, 1979), 56; and Lohmann Villena, *El corregidor de indios*, 188, 204–230, 509–564.

15. Hemming, *Conquest of the Incas*, 395.

16. Escobedo, *El tributo indígena*, 23–25, 34–50, 57. The *ayllu* formed the basic kin unit in Andean society after 1532; it regulated access and title to lands and organized community labor and tax functions.

17. Ibid., 104.

18. According to a contemporary in 1632, a breakdown of the 1,384,228 pesos collected in tribute revenues in Peru was as follows: 8,614 pesos (0.6%) for local charities, 53,920 pesos (4%) for salaries of the *kurakakuna*, 181,305 pesos (13%) for the *corregidores* and their lieutenants, 280,840 pesos (20%) for clerical rents, and 859,540 pesos (62%) for the treasury and the *encomenderos*. López de Caravantes, "Noticia general," 1634, folio 182, Biblioteca del Palacio Real; Lohmann Villena, *El corregidor de indios*, 89–90; Escobedo, *El tributo indígena*, 104, 119–126.

19. Lohmann Villena, *El corregidor de indios*, 285–288, 290.

20. Cole, *Potosí Mita*, 8.

21. Ibid., 8–15; and Bakewell, *Miners of the Red Mountain*, 62–71.

22. Arthur P. Whitaker, *The Huancavelica Mercury Mine* (Cambridge, Mass., 1941), 12; Guillermo Lohmann Villena, *Las minas de Huancavelica en los siglos XVI y XVII* (Seville, 1949), 371, 453–455; and a newer study of Huancavelica, by Carlos Contreras, *La ciudad del mercurio: Huancavelica, 1570–1700* (Lima, 1982).

23. Karen Spalding, "Exploitation as an Economic System: The State and the Extraction of Surplus in Colonial Peru," in *The Inca and Aztec States, 1400–1800:*

Anthropology and History, edited by George A. Collier, Renato I. Rosaldo, and John D. Wirth (New York, 1982), 325. Spalding argues that this exploitative political system actually controlled the economic development of Peru. I disagree. Although the structures of the colonial state were created by Toledo to achieve this end, I believe they failed from the outset.

24. A thought-provoking discussion of the changing role of the *kurakakuna* under colonial rule may be found in Karen Spalding, *"Kurakas* and Commerce: A Chapter in the Evolution of Andean Society," *Hispanic American Historical Review* 53 (November 1973): 581–599.

25. Hemming, *Conquest of the Incas,* 395.

26. The corruption of the *corregidores* and its impact are summarized in Kenneth J. Andrien, "El corregidor de indios, la corrupción y el estado virreinal en Perú, 1580–1630," *Revista de Historia Económica* 4 (Fall 1986): 499–500.

27. *Recopilación de leyes de los reynos de las Indias* (Madrid, [1680] 1973), bk. 6, título 5, leyes 24, 37, 45, 51.

28. For a more detailed description of the provinces and *repartimientos* under the jurisdiction of the Lima treasury office, see Andrien, "El corregidor de indios, la corrupción," 501–502.

29. The population data used to compile graph 1 may be found in the following works: Noble David Cook, "The Indian Population of Peru, 1570–1620" (Ph.D. diss., University of Texas at Austin, 1973), 352–353; and idem, "Population Data for Indian Peru: Sixteenth and Seventeenth Centuries," *Hispanic American Historical Review* 62 (February 1982): 73–75, 115–120. See also Andrien, "El corregidor de indios, la corrupción," 502.

30. The only entry in the colonial treasury accounts of Lima that record yearly remissions of tribute from the *corregimientos* is *tributos reales.* Although these funds represent only a fraction of the total tribute monies collected in the district, they still should have fluctuated according to the numbers of tributaries living in the district. For a detailed discussion of this methodological problem, see Andrien, "El corregidor de indios, la corrupción," 502–507. These impressionistic conclusions about the lack of a relationship between tribute returns and population figures can be confirmed statistically by using the SPSSX subprogram multiple regression. The result was an insignificant correlation coefficient of 0.2656; a coefficient of 0.5 or above is considered significant.

31. López de Caravantes, "Noticia general," 1634, folio 182, Biblioteca de Palacio Real; also cited in Andrien, "El corregidor de indios, la corrupción," 508.

32. Archivo General de Indias, Lima, 280, Nicolás Polanco de Santillána to crown, Lima, 31 July 1663.

33. Cole, *Potosí Mita,* 57–64.

34. Lohmann Villena, *Las minas de Huancavelica,* 453–455.

35. Bakewell, *Miners of the Red Mountain,* 151; and Cole, *Potosí Mita,* 30.

36. Bakewell, *Miners of the Red Mountain,* 142–156; and Cole, *Potosí Mita,* 23–33.

37. Stern, *Peru's Indian Peoples,* 114–138.

38. Cole, *Potosí Mita*, 56–58; and Bakewell, *Miners of the Red Mountain*, 123–124, 162–163.

39. Javier Tord and Carlos Lazo, *Haciendas, comercio, fiscalidad, y luchas sociales (Perú colonial)* (Lima, 1981), 93.

40. According to some critics of the system, all of the Peruvian *corregimientos* except Trujillo, Arequipa, Huamanga, Cusco, Chucuito, La Plata, and La Paz were controlled by the viceroy by 1588 and were frequently handed over to vice-regal retainers (*criados*) or sold outright. Alfredo Moreno Cebrián, *El corregidor de indios y la economía peruana del siglo XVIII (los repartos forzosos de mercancías)* (Madrid, 1977), 30; and Alfredo Yalí Román, "Sobre alcaldías mayores, y co-rregimientos en Indias: Un ensayo de interpretación," *Jahrbuch für Geschichte von Staat, Wirtschaft, und Gesellschaft Lateinamerikas* 9 (1974): 26–29. *Corregimientos* were not officially sold until 1678. Lohmann Villena, *El corregidor de indios*, 125.

41. Fernando de Santillán, "Relación del orígen, descendencia, política, y gobierno de los Incas," in *Relaciones geográficas de Indias, Perú*, edited by Marcos Jiménez de la Espada (Madrid, 1965), 2:319–320.

42. Nicolás Sánchez Albornoz, *Indios y tributos en Alto Perú* (Lima, 1978), 70; and Escobedo, *El tributo indígena*, 86–87.

43. Karen Spalding, "Social Climbers: Changing Patterns of Mobility Among the Indians of Colonial Peru," *Hispanic American Historical Review* 50 (November 1970): 646–647.

44. Archivo General de Indias, Lima, 37, Marqués de Montesclaros to crown, Lima, 7 December 1615; and Cook, *Demographic Collapse*, 146–150.

45. For a full discussion of the fiscal crisis in seventeenth-century Peru and the largely unsuccessful royal reform efforts to check this decline in the state's financial power, see Kenneth J. Andrien, *Crisis and Decline: The Viceroyalty of Peru in the Seventeenth Century* (Albuquerque, N.M., 1985).

46. Jeffrey Austin Cole, "Viceregal Persistence versus Indian Mobility: The Impact of the Duque de la Palata's Reform Program in Alto Peru," *Latin American Research Review* 19 (1984): 37–50; and Sánchez Albornoz, *Indios y tributos*, 32.

47. Karen Spalding, ed., *Essays in the Political, Economic, and Social History of Colonial Latin America* (Newark, Del., 1982), viii. A number of scholars have dealt directly or in part with the evolution of the colonial state in the Andes during the sixteenth and seventeenth centuries. The research involved has been varied, and much of it has focused on elites or economic issues rather than the en-counter between Spaniards and Andeans. It is beyond the scope of this essay to review all of these contributions, but the examples chosen from publications of the last fifteen years do reveal the parameters of such studies and the possibilities for future productive research.

48. James Lockhart, *Spanish Peru, 1532–1560: A Colonial Society* (Madison, Wisc., 1968); idem, *The Men of Cajamarca: A Social and Biographical Study of the First Conquerors of Peru* (Austin, Tex., 1972); Teodoro Hampe Martínez, "La mi-sión financiera de Agustín de Zárate, contador general del Perú y Tierra Firme (1543–1546)," *Ibero-Amerikanisches Archiv* 12, 1 (1986): 1–26; and Inge Buisson,

Gunter Kahle, Hans Joachim Konig, and Horst Pietschman, eds., *Problemas de la formación del estado y de la nación en Hispanoamérica* (Bonn, 1984).

49. Fred Bronner, "Peruvian Encomenderos in 1630," *Hispanic American Historical Review* 57 (November 1977): 633–659; Manuel Burga, *De la encomienda a la hacienda capitalista: El valle de Jequetepeque del siglo XVI al XX* (Lima, 1976); Keith A. Davies, *Landowners in Colonial Peru* (Austin, Tex., 1984); Luis Miguel Glave and María Isabel Remy, *Estructura agraria y vida rural en una región andina: Ollyantaytambo entre los siglos XVI y XIX* (Cusco, 1983); Waldemar Espinoza Soriano, *Huaraz: Poder, sociedad, y economía en los siglos XV y XVI* (Lima, 1978); Robert G. Keith, *Conquest and Agrarian Change: The Emergence of the Hacienda System on the Peruvian Coast* (Cambridge, Mass., 1976); Susan Ramírez, *Provincial Patriarchs: Land Tenure and the Economics of Power in Colonial Peru* (Albuquerque, N.M., 1986); Efraín Trelles Aréstegui, *Lucas Martínez Vegazo: Funcionamiento de una encomienda peruana inicial* (Lima, 1982); and Rafael Varón Gabai, *Curacas y encomenderos: Acomodamiento nativo en Huaraz, siglos XVI-XVII* (Lima, 1980).

50. Lohmann Villena, *El corregidor de indios*; Andrien, "El corregidor de indios, la corrupción"; Moreno Cebrián, *El corregidor*; Tord and Lazo, *Hacienda, comercio, fiscalidad*; and Yalí Román, "Sobre alcaldías."

51. At present Peter J. Bakewell has undertaken to write a new biography of Francisco de Toledo.

52. Cole, *Potosí Mita*; Escobedo, *El tributo indígena*; and Thierry Saignes, "Notes on the regional contribution to the mita in Potosí," *Bulletin of Latin American Research* 4 (1985): 65–76.

53. Some excellent information on the *mit'a* of Huancavelica may be found in Stern, *Peru's Indian Peoples*; and in an older study by Luis Basto Girón, *Las mitas de Huamanga y Huancavelica* (Lima, 1954). An older work on Andean public officials is Waldemar Espinoza Soriano, "El alcalde mayor indígena en el virreinato del Perú," *Anuario de Estudios Americanos* 17 (1960): 183–300. Alejandro Málaga Medina, "Las reducciónes del Perú (1532–1600)," *Historia y Cultura* 8 (1974): 155–167. For some regional studies that treat the *reducciones* in their local context see also Larson, *Colonialism and Agrarian Transformation*; and Ramírez, *Provincial Patriarchs*.

54. Steve J. Stern, "The Social Significance of Judicial Institutions in an Exploitative Society: Huamanga, Peru, 1570–1640," in Collier, et al., *Inca and Aztec States*, 289–312, deals with these issues most directly, but see also Larson, *Colonialism and Agrarian Transformation*, and Spalding, *Huarochirí*.

55. Karen Spalding, "*Kurakas* and Commerce"; María Rostworowski de Diez Canseco, *Curacas y sucesiones: Costa norte* (Lima, 1961); idem, *Etnía y sociedad: Costa peruana prehispánica* (Lima, 1977); idem, *Estructuras andinas del poder: Ideología religiosa y poder* (Lima, 1983); Susan Ramírez, "Social Frontiers and the Territorial Base of Curacazgos," in *Andean Ecology and Civilization: An Interdisciplinary Perspective on Andean Ecological Complementarity*, edited by Shozo Masuda, Izumi Shimada, and Craig Morris (Tokyo, 1985), 423–442; idem, "The *Dueño de Indios*: Thoughts on the Shifting Bases of Power of the *Curaca de los Viejos*

Antiguos under the Spanish in Sixteenth-Century Peru," *Hispanic American Historical Review* 67 (November 1987): 575–610.

56. Sabine MacCormack, "The Heart Has Its Reasons: Predicaments of Missionary Christianity in Early Colonial Peru," *Hispanic American Historical Review* 67 (1985): 443–466; idem, "Antonio de la Calancha, un agustino del siglo XVII en el Nuevo Mundo," *Bulletin Hispanique* 84 (1982): 60–94; Antonio Acosta, "Religiosos, doctrinas, y el excedente económico indígena en el Perú a comienzos del siglo XVII," *Histórica* 6 (1982): 1–34; Berta Inés Qucija, "Las danzas del los indios: Un camino para la evangelización del virreinato del Perú," *Revista de Indias* 44, 174 (1984): 445–463; Olinda Celestino "La religiosidad de un noble cañare en el valle del Mantaro, siglo XVII, a través de su testamento," *Revista de Indias* 44, 174 (1984): 547–557; Teodoro Hampe Martínez, "La actuación del obispo Vicente de Valverde en el Perú," *Historia y Cultura* 13/14 (1981): 109–153; Lorenzo Huertas Vallejos, *La religión en una sociedad rural andina (siglo XVII)* (Lima, 1981); Luis Millones, "La religión indígena en la colonía," in *Historia del Peru*, edited by J. Mejía Baca (Lima, 1980), 5:423–497; idem, "Shamanismo y política en el Perú colonial," *Histórica* 8 (1984): 131–149; and Rafael Varón Gabai, "Cofradías de indios y poder local en el Perú colonial: Huaraz siglo XVII," *Allpanchis* 17 (1982): 27–46.

57. Frederick Bowser, *The African Slave in Colonial Peru, 1524–1650* (Stanford, Calif., 1974).

58. No study of colonial crime and other forms of antisocial behavior has been published to compare with William B. Taylor's study of colonial Mexican villages: *Drinking, Homicide, and Rebellion in Colonial Mexican Villages* (Stanford, Calif., 1979). For a discussion of crime and punishment under the Inca, see Sally Falk Moore, *Power and Property in Inca Peru* (New York, 1958); Edmundo Guillén Guillén, "Titu Cusi Yupanqui y su tiempo, el estado imperial Inca, y su trágico final, 1572," *Historia y Cultura* 13/14 (1981): 61–99; and Liliana Regalado de Hurtado, "De Cajamarca a Vilcabamba: Una querella andina," *Histórica* 8 (1984): 177–196.

59. Larson, *Colonialism and Agrarian Transformation*; Glave and Remy, *Estructura agraria*; Thierry Saignes, "Políticas étnicas en Bolivia colonial, siglos XVI–XIX," *Historia Boliviana* 3 (1983): 1–30; Spalding, *Huarochirí*; and Stern, *Peru's Indian Peoples*.

60. Bakewell, *Miners of the Red Mountain*; Christiana Borchart de Moreno, "La transferencia de la propiedad agraria indígena en el corregimiento de Quito, hasta finales del siglo XVII," *Cahiers du Monde Hispanique et Luso-Bresilien* 34 (1980): 1–19; idem, "Composiciones de tierras en el valle de los Chillos a finales del siglo XVII," *Cultura* 5 (1980): 139–178; idem, "Composiciones de tierras en la audiencia de Quito: El valle de Tumbaco a finales del siglo XVII," *Jahrbuch für Geschichte von Staat, Wirtschaft, und Gesellschaft Lateinamerikas* 17 (1980): 121–155; Cole, *Potosí Mita*; Davies, *Landlords in Colonial Peru*; Mary Burkheimer LaLone, "Indian Land Tenure in Southern Cuzco, Peru: From Inca to Colonial Patterns" (Ph.D. diss., University of California at Los Angeles,

1985); Segundo E. Moreno Yánez, "El formulario de las ordenanzas de indios: Una regulación de las relaciones laborales en las haciendas y obrajes del Quito colonial y republicano," *Ibero-Amerikanisches Archiv* 3 (1979): 228–241; Ramírez, *Provincial Patriarchs*; Silvia Rivera C., "Del ayma a la hacienda (cambios en la estructura social de Caquiaviri)," in *Estudios bolivianos en homenaje a Gunnar Mendoza L.*, edited by Martha Urioste de Aguirre (La Paz, 1978), 249–264; and Miriam Salas de Coloma, *De los obrajes de Canaria y Chincheros a las comunidades indígenas de Vilcashuamán* (Lima, 1979).

61. Andrien, *Crisis and Decline*; Carlos Sempat Assadourian, *El sistema de la economía colonial: Mercado interno, regiones, y espacio económico* (Lima, 1982); Olivia Harris, Brooke Larson, and Enrique Tandeter, eds., *La participación indígena en los mercados surandinos: Estrategias y reproducción social, siglos XVI-XX* (La Paz, 1987); Fernando Iwasaki Cauti, "Ambulantes y comercio colonial: Iniciativas mercantiles en el Virreinato del Perú," *Jahrbuch für Geschichte, von Staat, Wirtschaft, und Gesellschaft Lateinamerikas* 24 (1987): 179–211; Raul Rivera Serna, "El trigo: Comercio y panificación en las áreas de Lima y Huamanga (siglo XVI)," in *Historia, problema, y promesa: Homenaje a Jorge Basadre*, edited by Francisco Miró Quesoda, Franklin Pease, G. Y., and David Sobrevilla A. (Lima, 1978), 533–545. A burgeoning literature using the fiscal accounts of the royal treasuries has also developed; the pioneers of this approach are John J. TePaske and Herbert S. Klein. For a recent survey of this literature, see Herbert S. Klein and Jacques A. Barbier, "Recent Trends in the Study of Spanish American Colonial Public Finance," *Latin American Research Review* 23 (1988): 35–62.

62. Suzanne Austin Browne (Alchon), "The Effects of Epidemic Disease in Colonial Ecuador" (Ph.D. diss., Duke University, 1984); Cook, *Demographic Collapse*; Brian M. Evans, "Census Enumeration in Late Seventeenth-Century Alto Perú: The Numeración General of 1683–1684," in *Studies in Spanish American Population History*, edited by David Robinson (Boulder, Colo., 1981), 25–44; Javier Ortiz de la Tabla y Ducasse, "La población ecuatoriana en la época colonial: Cuestiones y cálculos," *Anuario de Estudios Americanos* 37 (1983): 235–277; Thierry Saignes, "Valles y Punas en el debate colonial: La pugna sobre los pobladores de Larecaja," *Histórica* 3 (1979): 141–164; idem, "Algún día todo se andará: Los movimientos étnicos en Charcas (siglo XVII)," *Revista Andina* 6 (1985): 425–450; idem, *Caciques, Tribute, and Migration in the Southern Andes*, Institute of Latin American Studies Occasional Papers (London, 1985); Robson Brines Tyrer, "The Demographic and Economic History of the Audiencia of Quito: Indian Population and the Textile Industry, 1600–1800" (Ph.D. diss., University of California at Berkeley, 1976); Ann Margaret Wightman, *Indigenous Migration and Social Change: The Forasteros of Cuzco, 1570–1720* (Durham, N.C., 1990); Ann Zulawski, "Labor and Migration in Seventeenth-Century Alto Perú" (Ph.D. diss., Columbia University, 1985); "Wages, Ore Sharing, and Peasant Agriculture: Labor in Oruro's Silver Mines, 1607–1720," *Hispanic American Historical Review* 67 (August 1987): 405–430.

PART THREE

Cultural and Artistic Encounters

SIX

Guaman Poma and the Art of Empire: Toward an Iconography of Inca Royal Dress[1]

R. Tom Zuidema

I. INTRODUCTION

The dearth of written sources on Inca civilization at the time of the Spanish invasion poses daunting problems for scholars attempting to gain a coherent picture of Andean culture. The Inca capital of Cusco had lost its splendor even before the Spaniards entered in 1534. When Juan de Betanzos[2] and Pedro Cieza de León[3] wrote their chronicles, they already had lost direct access to most of the ritual and intellectual aspects of Andean civilization. Alphabetic writing as practiced either in the Old World or in Mesoamerica did not exist. *Tucapus*—square and mostly abstract signs, used on Inca textiles and in other media—were part of a complicated system of graphic communication, but no chronicler ever reported on it directly. Chroniclers, and modern students following in their steps, reduced a sophisticated state calendar to an impoverished sequence of month names in terms of their supposedly Western equivalents. When later indigenous intellectuals began to write, they had to express themselves within the framework of the dominant culture of colonial Peru of their times.

One way to gain access to pre-Columbian culture is to confront our written sources with specific examples of Inca art. A bridge between the two can be built by making use of the few graphic representations in the chronicles, as well as indigenous art produced in colonial times. An important source for such an examination are the tunics (*uncus*) worn by the Inca kings and nobles, particularly those found in the work of the Andean chronicler Felipe Guaman Poma de Ayala. In addition to

Guaman Poma's four hundred drawings, many of which depict Incaic and colonial clothing and provide detailed descriptions of the social and ritual contexts for these patterns of indigenous dress, Joan de Santacruz Pachacuti Yamqui[4] provided four drawings of cosmological interest. Along with the work of the chronicler Martín de Murúa and the tunics actually preserved from the Incaic and Spanish periods, these materials can help to provide a link between clothing designs, patterns of Inca administration, and imperial social distinctions. The thrust of this article will be to identify a type of dress, as it was worn originally by the Inca king during initiation rituals of noble youths around the December solstice in Cusco. Although my approach involves studying how Guaman Poma depicted these textiles, my findings will prove similar to those of John H. Rowe[5] and Ann P. Rowe,[6] who applied the concept of standardization to Inca tunic designs.

Three sources form the basis for this study: (1) the drawings of Guaman Poma and Murúa of tunics, (2) the verbal descriptions of tunics in mythic or ritual contexts, as given by native informants or Spanish ethnographers, and (3) the woven tunics preserved from colonial or pre-Hispanic times. The design and layout of the tunics depicted by Guaman Poma provide important insights into Incaic political and social distinctions. The verbal descriptions of tunics focus on the repetitive use of certain motifs and provide information about the social, ritual, mythical, temporal, and even affective role of these designs. Finally, the tunics preserved from Inca and colonial times yield important information on the context, meaning, and iconography of Andean dress.

II. THE "PICTURED" TUNICS

II.I The Layout of Tunics (uncu)

Guaman Poma's drawings define four key rules governing the layout of male tunics (uncus), each corresponding to certain social distinctions. The *first rule* concerns the distinction between Incas and non-Incas. Incas were all the peoples residing in the Cusco valley, who traced their lineage through the male line to the mythical conqueror Manco Capac. These males were accorded the privilege of using *tucapu*-signs on their *uncu*. Nobles of the Incas-by-privilege class could be given the personal use of certain other distinctions of Inca rank. The case of female dress is different from the male one.

Female dress differed, and the *second rule* affects the distinction of decoration between male and female dress. This difference is illustrated by the description of a ritual (called *sucullo*), given by Ludovico Bertonio[7] for the Aymara living around Lake Titicaca. During a harvest ritual celebrated in June, infants born during the previous year were presented to society in the public plaza. The male babies wore a black shirt (*sucullo ccahua*), with three threads interwoven from above to below on front and back. The skirts of the female infants were similar, but their threads were woven horizontally, a little bit lower than where grown-up women wore their belt. Bertonio compared the horizontal threads woven into the skirt of a girl to the girdle that women used at a later age as an additional element in their dress.

Guaman Poma, on the other hand, represented *all* women and girls, from the age of one year onward, with a girdle (*huaka* in Aymara, *chumpi* in Quechua) or with its design woven into the skirt. The design consisted of squares, a plain checkerboard pattern, or it could be filled with *tucapus* in a checkerboard or diagonal design. He did not use these differences to distinguish Inca from non-Inca women, or to distinguish their ranks, though non-Inca women seem to have used *tucapus* rarely. In his drawings, Inca men wore a waistband, or a waistband design woven into their *uncu*; non-Inca men did not.[8]

The *third rule* consists of Guaman Poma's application of the horizontal/vertical distinction to differentiate between Incas and non-Incas. Decoration in tunics of the non-Incas was only of the vertical type, as single lines or narrow bands with a non-*tucapu* design. The most important distinctions made here correspond to the four provinces, or *suyus*, of the whole empire outside the valley of Cusco.

The *fourth rule* that we can abstract from Guaman Poma's drawings assigns different design motifs to the upper and the lower parts of an *uncu*. This practice will be of special interest in discussing the additional motifs that two kings and some Inca nobles employed in their *uncus*. But beyond this particular use, the practice had a wider significance for making hierarchical distinctions and defining the social role of the owner.

When illustrating the dress of men of the four *suyus* of the empire, for example, Guaman Poma assigned to those of Chinchaysuyu (*suyu* I) a tunic with a thin horizontal line in the middle of some four or five vertical lines or decorated bands on the lower part of the *uncu* (fig. 1). Noblemen of Chinchaysuyu added *flecos* (or *fluecos*), tassels of wool, to the upper part (figs. 1, 3). Guaman Poma claimed for himself a descent from kings whose territory had become integrated into this part of the empire as the province of Huánuco. He adopted for himself Spanish trousers, which are always decorated with a pattern of stars (fig. 1). Normally, he combined the trousers with the upper part of the pre-Hispanic

Figure 1. Upper and lower halves of an *uncu*: the example of Chinchaysuyu.
(a) Guaman Poma, *Nueva corónica*, 322. (b) Guaman Poma, *Nueva corónica*, 434.
(c) Guaman Poma, *Nueva corónica*, 368. (d) Guaman Poma, *Nueva corónica*, 975.

uncu. In two cases, however, he assigned to himself the reduced version of the whole pre-Hispanic *uncu* as the upper part of his dress (fig. 1). He applied a process of progressive halving in the upper half of the *uncu.*

Guaman Poma used various narrative contexts to exhibit his material, making it necessary to discuss three different models of society: the ancestral, the calendrical, and the administrative. The ancestral model includes the lists of kings, queens, and captains. I do not know the sources of Guaman Poma's knowledge of the dress code; he may have seen actual Inca mummies, or drawings of them, when they were discovered and exhibited, first in Cusco and later in Lima.[9] But it is also possible that his knowledge derives from the integration of this ancestral model with the other two.

According to the calendrical model, royal ancestors were worshiped each in his own month, and their cult was tended by those who considered themselves their respective descendants. For example, just as the king would wear the local dress of a province when visiting it,[10] a royal mummy might have worn the tunic of his descendants, who were in charge of certain rituals carried out for the good of Cusco society in general.

The administrative model is best described by Guaman Poma, and he alone illustrated it. He distinguished ranks of high and low Inca nobility, including different groups of Incas-by-privilege, a Spanish term for non-Inca peoples living around Cusco within a radius of up to 150 kilometers, whose lords were given certain rights of Inca nobility. He also described non-Inca peoples living farther away; he depicted and described the latter almost exclusively in terms of a division of the whole empire into four provinces (*suyu*). I enumerate these as follows to demonstrate their relative ranking (diagram 1):

NW	Chinchaysuyu	I	III	Antisuyu	NE
SW	Condesuyu	IV	II	Collasuyu	SE

Diagram 1. The four *suyus*

An office or rank could be occupied by a low Inca noble, or by a noble of the Incas-by-privilege, or by one of the four imperial divisions or *suyus.*[11] Thus, each of these three models was integrated into a coherent imperial system.[12]

When Guaman Poma wrote about Inca political hierarchy, he mentioned, after the king and queen, the high nobility, the low nobility divided into *Hanan* and *Hurin* (see II.2), the nobles of the Incas-by-privilege divided according to the four *suyus,* and finally the nobles of the four *suyus* outside the territory of the latter.[13] The hierarchical distinctions generally are reflected in the dress code, but they may be applied in the drawings somewhat differently from the categories outlined in the text.[14]

II.2 The Ancestral Context:
Kings, Captains, and Queens and Ladies

The Valley of Cusco was divided into two parts or moieties, one north of its river, called *Hanan,* "upper," and one south of it, called *Hurin,* "lower." Each moiety was subdivided again into five sections called *panacas,* one of whose tasks was the care of the rituals, each in one month of the Inca year. The administration of these *panacas* was taken care of by royal relatives who became identified first with the respective ancestors of the various *panacas*[15] and later with the ancestors in the royal dynasty itself.[16] The first ten so-called kings represent the sociopolitical organization of Cusco and its valley more than the course of Inca history. Only the eleventh king, Huayna Capac—the last to die in preconquest circumstances—is represented as a ruler of the empire. In this way, Guaman Poma confirmed the texts of the Spanish chroniclers by representing Huayna Capac spatially with the whole empire—Tahuantinsuyu (Tawantinsuyu), "the empire of the four *suyus.*" The governors of the four *suyus* were called his captains.[17]

I have placed Guaman Poma's first ten "kings" in one figure (fig. 2) and as representatives of their respective *panacas.*[18] The descending hierarchy of the various *panacas* is with *Hanan* above and *Hurin* below, and from the higher-ranked *panacas* on the left to the lower-ranked ones on the right. Thus, we can appreciate the internal organization of the dress code. The *uncu* of Huayna Capac (11), not included here, is different from those of the rest of the "kings." A study of its calendrical context will relate it to the motifs added to the *uncus* of the second and the fourth "kings." The last four of the ten "kings" are dressed more richly than the others. The six earlier kings are all distinguished by a waistband of a type belonging to them only, which might point to a matrilateral connection of their persons, as the administrators in *Hurin* (those who became identified with the "kings" there) were the offspring of alliances with non-Inca realms. While I have not explained why the sixth "king" has a waistband,[19] there is an overall correspondence be-

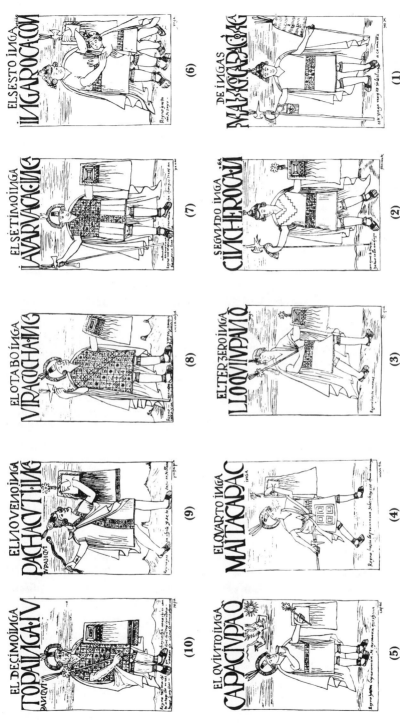

Figure 2. The first ten kings in the Inca dynasty. The sequence goes from right to left and from the lower to the upper row. Guaman Poma, *Nueva corónica*, 86, 88, 96, 98, 100, 102, 104, 106, 108, 110.

tween Guaman Poma's distinction of the first six kings and the later four kings and the *Hurin* (first five)/*Hanan* (last five) distinction as applied to the legendary dynasty.[20] The most commonly accepted list of "kings" is the following:

Hurin-Cusco	*Hanan-Cusco*
Manco Capac (1)	Inca Roca (6)
Sinchi Roca (2)	Yahuar Huacac (7)
Lloque Yupanqui (3)	Viracocha Inca (8)
Mayta Capac (4)	Pachacuti Inca (9)
Capac Yupanqui (5)	Tupac Yupanqui (10)

Huayna Capac (11)

Atahualpa   Huascar

The system of captains in Guaman Poma is similar to that described by Pedro Sarmiento de Gamboa. Whereas Sarmiento mentioned that each of the first ten "kings" had a secondary son, who became the head of his father's *panaca*, Guaman Poma recognized these sons as captains of their fathers' armies (fig. 3). In the case of Huayna Capac, however, he jointly listed the four governors of the *suyus* of the empire, instead of the one captain, and represented them as being of non-Inca origin (fig. 4). In this way, he confirmed the opinion of other chroniclers about Huayna Capac's close association with the people of the four *suyus*.[21] In addition, the tunics of the captains of the first ten kings do not express the same *Hanan/Hurin* distinction as do the royal tunics.

The queens follow the same sequence as their husbands, but without any *Hanan/Hurin* distinction (fig. 5).[22] Only two queens (numbers one and nine) stand out in their dress and ornaments, and they will be of special interest for their calendrical importance. For the captains, Guaman Poma mentions only the wives of the four who were non-Inca (numbers twelve through fifteen).

II.3 The Calendrical Context: The Two Series of Months

Although Guaman Poma presented the Inca months as corresponding to the European calendar, his references to the sequence of Andean rituals remains important to understanding patterns of dress. The *first series* considers the calendar as celebrated by the nobility in Cusco (fig. 6). The king himself is recognizable in nine months (February, March, April, June, July, August, December, and, probably, January and October). In three months (September, November, and May), the central figure clearly is *not* the king. Except for the months of December and

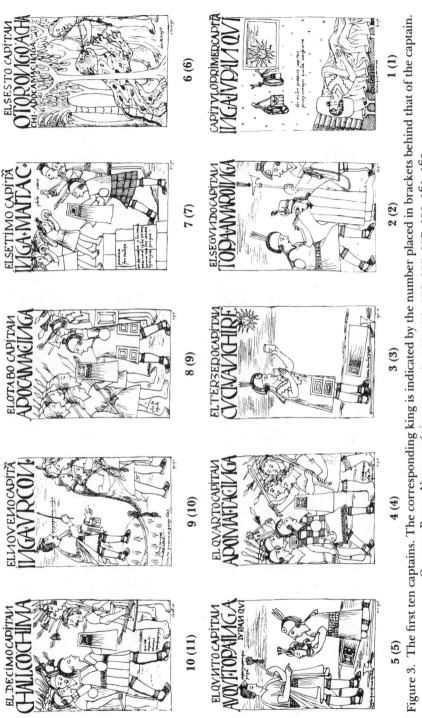

Figure 3. The first ten captains. The corresponding king is indicated by the number placed in brackets behind that of the captain. Guaman Poma, *Nueva corónica*, 145, 147, 149, 151, 153, 155, 157, 159, 161, 163.

ELDO 3 E CAPÍTAN
CAPACAPOGVAMAN
CHAVA

(b)

EL TRE 3 E CAPÍTAN
CAPACAPONIIAR
VA

(d)

EL ONZENOINGA
GVAINACAPAC

(a)

EL QVN 3 E CAPÍTAN
MALLCOMVLLO

(e)

ELCATOR 3 E CAPÍTAN
MALLCO CASTILLA
PARI

(c)

Figure 4. Huayna Capac, the eleventh king, with the governors of the four *suyus*. Guaman Poma, *Nueva corónica*, 112, 167, 171, 169, 173.

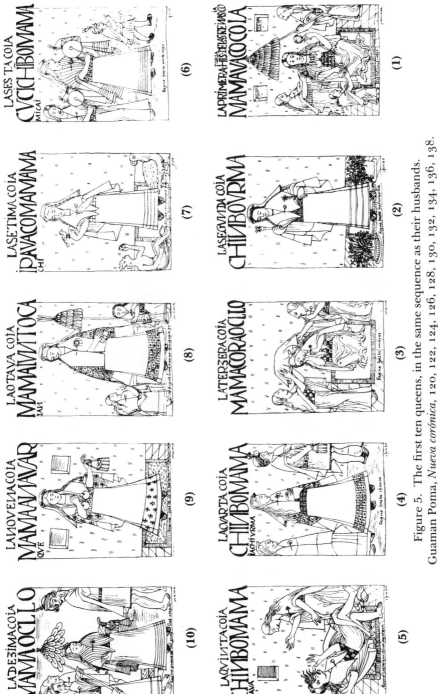

Figure 5. The first ten queens, in the same sequence as their husbands. Guaman Poma, *Nueva corónica*, 120, 122, 124, 126, 128, 130, 132, 134, 136, 138.

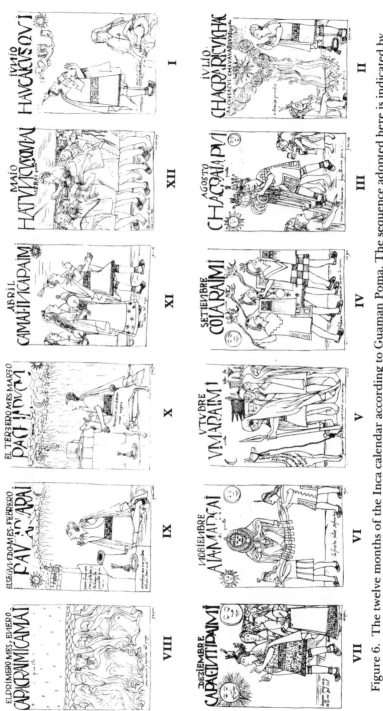

Figure 6. The twelve months of the Inca calendar according to Guaman Poma. The sequence adopted here is indicated by the Roman numerals. Guaman Poma, *Nueva corónica*, 248, 250, 252, 254, 256, 258, 260, 238, 240, 242, 244, 246.

August, where there are added motifs on the royal *uncus,* these are plain, with only a normal kind of waistband.[23]

In the *second series* Guaman Poma described primarily agricultural activities. The *uncus* of the men are undecorated, except for that of the principal figure for August, who has the same *uncu* as the king's in the first series.[24]

II.4 Guaman Poma's Combination of Space and Time

Betanzos and an anonymous chronicler[25] had indicated that an integrated system of space and time existed in the political organization of Cusco; Guaman Poma gives pertinent details about that integration through his drawings of kings, captains, queens, and months.

The original Inca calendar did not account for a period of thirty-seven days (3 May to 9 June), during which no agricultural activities were carried out. The main part of the year—328 days—was organized into twelve monthlike periods of unequal length. The Spanish chroniclers, who were not aware of this system of thirteen named periods, depicted it as corresponding to their own system of twelve months. Thus, Betanzos and the anonymous chronicler mentioned how the population of Cusco was divided into twelve parts, each being assigned the direction of the rituals for one month. Ten of these were the *panacas.* The months of planting (IV) and harvest (XII) belonged to the original population of the valley, conquered by the Incas. Both months were associated with a female ancestor who also became integrated in the dynasty as a queen (nine and one, respectively).[26]

Guaman Poma identified the months of planting and harvest as September (IV) and May (XII), respectively. While in most pictures (months I–III, VII, IX–XI), the central person is recognizable as the king, in others it is either an Inca nobleman (months IV–V, VII) or a non-Inca lord (VI). This leaves the thirty-seven day period as a thirteenth month (XIII) when non-Inca lords of the four *suyus* brought their presents to the king and left with others. The references of Guaman Poma to an association of this period with Huayna Capac and his queen are especially convincing. Figure 7 reflects the integration of space and time by placing the "kings" and "queens" according to the "months" that they represent as ancestors to the *panacas* and the three other groups. We realize that their place in the calendrical sequence is not the same as in the "dynastic" sequence. Thus, Guaman Poma's drawings will illustrate an integrated system of time-space that he never explicitly mentioned in his text; he serves to confirm and correct the information of other written sources of which he may not have been aware.

Figure 7. The integration of space and time in the original Inca calendar recognizing thirteen months. The Roman numerals represent the months; the Arabic numerals within brackets represent the eleven male royal ancestors and the two female royal ancestors. Guaman Poma, *Nueva corónica*, 96, 100, 98, 136, 86, 88, 110, 112, 120, 104, 106, 102, 108.

II.5 The Administrative Context: The Head Ornaments

Guaman Poma prepared two elaborate, illustrated descriptions of ranks and offices which included (1) high nobility, (2) low nobility as divided into *Hanan* and *Hurin*, (3) various groups of Incas-by-privilege, and (4) non-Inca lords of the four *suyu*.[27] For the second and third groups, he made no clear distinctions in the dress code for the moieties or *suyus*; he distinguished between lords through their head ornaments, which may be either rectangular or round. He did not, however, apply the device consistently. Apparently, the rectangular ornament indicated the higher rank in drawings in which both types were depicted.[28]

III. THE "WRITTEN"[29] TUNICS: THE THREE DESIGN MOTIFS—*AHUAQUI, CASANA,* AND *COLLCAPATA*

As we have seen, Guaman Poma used patterns of tunic design to make distinctions of rank and political organization in the Inca empire. I will concentrate on three that stand out for two reasons. First, Guaman Poma included them in his record of kings and nobles, and second, we have additional textual support from him and others.

III.1 Ahuaqui

Ahuaqui was a V-shaped design, made of squares and woven into the tunic as a yoke around the neck at front and back. A similar design, but of straight lines, could replace it or be combined with it; it is uncertain, however, whether the same name was applied to it.[30] Although the term *ahuaqui* alone remains open to different interpretations, its combination with the term *casana* defines the range of V-shaped yoke motifs to which it can be applied.[31] In the case of King Sinchi Roca (two), who is portrayed with a rose shirt with his *ahuaqui*, three rows of *tucapu*, with red below, Guaman Poma does not show the *casana* motif and indicates the *ahuaqui* only by its stepped inner and outer borders.[32] In other examples he shows the space filled with squares, but never in a checkerboard pattern. The *ahuaqui* occurs twice with a waistband, the latter either filled with *tucapus* or with a non-*tucapu* design; it is frequently combined with *casana*, but only once with *collcapata*.[33]

III.2 Casana

The *casana* motif consisted of four squares within a larger frame and occurred only on the lower half of a tunic. The combination of an *ahuaqui* and a *casana*, given in the term mentioned by Diego González Holguín, is confirmed by the survival of a woven tunic (fig. 9b).[34] Both

motifs also might be combined with the waistband. Guaman Poma illustrated them repeatedly and mentioned them by name when they belonged to a royal *uncu*. The king with this motif in his tunic was Mayta
Capac (four), and Guaman Poma described the design of his *uncu* as blue
above, three rows of *tocapo* in the middle, and *caxane* below in white and
green.[35]

III.3 Collcapata

Martín de Murúa was acquainted with the third motif, a checkerboard
pattern, as *collcapata*. Cristóbal de Molina referred to it by name in a
calendrical ritual, and Santacruz Pachacuti mentioned and illustrated it
in his cosmological drawing. Guaman Poma illustrated it repeatedly
without naming it. Although it occurs only twice in a pre-Hispanic
context as a pattern covering the whole tunic, the relationship to its
half-representation gives us the most important clue for analyzing the
meaning of all three motifs in their sociopolitical context.

Molina is the first author to refer to a tunic called *collcapata* in his
description of the rituals for the June solstice. On that occasion, the king
and noble lords went out to a hill, Mantucalla (Manturcalla), to dance
and drink, being served by *acllas*, "virgins of the sun," and burning wood
as a sacrifice to the sun.[36] Two golden statues were brought out, called
Inca ocllo and Palpa ocllo, which represented the wives of the sun. These
statues are mentioned in relation to three tunics, called *llancapata, collcapata,* and *paucar uncu*. It is not stated how the tunics were used, but I
assume from the ritual context that the *collcapata* belonged to, or was
associated with, the image of the sun or the scepter, *suntur paucar*, in
symbolic representation of the sun and the king.[37] Murúa mentioned the
uncus llancapata and *collcapata* as male tunics and says that the latter had
a checkerboard pattern.[38] The name *collcapata,* however, is of interest for
understanding the pattern in general. Let us explore its use, function,
and meaning.

In Cusco, the toponym *collcapata* was given to the hill above the city
where the fortress of Sacsayhuaman was considered to be another temple of the sun. Santacruz Pachacuti presented his temple of the sun as
standing on Collcapata, "the hill of terraces with storehouses," and illustrated the latter as a rectangular grid pattern. He may have intended a
checkerboard pattern, and the metaphorical use of the word *collca* supports such a view. Andean peoples had various kinds of storehouses, but
only the stone ones—used by the state (González Holguín) and the army
(Bertonio)—were called *collca*. Bertonio added to his description the
words *collca huahuani,* "one who has many children (sons)," and *collca*

haque, "to be many in a house, family, relatives." Apparently, tunics with a checkerboard pattern were compared to the repetitive pattern of storehouses in parallel rows, expressing similar ideas about state administration. Storehouses and checkerboard tunics belonged to the base of a hierarchical structure upon which higher forms of organization and composition were built.

III.4 The Social Contexts of the Three Motifs

Guaman Poma gave no explanation of the fact that two kings had the *ahuaqui* or the *casana* motifs on their tunics. Yet there must have been a symbolic reason, independent of the person's social position. The *collcapata* motif occurs in a royal context only in the tunic of King Huayna Capac (eleven), covering the whole dress and including the use of two *tucapus* within this pattern. In his depictions of people other than kings during the pre-Hispanic period, Guaman Poma used *ahuaqui* frequently with *casana,* but only once with *collcapata.* Moreover, the latter pattern occurs only within the dual relationship of two men, the other having *casana.* Although this seems to give a preponderance to *casana,* *ahuaqui* gains a central meaning in the royal *uncu* used during Capac raymi, the design of which is an elaboration upon the combination of *ahuaqui* with the waistband.

In order to elucidate the contrasting meanings of *collcapata* and *casana,* I will first indicate their use in Guaman Poma's series of captains. The juxtaposition of *casana* and *collcapata* within each moiety (captains three and four, and seven and nine, respectively) stands out; each juxtaposition occurs in the context of a third captain (five and nine, respectively) who has a waistband. The latter, of higher rank, has either a crown, *masca paycha* (captain five; but without the upper part as found with kings), or a rectangular headband ornament (captain nine) with the two feathers indicating high nobility.[39] Even though captains seven, eight, and nine are attached to different kings, they are discussed as a group, being contemporaneous and fighting together.[40]

Guaman Poma also juxtaposed the *casana* and the *collcapata* motifs in his pictures of the months of planting and after-harvest. He referred to the calendrical context only indirectly in depicting the tunic of *collcapata* during the feast of Inca raymi (after-harvest). He discussed two officers, who served their king in a police function, imprisoning the non-Incaic lords who failed to bring presents to Cusco and pay their respects to the king.[41] The first officer, of *Hanan,* carries the royal crown on a stick (fig. 8b). He also replicates in the lower part of his tunic the design used by the king in Inca raymi, which Guaman Poma depicts in a second de-

Figure 8. Huayna Capac (eleven), his queen Raua Ocllo, and the month
of Inca raymi (XIII). Guaman Poma, *Nueva corónica*, 320,
344, 346, 112, 318, 140.

scription of these rituals (fig. 8a). The second officer, of *Hurin,* carries the royal sandals and *chuspa* (bag), and his tunic is of the *ahuaqui-casana* type (fig. 8c). Moreover, he has a rope for tying prisoners, in contrast to his companion giving the orders. The crown and the sandals indicate their respective links to *Hanan* (upper) and *Hurin* (lower).[42]

Elsewhere I have argued for an identity of the ancestral king Huayna Capac (eleven) with the ruling king during his ritual functions in Inca raymi.[43] Guaman Poma shows them both wearing the same kind of *uncu* with the checkerboard pattern of two *tucapus* covering the whole field (figs. 8d, 8a).[44] As this identity is central to my argument, let me review briefly the evidence on Huayna Capac. Even though he was not represented spatially within the valley of Cusco, he received a time slot in the calendar. Other chroniclers, before Guaman Poma, already had either linked the king with the lords of the four *suyus* during the celebrations after harvest or mentioned the coronation of Huayna Capac in that context. Guaman Poma likewise presented Huayna Capac in such a role during the month of Inca raymi.

This correlation applied to Huayna Capac as king, but can be demonstrated more definitively for his queen. Guaman Poma identified Raua Ocllo (eleven), the wife of Huayna Capac, unambiguously with the queen in the month of Inca raymi.[45] When at that time the king sang in duo with a llama, both imitating the water that returned to the irrigation canals, the queen in her calendrical role, as well as Raua Ocllo, carried out a ritual with similar intent. Raua Ocllo was said to have had many musicians at her court who sang *haravi,* love songs, in the place called Huaca Punco—still well known, where the Huatanay River enters Cusco—and they played the *pincullu,* a flute, in Pincollona Pata, in Cantoc, and in Viroy Pata (and) Cinga Urco.

The songs were transcribed later, as those directed to a "queen" in the month of Inca raymi. This text is combined with a drawing where young men play the *pincullu,* sitting on the mountains Cenca and Pincullonapata, and where girls with loose hair swim in the water, called Uatanay mayu (the river Huatanay), Cantoc uno (the water of Cantoc), Collquemachacuay, and Viroy paccha (waterfall of Viroy) (fig. 8e). Not only are the same place names used again, but two other factors support Raua Ocllo's identification with the queen in Inca raymi. She is shown washing her abundant hair, the water gushing down into a basin (fig. 8f), while in the other drawing the long hair of the sirens forms part of the waves in the river. This last drawing with its text introduces that of the king singing with a llama; there, the description of the love songs to a "queen" is continued. Drawings and texts form part of a single entity. While the second text would not have identified Huayna Capac immediately as the king of Inca raymi, his *uncu* and the information on his wife do.

With this identity established, it now seems possible to link the name Collcapata to Huayna Capac's *uncu* and to that of the Inca in Inca raymi. One of the best-known names for the stars of the Pleiades was, and still is, Collca. They disappear from sight during the time when harvest is stored, that is, when seed disappears from sight until it can be used again for planting during the next agricultural season.[46] *Uncus* with a checkerboard pattern, of a simpler version than Huayna Capac's were worn by soldiers.[47] We might suggest that they were also an attribute of the farmers when they brought in the harvest, singing the songs *aucaylli* (*auca*, "warrior, enemy"; *aylli*, "victory song"), as is mentioned by Guaman Poma in this context.[48]

The other occasion on which Guaman Poma used the *collcapata* and *casana* patterns in a complementary way is for the month of planting, "September," when the moon and women in general were honored in the "feast of the Queen," Coya raymi. Guaman Poma showed how warriors with torches chased evil and illnesses out of the valley (fig. 6: month IV). The leading captain's tunic is covered with a butterfly design, otherwise used only by the ancestral queens associated with the months of planting and harvest (fig. 6: IV and XI) and by women in bridal dress during their wedding (fig. 13b).

The captain is an Inca noble, recognizable by his pierced ears, but he has on his helmet the emblem of the non-Inca nobles of Collasuyu (II). One of the two other noble warriors has the *collcapata* in the lower part and a nonstepped *ahuaqui* in the upper part of his tunic,[49] and he carries the rectangular emblem on his helmet. The other warrior has the *ahuaqui-casana* design and the circular emblem. In their cases, then, the two emblems probably imply a *Hanan/Hurin* distinction of the *collcapata* and *casana* motifs.

The warriors were at the service of a female interest, as Coya raymi had to be a month of peace propitious for planting. This fact is most evident in the *uncu* of the leading captain using a female symbol. First of all, he represents the queen, and we may ask the question: where was the king at this time? The male rituals of plowing are the ones that introduce the female ones of planting in September. The king in August is presented without the waistband of nobility, and he carries the *casana* motif (fig. 6: III). Mayta Capac (four)—the ancestral king whose *panaca* is in charge of the month of August and thus of the plowing rituals—has the same *casana* motif in his *uncu*, according to Guaman Poma as well as to Murúa (fig. 7: III). He does not have the *ahuaqui* but instead exhibits the waistband.

Apart from these calendrical reconstructions, the mythology about Mayta Capac depicts his close association with the thunder god.[50] Mayta Capac was the prototype of a man in the act of plowing, singing again the victory songs called *aucaylli* (fig. 6: III), as had been done in the post-harvest rituals. He is compared to the class of young, initiated warriors—those still without the responsibilities of administrative office customarily given to married men. Guaman Poma referred to them repeatedly and gave them all an *uncu* with the *casana* motif.[51]

With this information we can understand the role of the king who, in August, ritually opened the earth with the plowstick, *chaqui taclla*. The act of piercing (*casay*) explains the use of the word *casana* for the earth itself, divided as it is in four *suyu* or quarters, at the time of the year when it is to be pierced. The men who in August were assisted by their wives in plowing served during September in the female act of planting. The *casana* motif played a particular role in the months of August and September.[52]

In the third critical period in the agricultural calendar, called Capac raymi (before and after the December solstice), the ritual interest changed from sowing to preharvest activities.[53] Although Guaman Poma said nothing about the role of the tunics in Capac raymi, Murúa's work allows us to develop an argument identifying all three *uncus*.[54]

After Tupac Yupanqui's (ten) conquests in Ecuador as a crown prince, and before the abdication of his father, Pachacuti Inca, he was brought to the temple of the sun during the feast of Capac raymi and given the royal paraphernalia of the crown, *masca paycha*, the tunic, *Capac uncu tarco huallca*, the scepter, *suntur paucar*, the halbard, *tupa yauri*, and the golden beaker, *tupa cusi*.[55] This account by Murúa is confirmed by Sarmiento, who indicated that the older brother of Tupac Yupanqui, Tupac Amaru, also played an essential role. Santacruz Pachacuti best clarifies the ritual relationship among the three family members on this occasion, however, by describing how Pachacuti Inca sat with both his sons on three equal thrones.[56] All three wore the *masca paycha*, but they carried different objects as their scepters: Pachacuti Inca the *suntur paucar*, Tupac Yupanqui the *tupa yauri*, and Tupac Amaru the *champi*, a club. Pachacuti Inca then abdicated.[57]

The similarity of the three accounts, with their richness of detail regarding royal dress and paraphernalia, makes clear that the story represents the traditional importance of Capac raymi. Murúa's drawing illustrates the abdication (fig. 9a). Pachacuti Inca wears the *Capac uncu*

(b)

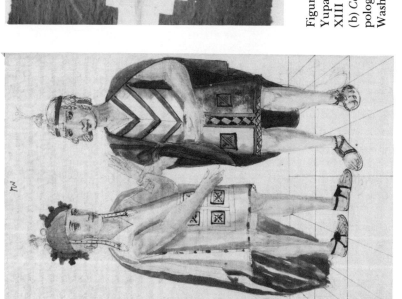

(a)

Figure 9. (a) Pachacuti Inca with the *Capac uncu tarco hualla* and Tupa Yupanqui with the *casana uncu*. Fray Martín de Murúa, f. 44v, Ms. Ludwig XIII 16 (83.MP.159). J. Paul Getty Museum, Santa Monica, California. (b) *Casana uncu*. Photo R. T. Zuidema. Catalog no. 307655, Dept. of Anthropology, National Museum of Natural History, Smithsonian Institution, Washington, D.C.

Figure 9. (continued)

(c) Black and white checkerboard tunic. No. 471097, Museum of Fine Arts, Boston.
(d) Inca key checkerboard tunic. No. 91147, Textile Museum, Washington, D.C.

tarco huallca, and Tupac Yupanqui is dressed in the *Casana uncu.*[58] Although Tupac Amaru is not presented in this drawing, it is reasonable to suggest that he was associated with the *collcapata uncu.*[59]

If we can accept, then, that a triad of persons was represented in Capac raymi, as in the two other feasts, the tunic *Capac uncu tarco huallca* becomes particularly interesting. The king who wears it is placed at that time most visibly in the center of Cusco's hierarchy, and we may expect that the design of his *uncu* best expresses that position.

The *huallca* (in Quechua), or *sipi* (in Aymara), was a "plumage of various colors" worn around the neck (Bertonio). Guaman Poma confirms Bertonio's information that in feasts it was worn by people from Chinchaysuyu around the head (fig. 1a). But neither he nor Murúa ever shows it in the more normal position, around the neck.[60] The feather necklace was undoubtedly a feature of Inca dress, and paintings of Inca nobles show it in combination with the *ahuaqui* (IV.4).[61]

Sarmiento and Santacruz Pachacuti provide clues about the symbolic significance of the *ahuaqui* and *huallca* for Capac raymi. Both authors underscored the fact that the *Capac uncu tarco huallca* was worn during Capac raymi. A feast, called Itu, in November already opened the sacred time related to Capac raymi—a ritual that could be celebrated only by the king and high nobility in Cusco, and by some royal relatives outside the town to whom special permission had been granted. As the Itu was primarily a royal imploration to the sun for rain, its meanings in Aymara suggest three reasons that it was used as nomenclature for the festival: (1) a circle around the sun appears mostly when there is moisture in the air, something expected in November; (2) the circle with its colors was compared to the necklace of the king, be this the *ahuaqui* or the *huallca* in different colors; and (3) the circle symbolized the subjects of the king organized around his person.[62] While the Itu feast had a cosmological purpose, it was primarily a manifestation of adherence by the nobility to the king. The ancestral king Sinchi Roca (two), associated with the month of November, also wore the *ahuaqui,* and he may have been the ancestor representing the young men dancing in the Itu. But it was the king himself who wore the *Capac uncu tarco huallca,* including the *ahuaqui* and the *huallca.*

IV. SURVIVING *UNCUS* AND THE PRE-HISPANIC PAST

Although Guaman Poma probably used his knowledge of pre-Hispanic tunics, as well as later ones, to present his textile code, he may have transposed colonial contexts to pre-Hispanic situations. J. H. Rowe's[63]

and A. P. Rowe's[64] examination of the existing pre-Hispanic tunics indicates four standardized designs that allow us to compare their classification with that offered by Guaman Poma. The two principal standardized
types studied by J. Rowe are the "black and white checkerboard" tunic
and the "Inca key checkerboard" tunic (figs. 9c, d).[65] The first type combines a stepped and triangular yoke part, in red, with a black-and-white
checkerboard pattern going down to the bottom. The yoke part cuts into
the upper five rows of the ten on the tunic. In the second type, the
checkerboard pattern covers the upper two-thirds part, without a yoke,
and leaves the lower one-third part open for six alternating stripes in
red and blue. All squares are filled with one *tucapu* pattern in alternating
colors that Rowe calls the "Inca key." Rowe gives evidence that the two
types of *uncu* were used in close relationship to one other. Perhaps they
corresponded to two of the versions that Guaman Poma shows of *collcapata,* with the design either in the upper or in the lower half.[66]

On the basis of Guaman Poma's record we have to assume that the
(ahuaqui-)casana uncu and the *ahuaqui uncu* were two other standardized
types. I know of only two actual *uncus* in public collections that demonstrate the *casana* motif.[67] One (fig. 9b) conforms closely to Guaman
Poma's renderings of the *ahuaqui-casana,* but the colors of red, black, and
yellow are different from those mentioned by Molina for the *uncu* with
the cross.

Guaman Poma's classification of tunics allows us to make some sug-
gestions as to the social function of Rowe's standardized types. The
ethnohistorical and pictorial information that I just reviewed on the
three triadic relations between a king and his two sons or officials, or
between a higher official and two lower ones, offers a means to study
some extant tunics with intricate iconographic patterns in the context of
the standardized types. At the moment I am not aware of any existing
uncu with the butterfly motif, similar to Guaman Poma's captain in Coya
raymi (September). The two other triads offer better possibilities for
analysis.

IV.1 The Uncu *of Inca Raymi and of Huayna Capac*

Guaman Poma[68] described the *uncu* of Huayna Capac as green and
orange from the middle up and blue and white from there down, in a
checkerboard pattern. His drawing of the *uncu* shows two *tucapus* alternating in a checkerboard pattern. The design of one is a letter Z with
two circles on a light background, probably referring to the Inca key
motif, and that of the other a diamond motif on dark background.

The surviving tunic pictured in figure 10a combines the themes of

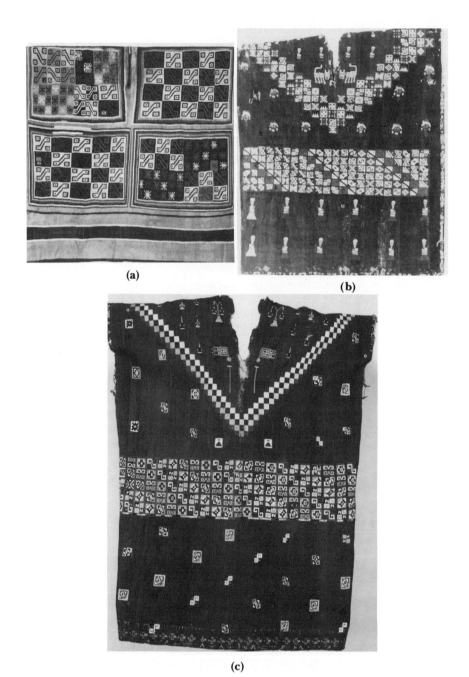

Figure 10. (a) *Uncu* combining *casana* and *collcapata* motifs, No. 91282, Textile Museum, Washington, D.C. (b) *Poli uncu.* Poli Collection, Lima, Peru. (c) *Uncu.* No. 332143, American Museum of Natural History, New York.

the Inca key checkerboard and the *casana*. The upper part is divided into four quarters, separated from one another by red lines. Two diagonally opposed quarters are filled with the Inca key checkerboard pattern. The other quarters apply a second-level quartering.[69]

There is an important difference between Huayna Capac's *uncu* and the tunic photographed in figure 10a. We have no evidence from any extant *uncu* of two different *tucapu*-signs used in an alternating way, instead of one in different colors. Nonetheless, the similarity between the two examples is close enough—their lack of an *ahuaqui*; *tucapus* in a checkerboard pattern; and the use of the Inca key *tucapu*—to make an iconographic comparison profitable. While the similarity between Huayna Capac and the king in Inca raymi initially helped me to discover the importance of the theme of the four *suyus,* the actual tunic now serves to uncover the iconographic connection of Huayna Capac's *uncu* with those of the two officials serving their king in Inca raymi. The *uncu* of the *Hanan* official had a lower part similar to Huayna Capac's, while the *Hurin* one included the *casana* motif. The actual *uncu* integrates into one design an interest in both motifs.[70] While it may have been used ritually by a person in a position similar to Huayna Capac's and to the king's in Inca raymi, it suggests that Guaman Poma did follow a pre-Hispanic precedent by bringing together *collcapata* and *casana*.

IV.2 The Capac Uncu Tarco Huallca
("Royal Tunic with the Feather Collar")

Now let us proceed to a special class of surviving tunics that expresses more explicitly the idea of royalty and political hierarchy. Apparently, this "royal" *uncu* became popular in colonial times, worn by people who either claimed royal descent or were allowed to represent the royal position at specific times of the year. The design of this royal *uncu* clearly goes back to Inca and even pre-Inca times. Here I shall describe the actual pieces, concentrating on the design of one of them, and identify the royal *uncu* in colonial paintings. In my conclusion, I shall discuss Murúa's version of the royal *uncu* and suggest an iconographic interpretation of the actual royal *uncus* as belonging to the pre-Hispanic class of *Capac uncu tarco huallca.*

IV.3 Royal Uncus, *Extant Examples*

The royal *uncu* consisted of two standardized features: a waistband, normally broader than three rows, and an *ahuaqui* yoke, consisting of four diagonal rows of squares on each side, each row in a different color, or of *tucapus* replacing the squares. The tunics also had two special features: four felines within the *ahuaqui* facing the neck opening (and thus the person wearing the *uncu*) and a dispersed pattern of *tucapus*, combined with, or being replaced by, naturalistic representations occupying similar spaces, occurring inside the *ahuaqui* and above and below the waistband.

So far, I have examined only three extant examples of the royal *uncu* and three additional examples where the felines are moved to the lower part as a colonial development of the design. The example pictured in figure 10b—from the Poli collection in Lima—is the most elaborate and distinctive one. It is apparently an early colonial piece.[71] The second example, from Copacabana and now in the American Museum of Natural History in New York, has the feline motif replaced by the *casana* motif (fig. 10c). It has a blue or purple background like the Poli piece. The third *uncu* is on one side dark red (which part belongs to the Archaeological Museum of the University of Cusco) and on the other side blue (now in the Cleveland Museum of Art). All three pieces have a red field within the *ahuaqui* border—such as is found in some other elaborately decorated *uncus* without the felines—and they have this characteristic in common with the standardized type of the black and white checkerboard *uncu*. While the felines and extra decorations enable us to identify all three pieces as royal, the *ahuaqui* and waistband are their "frame of reference."

The *ahuaqui* on the Poli tunic of Lima can be described best considering the front and back parts of the *uncu* together, forming one diamond-shaped design. While in the other two pieces the four rows of squares on each side of the diamond are in different colors, the squares in the Poli *uncu* are filled with *tucapus* of seven different kinds. The *tucapus* are used to establish a pattern of diagonals toward the center (the diagonals standing perpendicular on the rows), each diagonal consisting of two identical *tucapu* pieces. Taking into account some irregularities at the corners of the design, there is a total of eighty diagonals of paired *tucapus*. The waistband consists of twenty-three columns of six *tucapus* on one side and twenty-two columns on the other. The waistband uses five of the seven *tucapus* that occur in the *ahuaqui*, combined with five extra ones. Each *tucapu* is diagonally repeated.[72]

The lower half on each side of the Poli *uncu* also contains two rows of six crowns or *masca paychas*; five in each row have a red lower fringe, and one has yellow. The *masca paycha* as worn by the king consisted of three parts: two feathers or a miniature scepter (*suntur paucar*) for the upper part, a square golden plaque called *tupa cochor* for the middle part, and a fringe of red woolen threads for the lower part. It was the fringe that gave the whole crown its name. Cieza and Murúa tell us that each thread of the fringe represented an enemy slain by the king. Thus, we might associate the five red *masca paychas* in each row of the *uncu* with the five trophy heads as found on each side of the *ahuaqui* above the waistband. According to Garcilaso, the crown prince had a yellow *masca paycha*, perhaps indicating that he had not slain an enemy yet.[73] Thinking of the probable use of this *uncu*, I propose that the ten red *masca paychas* on each side represented the ten *panacas* of the organization of Cusco and the two yellow ones the noble initiates at the time of Capac raymi. While this proposition is conjectural, it makes us aware that the *uncu* was used for a precise political purpose.[74]

One of the first Spanish conquerors to enter Cusco, Juan Ruiz de Arce,[75] mentions that the Inca king had the decoration of a lion on his golden beakers and other objects belonging to him, and that the crown prince had the head of a lion in such a location. A wooden beaker of early colonial origin, found during a well-controlled excavation in Ollantaytambo near Cusco, has inlays of eight painted felines. Thomas Cummins[76] argues that the way of representing them on the beaker goes back to an Inca tradition and that their style is similar to that of the felines on the royal *uncu*. The four felines as found within the *ahuaqui* of the Poli tunic can be seen as one another's mirror images. A pre-Hispanic *uncu*, described as (provincial) Inca from the coastal Ica valley, has an upper red field with four black felines facing one another. Two late but pre-Hispanic *uncus* with feather decoration have the four felines just outside an *ahuaqui* design (fig. 11a).

While the iconographic element of four felines was known in late pre-Hispanic times, it is only from the art of the much earlier Huari empire that a group of four tunics is known, each exhibiting four felines within the design of a yoke (fig. 11b). Series of figures are running toward the center in the rest of their fields. There is a great stylistic difference between the Huari and the examples of the royal *uncu* discussed here, as well as a great similarity between their probable political purposes. The feature of four felines within a yoke design also is found in the decoration on the shoulder of some large Huari face-neck jars (fig. 11c). The tunics of both Huari and Inca cultures cannot be understood without imagining the presence of the lords wearing them. The iconographic whole was the lord, including his royal paraphernalia, body decorations, and tunic. The ethnohistorical data on men wearing a puma head and skin help explain the presence of the felines on both the Huari and the Inca tunics.[77]

This information, which is pertinent for placing the royal tunics in

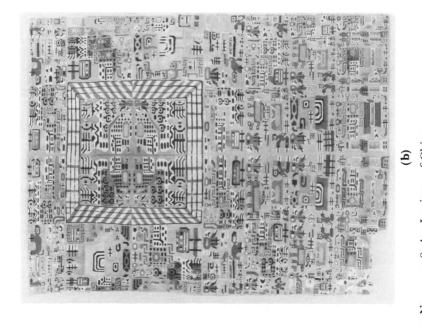

(b)

(a)

Figure 11. (a) *Uncu* with feathers, Inca valley. No. 551778, Art Institute of Chicago.
(b) Huari *uncu*. No. B501TT, Museum of Dumbarton Oaks, Washington, D.C.

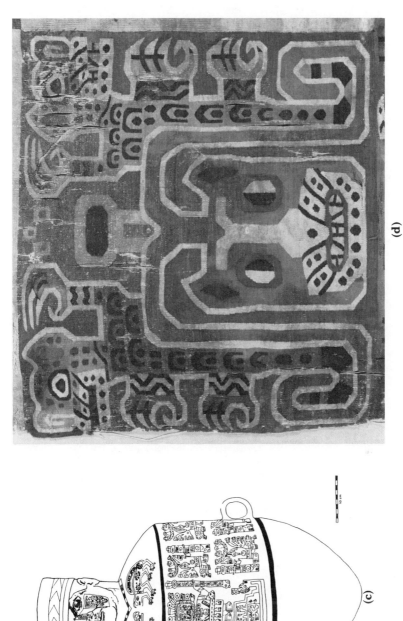

(d)

(c)

Figure 11. (continued)

(c) Huari face-neck jar, Ayacucho. Anita G. Cook, "The Político-Religious Implications of the Huari Offering Tradition," *Diálogo Andino* 4 (1985): 219, fig. 3. (d) Detail of a Huari tapestry. No. 1950.12, Syracuse University Art Collections, Syracuse, New York.

an Inca ritual context, discusses the last days of the feast of Capac raymi as celebrated in the plaza of Cusco. The boys to be initiated were presented to their noble sponsors, who were dressed with a puma head and skin over their own head and back and who played four large drums. Normally these drums of war were used at political borders, but here they belonged to the political center. We remember how the defense of Cusco against outside attack was commemorated by a prince who was going through this rite of passage. He had worn the puma skin and had been compared to the head of a puma, as a ruler of the state of which his subjects were the body.[78]

Although no known examples of Inca art represent a man with a puma head and skin over his own head, such representations are well known in Huari art. Two tapestry fragments show a repetition in checkerboard fashion of a frontal feline head (fig. 11d).[79] Each head has two other felines, seen in profile position, on its two sides. They are mirror images of one another and together can be considered as the split representation of one feline skin worn over the head of the owner. The profile felines are shown in a color opposition, as shown in the Huari tunics with the feline yoke part. Therefore we can compare this design to the feline skin worn by the ruler. It does not represent four different felines, but four views of a single one.[80] With such an argument available for Huari art, we can suggest that the four felines present in the Inca royal *uncus* represented the puma skin as worn over the head of the king and the men playing the drums.

Regarding the two other royal *uncu* displayed in New York and Cleveland, we observe in the tunic from the American Museum of Natural History (fig. 10c) six flowers and two yellow *masca paychas* inside the *ahuaqui*; fifteen *tucapus,* including two red *masca paychas,* in the upper field; and twenty *tucapus* in the lower field. This *uncu* also replaces the four felines by four flags with the *casana* motif. The Cusco-Cleveland *uncu* has flowers, insects, and shields instead of *tucapus*. There is, moreover, a lower border of flowers. The *uncu* from the Poli collection and the one from the American Museum of Natural History represent royalty and may have used the difference between the red and the yellow *masca paychas* as a reference to the initiation of a "crown prince" during Capac raymi. Nevertheless, even if all *uncus* are of colonial manufacture, they express the concept of royalty of the *uncu* of pre-Hispanic times.

IV.4 Colonial Paintings of the Royal Uncu

Two groups of colonial paintings depicting the royal *uncu* provide additional insights into social and ritual contexts of Inca dress. I will focus on four of the fifteen paintings of the celebration of Corpus Christi in Cusco, probably executed around the year 1680, and two paintings found in the churches of the towns of Juli and Ilave on Lake Titicaca.[81]

The Cusco paintings reflect the tradition that in the celebration of Corpus one or two of the descendants of the royal *panacas* were chosen to represent the Inca king in the procession (fig. 12a). Around this time of the year, the harvest feast was celebrated; Cusco today still celebrates Corpus Christi as its most important feast, maintaining this connection to harvest. In the paintings, the royal dress and other regalia, especially the *masca paycha*, have become very fancy, adapting to colonial taste. Yet the *uncu* retains the essential elements of the royal tunics, with its waistband and with the various *tucapus* dispersed over the whole field. Since the "king" wears a wide necklace of feathers, the *huallca*, around the neck, we cannot detect the possible presence of an *ahuaqui* or the four felines. Here the paintings from Juli and Ilave on Lake Titicaca are helpful, for they show the same kind of *uncu* with an *ahuaqui* (fig. 12b, c). I will deal here with three issues making it plausible to accept the actual *uncus* as *Capac uncu tarco huallca*: (1) their calendrical use, (2) the existence of the *ahuaqui*, and (3) the significance of the feline masks in the paintings attached to the shoulders of the "king."

Polo mentions how one particular form of the Itu feast, otherwise held in November, could be celebrated by all people during harvest (around April–May) and that in his time it was celebrated during Corpus Christi. He calls the feast "Ayma," which means in Aymara, according to Bertonio: "*Aymatha*: To dance in the old way, especially when [people] go to [work in] the fields of their lords." Thus, one can argue that the use of the *Capac uncu tarco huallca* was preserved on Corpus Christi, this being the only occasion on which the Inca nobility was allowed to remember its glorious past.

The two paintings of Juli and Ilave also strongly suggest that the connection between the *Capac uncu* and Capac raymi may not have been totally lost. Here each of the Three Kings visiting the Christ-child represents a continent of the world—America, Europe, and Africa. In the Ilave painting, the Inca as the American king wears a royal *uncu* with a narrow collar of feathers that still allows us to see the presence of an *ahuaqui* (fig. 12c).[82] In the Juli painting, the Inca king wears a long robe with a (probably golden) chain around the neck (fig. 12b). Of particular interest is the *ahuaqui* consisting of at least three detectable rows of stepped squares, each row in a different color. This *ahuaqui* is close in execution to those of the American Museum of Natural History and Cusco–Cleveland *uncus*. The Inca king in both paintings has a royal

Figure 12a. Detail of painting of Inca noble representing king during the feast of Corpus Christi, approximately 1680. Museum of the Archbishopric, Cusco.

Figure 12b. Detail of painting with Inca king representing one of the Three Kings. Church of Juli, Peru.

Figure 12c. Detail of painting with Inca king representing one
of the Three Kings. Church of Ilave, Peru.

function in a Christian setting, related to the December solstice and to a rite of passage (the birth of Christ).[83] Given their similarity to the Juli–Ilave paintings, we may conclude that the feather collar, the *huallca,* in the Cusco paintings probably hid the presence of an *ahuaqui.*[84]

The last issue concerns the possible existence of felines within the royal *ahuaqui.* None of the paintings shows them woven into the dress, either because the feathers may have covered them completely or because the *ahuaqui* may have come too close to the neck. Nonetheless, the Andean use of the European heraldic lion makes clear that the interest of representing felines close to the neck is still present. The large face of a golden lion without a lower jaw is seen in the Corpus paintings and in that of Ilave, loosely positioned on the shoulders of the king and over the feather necklace.[85] We are dealing with a Renaissance convention (e.g., on European armor), but it was in the interest of the Inca "king" to replace with the lion heads the now invisible felines woven into the tunic.

V. CONCLUSION

For the three principal feasts or *raymi* of the year, Capac raymi (December), Inca raymi (May), and Coya raymi (September), we observed how in each case a ritual was enacted where an *uncu* with a singular pattern was used in combination with two others—the *collcapata* and *casana,* related to the moieties of Hanan- and Hurin-Cusco. A similar hierarchical pattern was exhibited also by three successive captains in Hanan- as well as in Hurin-Cusco. Here the highest-ranked captain had a *tucapu* waistband as found in the *Capac uncu.* The triadic pattern of each of these cases was replicated on a higher level by the three singular *uncus* themselves—defined by the kinds of oppositions established by their feasts (diagram 2).

In the first opposition, Capac raymi was the feast celebrated only by the Inca nobility, while the other two feasts established relations with the outside. During Inca raymi, the king ate and drank in the plaza with people of all classes: the nobility, the Inca commoners, and the Incas-by-privilege. The term "Inca" did not refer to the king alone, but to his commonality with all the people called Incacuna, "the Incas." During Coya raymi, all people, rich and poor, high and low, invited one another to eat and drink together, keeping the peace needed for planting. The second opposition was of Coya raymi to Capac raymi and Inca raymi, where the term *coya,* "queen," expressed the exclusive female character of the feast, all women being honored at that time.[86] The last opposition

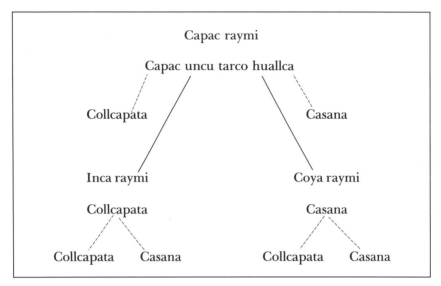

Diagram 2. Hierarchy of feasts and *uncus*

was of Inca raymi to Coya raymi and Capac raymi. Here the iconographic contrast between the *uncu* with the *collcapata* pattern, used by
the king in Inca raymi (for brevity's sake called "Inca" *uncu*), and the
one of the captain in Coya raymi (called "Coya" *uncu*) and the *Capac uncu*
indicates that the first lacks all the naturalistic decorations of the second
and the third. In all likelihood, not only the depictions of butterflies in
the *uncu* of the captain but also those of insects and flowers in the *Capac
uncu* had a primarily female meaning.

Although expected in the first example, why do they occur in the
Capac uncu? An answer might be found in the role of Capac raymi as a
period of transition. Its first part was dedicated to the end of the planting season; the second began with a concern for the ripening of the
plants. The initiation rituals and the contact with the ancestors supported such interests, procuring a transference of the fertility of the parents to that of the child. As a political statement, Capac raymi was a feast
of the Inca nobility, including male and female. The *Capac uncu,* combining abstract and figurative elements, probably represented a male-
female interest as against a male interest of the "Inca" *uncu* without
figurative elements. Although we might interpret the captain's *uncu* with
butterflies as the "Coya" *uncu,* the king's *uncu* at that time seems to have
been identified more with the *casana uncu.* The king wore the latter in

August, during plowing, making the earth ripe to receive the seeds. As such he placed himself at the service of the queen, then and in Coya raymi.[87]

The Inca interest in combining a concentric spatial model, like that of the *ceque* system, with a nonconcentric one, such as a rectangular grid pattern, provides clues to an understanding of the specific messages conveyed by the "Coya," "Inca," and *Capac uncus*.[88] With Inca raymi, Cusco became an open city till the time of planting; it received the tribute for its many *collca*, "storehouses," from the four *suyus* of the empire. The king communicated with people of all classes and ranks, including those from the outside called "of the four *suyus*." The design motifs of *casana* and *collcapata* gave best expression to those ideas of noncentrality; the actual *uncu* that combined those motifs into one, the "Inca" *uncu*, had no *ahuaqui*. In contrast, the *Capac uncu* was organized around the concept of the center. The *ahuaqui* excluded an outer field from an inner one in which the felines symbolized the king and the noble puma-men. The *Capac uncu*—as shown in the Poli example—represented the royal *panacas*, identified by their respective *masca paychas*, as conquerors and as hunters of trophy heads. It was used in Capac raymi to symbolize succession to royalty. But in the two other feasts, the king communicated with men from the outside or women and adopted for his own use a royal version of the *uncus* representing them.

The *ahuaqui* probably did not serve only as a border. As the *Capac uncu* was used in the context of succession to the office of royalty, the *ahuaqui* may also have symbolized the transition from outside to inside, expressing a hierarchical chain of command either by way of the rows of colors, used in most of the *ahuaqui*, or by way of the diagonals of equal *tucapus* in the Poli *uncu*. We observe the parallel with the political and cosmological model of which the *ceque* system in Cusco, with its forty-one directions going out from the temple of the sun in town, is the best documented example.

One troubling question remains: Why, in the colonial context, did representations of the "Coya" *uncu* disappear? Though the female role of the months of August and September remains alive today—witness the feasts of the Virgins of Copacabana (5 August), Asunción (15 August), Santa Rosa (30 August), and the Nativity or Cocharcas (8 September)—the triadic system of principal feasts and of times of paying tribute[89] was transformed by the Ordenanzas of Viceroy Francisco de Toledo (1572) into a dual one, where the European custom of the solstices (Christmas and the feast of St. John) was central. Guaman Poma still remembered the link of the "Inca" *uncu* to the original feast of Inca raymi, celebrated in early May. But it seems that later the *Capac uncu tarco huallca* replaced its function during Corpus Christi (a movable feast, sixty days after Easter, sometime between 21 May and the end of June), as evidenced by the Corpus paintings from Cusco. Although Betanzos, Sarmiento, and Santacruz Pachacuti placed *Capac uncu tarco huallca* in its ritual context, only Murúa attempted to illustrate it. Moreover, it was not depicted in paintings until around 1660. Its design emerges fully only in colonial society. In fact, Murúa's drawing allows us to identify the *Capac uncu tarco huallca* only by its use of the V-shaped yoke pattern as an *ahuaqui*; we can assume that the symbolic function of the *ahuaqui* was similar to that of the *huallca* and that the word *tarco huallca* applied to both. The other part of Murúa's design does not correspond to the evidence of the surviving royal *uncus*.

Even more problematic is the iconographic link between the *uncu* assigned by Guaman Poma to the king in the feast of Capac raymi and the extant *uncus*. Why does he not show the *Capac uncu,* and why does he depict an apparently different kind of *uncu?* To answer these questions, we must go back to his depictions of King Tupac Yupanqui (ten) and of the king in Capac raymi (figs. 2: 10; 6: VII). We could have expected to see the *Capac uncu* during this feast, as we saw the "Inca" *uncu* in Inca raymi, worn by Huayna Capac. But Tupac Yupanqui's *uncu* is different, although his kind of *uncu* also belongs to the king in his council of lords of Hanan- and Hurin-Cusco and the four *suyus* (fig. 13a). Later, when in a similar drawing Guaman Poma places himself in the position of king, he relegates the *uncu* of Tupac Yupanqui to the lord of Hanan-Cusco; he shies away from assigning this royal *uncu* to himself (fig. 1c). The *uncu* is later worn by Inca kings interacting with a viceroy and an archbishop (fig. 13b), and by Tupac Amaru when, in 1572, he is taken prisoner. But we do not know its name, and we have no access to a calendrical or ritual interpretation or to its representation in a colonial painting.[90] Guaman Poma depicted the *uncu* of the king in Capac raymi with a waistband and a scroll design similar to that found on the mantle of the pope (fig. 13c). Cusco was for Guaman Poma the "pontifical city," in the center of the world's "upper moiety," and as such it was included in his chapter dedicated to the popes (fig. 13d). A comparison was made between the Inca king in Capac raymi and the pope.[91] With the freedom of style that he implied in his depiction of the king's *uncu* in Capac raymi, he may have thought of a comparison with the actual *Capac uncu tarco huallca*.

The *Capac uncu tarco huallca* represented sacred kingship in Peru. Its connection to the *casana* and *collcapata uncu* allowed the integration of

Figure 13. (a) The king in his council. Guaman Poma, *Nueva corónica*, 366.
(b) The archbishop Don Juan Solano, marrying Don Cristóbal Sayri Topa
Ynga and Doña Beatris, *coya* (queen). Guaman Poma, *Nueva corónica*, 444.
(c) Pope Leo III. Guaman Poma, *Nueva corónica*, 39–40.
(d) Cusco as the pontifical city. Guaman Poma, *Nueva corónica*, 42.

its own internal and vertical concept of hierarchy into the concepts of external and horizontal alliances as expressed by these other *uncus* during Coya raymi and Inca raymi. The royal puma motif entered into the general dress code through those of the waistband, *ahuaqui, casana,* and *collcapata.* Thus we can trace the roots of dress at the Inca court into pre-Columbian times.

The extensive mythical and ritual evidence found in the descriptions and illustrations of specific types of tunics is essential for an iconographic understanding of the Inca polity. As we have seen, the Incas had an elaborate dress code for making local, temporal, and hierarchical distinctions. When the king traveled through a province of his empire, he would wear a version of the local dress. Moreover, through the use of specific designs and motifs displayed on his tunics, he identified himself with specific ranks of people, such as those of a particular age-group or class, or certain ritual roles. Additional distinctions could be made by the quality and refinement of the garments worn. Beyond such general information, however, the surviving examples of royal and noble tunics offer much further data about the importance of symbolic representation in Inca dress. Given its ability to convey complex information iconographically, we may conclude that dress fulfilled a role similar to that of writing in other imperial administrations.

NOTES

1. I wish to thank the National Gallery of Art, Washington, D.C., and the Center for Advanced Study of the University of Illinois, Urbana, for their generous support of the research for this paper.

2. Juan de Betanzos, *Suma y narración de los Incas* (Madrid, [1551] 1987).

3. Pedro Cieza de León, *El señorío de los Incas* (Lima, [1551] 1967).

4. Joan de Santacruz Pachacuti Yamqui Salcamayhua, *Relación de antigüedades deste reyno del Pirú* (1613), reproduced in *Tres relaciones de antigüedades peruanas,* edited by Marcos Jiménez de la Espada (Asunción del Paraguay, 1950), 207–281.

5. John H. Rowe, "Standardization in Inca Tapestry Tunics," in *The Junius B. Bird Precolumbian Textile Conference,* edited by Ann P. Rowe, E. Benson, and A. L. Schaffer (Washington, D.C., 1980).

6. Ann P. Rowe, "Technical Features of Inca Tapestry Tunics," *Textile Museum Journal* 17 (1978): 5–28.

7. Ludovico Bertonio, *Vocabulario de la lengua aymara* (Cochabamba, [1612] 1984).

8. *Tucapu* patterns in male dress occur on the waistband, only in a diagonal and never in a checkerboard pattern. There is no known name for the waistband design.

9. See Teodoro Hampe Martínez, "Las momias de los Incas en Lima," *Revista del Museo Nacional* (Lima) 46 (1982): 405–418.

10. Betanzos, *Suma y narración*.

11. See R. Tom Zuidema, "Bureaucracy and Systematic Knowledge in Andean Civilization," in *The Inca and Aztec States, 1400–1800*, edited by George A. Collier, Renato I. Rosaldo, and John D. Wirth (New York, 1982), 419–458; idem, *Inca Civilization in Cuzco* (Austin, Tex., 1990).

12. Felipe Guaman Poma de Ayala, *Nueva corónica y buen gobierno*, edited by John V. Murra, Rolena Adorno, and Jorge L. Urioste (Madrid, [1615] 1987), title page, 14, 17, 167, 291, 322, 350, 368, 377, 434, 755, 769, 975. Page references are to the editors' pagination as corrected from Guaman Poma's original numbering. Similar *uncus* exist in the Archaeological Museum of Lima and in North American collections, although these have also a waistband not found in Guaman Poma's drawings except for the *uncu* of Challco Chima (ibid., 163). See A. P. Rowe, "Technical Features," figs. 31–32, and the preceding note.

13. Zuidema, *Inca Civilization in Cuzco*; and idem, "The Place of the Chamay Wariqsa in the Rituals of Cuzco," *Amérindia, Revue d'Ethnolinguistique Amérindienne* 11 (1986): 58–67.

14. I cannot detect any *suyu* differences in the dress of Incas-by-privilege, although they are mentioned in other ways. Fernando de Santillán, *Relación del origen, descendencia, política, y gobierno de los Incas* (1563), reproduced in *Tres relaciones de antigüedades peruanas*, edited by Marcos Jiménez de la Espada (Asunción del Paraguay, 1950), 47, mentions explicitly that the *suyukuna* only began outside the territory of the Incas-by-privilege, and Molina's description of Inca spatial hierarchy might lead us to the same conclusion; see Cristóbal de Molina, *Fábulas y ritos de los Incas*, edited by Francisco A. Loaysa (Lima, 1943) and R. Tom Zuidema, *The Ceque System of Cuzco: The Social Organization of the Capital of the Inca Empire* (Leiden, 1964), 5–7.

15. Betanzos, *Suma y narración*, pt. 1, chaps. 20, 32; El Inca Garcilaso de la Vega, *Los comentarios reales* (Buenos Aires, [1609] 1945), bk. 7, chap. 9; Zuidema, *Inca Civilization in Cuzco*; and idem, "The Moieties of Cuzco," in *The Attraction of Opposites: Thought and Society in the Dualistic Mode*, edited by David Maybury Lewis and Uri Almagor (Ann Arbor, Mich., 1989), 255–275.

16. See Pedro Sarmiento de Gamboa, *Historia de los Incas* (Buenos Aires, [1572] 1943), and later chroniclers; also Zuidema, *The Ceque System*; and Pierre Duviols, "La dinastía de los Incas, ¿monarquía o diarquía?: Argumentos heurísticos a favor de una tesis estructuralista," *Journal de la Société des Américanistes* 64 (1979): 67–83.

17. For Huayna Capac's connection with the empire and the four *suyus*, see figure 4, herein. Guaman Poma, *Nueva corónica*, 115, 389, represents Atahualpa and Huascar only as prisoners.

18. Guaman Poma, *Nueva corónica*, 86–89, 96–111.

19. For possible reasons for the nondistinctiveness of Inca Roca (six) in terms of *Hanan* and *Hurin*, see Zuidema, *The Ceque System*, 147–148, 222; and idem, "The Place of the Chamay Wariqsa," 59–61.

20. Guaman Poma, *Nueva corónica*, 142, 300. I suspect that Guaman Poma in all these examples refers to a different kind of *chumpi*, a narrow band wrapped various times around the body, thereby distinguishing these kings as of lower rank than the later ones. See, for example, Francisco López de Gómara, *Historia general de las Indias*, edited by P. Guibelalde and E. M. Aguilera (Barcelona, [1552] 1965), 219, 336. J. H. Rowe, "Standardization," 242, observed the rectangular shape of the *tucapus* in the *uncus* of kings one, two, and six, but not the brick pattern, and did not mention the other examples.

21. Betanzos, *Suma y narración*, 175–183 (pt. 1, chaps. 39–41), elaborates upon the relationship between this king and the governors of the four *suyus*. Huayna Capac depended very much on non-Inca generals and troops for his conquest of Ecuador; along this line see Sarmiento de Gamboa, *Historia de los Incas*, chap. 60, 241–247; Miguel Cabello Valboa, *Miscelánea Antártica* (Lima, [1586] 1951), 3:353–379 (chaps. 20–22). The name of his *panaca* was derived from that of the Ecuadorian town of Tumibamba; see Sarmiento, *Historia de los Incas*, 251 (chap. 62).

22. Guaman Poma, *Nueva corónica*, 120–143, 175–182.

23. Guaman Poma, *Nueva corónica*, 237–262.

24. Guaman Poma, *Nueva corónica*, 1140–1177.

25. Anonymous, "Discurso de la sucesión i gobierno de los Yngas" [c. 1565], in *Chunchos*, edited by V. Maurtua, vol. 8 of *Juicio de límites entre el Perú y Bolivia* (1906), 150. Preliminary reconstructions of the Inca calendar are given in a series of papers by R. Tom Zuidema: "South American Calendars," in *The Encyclopedia of Religion*, edited by Mircea Eliade et al. (New York, 1987), 3:16–21; "A Quipu Calendar from Ica, Peru, with a Comparison to the Ceque Calendar from Cuzco," in *World Archaeoastronomy: Selected Papers from the Second Oxford International Conference on Archaeoastronomy*, edited by A. F. Aveni (Cambridge, Eng., 1989), 341–351.

26. Guaman Poma's pictures support arguments for placing these two ancestral queens in the calendar.

27. Guaman Poma, *Nueva corónica*, 330–368, 752–774.

28. Guaman Poma, *Nueva corónica*, 115–116, 149–152, (fig. 5, captains three and four), 254–255 (fig. 6, September), 320 (fig. 8a), 344–347, 354 (figs. 8b, 8c), 366–367 (fig. 13a), 400–401; see also Juan M. Ossio A., "Guaman Poma: *Nueva Corónica* o carta al rey: Un intento de aproximación a las categorías del pensamiento del mundo andino," in *Ideología mesiánica del mundo andino*, edited by Juan M. Ossio A. (Lima, 1973), 155–213; and idem, "Myth and History: The Seventeenth-Century Chronicle of Guaman Poma de Ayala," in *Text and Context: The Social Anthropology of Tradition*, edited by Ravindra K. Jain (Philadelphia, 1977), 51–93.

29. I adopt this term from the concept of "written garment" as introduced by Roland Barthes, *The Fashion System* (New York, 1983).

30. Diego González Holguín, *Vocabulario de la lengua general de todo el Perú llamada lengua quichua o del inca* (Lima, [1608] 1952). The term *ahuaqui* could

derive from the verb *ahuay,* to weave. According to González Holguín, *ahua-quiuncu* means the shirt that is in a checkerboard pattern from the shoulders down to the breast. *Ahuaqui cassana uncu* is a shirt that has a checkerboard pattern on the shoulders and has a triangular shape.

31. González Holguín, *Vocabulario de la lengua general.*

32. Guaman Poma, *Nueva corónica,* 88–89.

33. For the combination of *ahuaqui* with waistband, see Guaman Poma, *Nueva corónica,* 402, 765. I suspect that the term *ahuaqui* also could be used for part of the actual *uncu* that J. H. Rowe, "Standardization," discusses under the term of "black and white checkerboard tunic" (IV.1, fig. 9c). This has a V-shaped part in red around the neck with a stepped border as formed by the checkerboard pattern of black and white squares outside it. Rowe, "Standardization," 245, does not mention González Holguín's combination of the words *ahuaqui* and *cassana.* Thus, he restricts unnecessarily the *ahuaqui* motif to examples where it is filled with *tucapus.* The term had a much wider application.

34. The *casana* motif occurs in Guaman Poma twice alone (*Nueva corónica,* 159, 258), but otherwise always with *ahuaqui* (ibid., 149, 196, 252, 254, 279, 283, 346, 354, 767, 818, 1163).

35. Guaman Poma, *Nueva corónica,* 98.

36. Molina, *Fábulas y ritos,* 27, 34, 49. Guaman Poma shows an *aclla* serving drink for the month of June and the king burning wood for the month of July. The hill of Manturcalla—given its name because of the red color of the earth there (*mantur,* "red achiote")—was the site of a temple of the sun, called Chuquimarca, from which the June solstice was observed; Anthony F. Aveni, "Horizon Astronomy in Incaic Cuzco," in *Archaeoastronomy in the Americas,* edited by Ray A. Williamson (Los Altos, Calif., 1981), 308–310; R. Tom Zuidema, "Comment," *Latin American Research Review* 16 (1981): 168–169.

37. Molina, *Fábulas y ritos,* 49, calls the dress *colca pata* and also *colca uncu.* It seems that the terms *pata,* "flat terrace on a hill," and *uncu* could replace each other in these circumstances. The terms *llanca* and *paucar,* for, respectively, any dark (brown, blue) and bright (red, yellow) color, distinguish the two *uncus* as a group from *collcapata.*

38. Fray Martín de Murúa, *Historia del orígen y genealogía real de los Reyes Incas del Perú,* edited by Constantino Bayle, (Madrid, [1590] 1946), 215 (bk. 3, chap. 21). Before Murúa, José de Acosta, *Historia natural y moral de las Indias,* Biblioteca de Autores Españoles 73 (Madrid, 1954), 136 (bk. 4, chap. 41), already had referred to Capachica as the place from which the Inca got his finest *cumpi* cloth.

39. Only the high nobility could carry the two feathers: Betanzos, *Suma y narración,* 110 (pt. 1, chap. 21), 150 (pt. 1, chap. 32). According to Bertonio's *Vocabulario,* the Aymara word for this distinction of rank was *Kausu:* "plumage of the Incas of two feathers in the front part of the hat or the *llawt'u* [headband]." This word was derived from *Kausu,* "curved like a horn," used in *Kausu yauri,* "pot-hook," and *Kausu pakhsi,* "moon, two or three days old with horns."

40. Captains three and four are also distinguished from each other by the

respective circular and rectangular emblems attached to their helmets. Guaman Poma probably intended to represent an ascending order in the sequence of the captains of each moiety. The first captains are related to wild animals: either compared to one (one), Guaman Poma, *Nueva corónica*, 146, or transformed into an *Otorongo Achachi*, "Jaguar grandfather" (six), ibid., 156. The next two captains have the *casana* and *collcapata*, respectively, and the last ones the *tucapu* waistband. If the two series of captains three-four-five and seven-eight-nine were to represent ranked sequences, these would be similar to the one discussed in section II.2.

41. Guaman Poma, *Nueva corónica*, 344–347; see also R. Tom Zuidema, "At the King's Table: Inca Concepts of Sacred Kingship in Cuzco," in *Kingship and the Kings,* edited by Jean-Claude Galey, special issue of *Anthropology and History* 4, 1 (1989): 249–274.

42. Zuidema, *Inca Civilization in Cuzco*; and see R. Tom Zuidema, "El Ushnu," *Economía y sociedad en los Andes y Mesoamérica: Revista de la Universidad Complutense* 28, 117 (1979): 331–342.

43. Zuidema, "At the King's Table."

44. The only other time that the same *uncu* is shown again as worn by the king is in one of the drawings of the colonial city of Potosí; Guaman Poma, *Nueva corónica*, 1065–1068.

45. Guaman Poma, *Nueva corónica*, 140–141, 317–321. I want to restate here that, in my reconstruction of the calendar, the month of Inca raymi does not correspond to "April" as claimed by Guaman Poma, but to "May" as the thirteenth monthly period, also called Hatun cuzqui.

46. Gary Urton, in modern Misminay near Cusco, identifies not only the Pleiades as Collca, "storehouses," but also the "Tail of Scorpio." They are observed, respectively, for the times when corn is stored and when it is taken out for planting again. See Gary Urton, *At the Crossroads of the Earth and the Sky: An Andean Cosmology* (Austin, Tex., 1981), chap. 6, 113–128.

47. Guaman Poma, *Nueva corónica*, 406, 462. He uses the type of *uncu* with a simple checkerboard pattern covering the whole field only for noble warriors in the context of the time of Spanish conquest.

48. Bruce Mannheim, "Poetic Form in Guaman Poma's Wariqsa Arawi," *Amérindia, Revue d'Ethnolinguistique Amérindienne* 2 (1986): 41–57, analyzed and translated the poems of the time of Inca raymi, while Zuidema, "The Place of the Chamay Wariqsa," discussed the words *huaricsa* and *aucaylli* for an understanding of their ritual and mythical importance at this time of the year.

49. This is the only place where the nonstepped yoke motif is shown independently from any stepped border. See the extant *ahuaqui-casana uncu* (fig. 9b).

50. Zuidema, *The Ceque System,* 137–139; idem, "The Sidereal Lunar Calendar" (1982): 94–99; idem, "The Pillars of Cuzco: Which Two Dates of Sunset Did They Define?" in *New Directions in American Archaeoastronomy,* edited by Anthony F. Aveni, BAR International Series 454 (1988), 143–169; and Pierre Duviols, "Rituel et Commémoration: L'Opposition Inca/Alcauiza, Prélude à la Guerre contre les Chanca," in *La Commémoration: Colloque du Centenaire de la sec-*

tion des Sciences religieuses de l'École Pratique des Hautes Études, edited by Ph. Gignoux (1988), 275–285.

51. Guaman Poma shows in both calendrical series the king in August with the *casana uncu.* I will deal with the aspect of *casana* related to young initiated warriors in more detail elsewhere; see Guaman Poma, *Nueva corónica,* 145, 149, 159 (fig. 5), 196.

52. The act of piercing the earth with the *chaqui taclla* was done not only for plowing (ibid., 252, 1163) but also for planting (1166, 1175) and harvesting (1157). The significance of the act is still remembered today by farmers on the first of August when the earth and the Earth Mother are said to be open. Only after that day is one allowed to plow and plant.

53. See Zuidema, "The Moieties of Cuzco," on the change of interest in the two months of Capac raymi. Pedro Pizarro, *Relación del descubrimiento y conquista de los reinos del Perú* (1571), edited by Guillermo Lohmann Villena with note by Pierre Duviols (Lima, 1978), 92, one of the first Spaniards to set foot in Cusco, describes how he saw in the courtyard of the temple of the sun the famous garden of small golden corn plants; he explains that the garden was set up only during the three times of the year mentioned. The custom clearly has to do with the division of the year into four-month periods; see John H. Rowe, "What Kind of Settlement was Inka Cusco?," *Ñawpa Pacha* 5 (1967): 59–76. Besides the early sources that Rowe mentions, Betanzos, *Suma y narración,* 97 (pt. 1, chap. 19); and Pedro Cieza de León, *El señorío,* 37 (chap. 12), report the custom. To these periods should be added, however, the extra, thirteenth month; see R. Tom Zuidema, "The Ritual Calendar of the Incas," unpublished manuscript. Duviols, "Rituel et Commémoration," 275–285, discusses the same division of the year, adducing other kinds of mythical and ritual data.

54. Fray Martín de Murúa, *Historia general del Perú* (1613), edited by Manuel Ballesteros-Gaibrois (Madrid, 1962), vol. 1, pl. 22 (same as pl. 25 in Juan M. Ossio, *Los retratos de los Incas en la crónica de Fray Martín de Murúa* [Lima, 1985]); see fig. 9a.

55. Murúa, vol. 1, chaps. 21–25. Tupac Yupanqui returned with much gold, of which the statues Palpa ocllo and Ynga ocllo were made. These were the statues used in the June solstice rituals together with the three tunics, one of them the *collcapata,* which Murúa mentioned as being woven in Capachica.

56. Sarmiento, *Historia de los Incas,* 192–205 (chaps. 38–42); Cabello Valboa, *Miscelánea Antártica,* 274 (pt. 3, chap. 11); Santacruz Pachacuti, *Relación de antigüedades,* 245–249.

57. The essential role of the older brother in the crowning of Tupac Yupanqui was explained first by Betanzos, *Suma y narración,* 123–132 (pt. 1, chaps. 24–27), although he does not mention the *Capac uncu.* For Betanzos, however, the older brother was not Tupac Amaru but Yamqui Yupanqui, a brother who had become king in his own right during his father's lifetime. Thus Betanzos observes how on one occasion Pachacuti Inca and his two sons wear three equal crowns. The representation of a central figure with two similar ones at his sides, each with his own distinguishing emblem, is an old iconographic pattern in

Andean art; see Anita G. Cook, "The Middle Horizon Ceramic Offerings from Conchopata," *Ñawpa Pacha* 22/23 (1984/1985): 50. I have used the description of Santacruz Pachacuti as an introduction for analyzing this theme: see R. Tom Zuidema, *Meaning in Nazca Art: Iconographic Relationships between Inca-, Huari-, and Nazca Cultures in Southern Peru* (Göteborg, Sweden, 1972): 35–54.

58. I draw this conclusion, observing the parallels with another drawing of Murúa where Manco Capac (one) invests his son Sinchi Roca (two) and with Guaman Poma's drawing of Inca Roca (six) and his son (fig. 3: 6). Molina, *Fábulas y ritos,* 59, describes their tunics as *uanaclla* (also *huanaclla*), of black and yellow color, and in the middle a red cross. Two other chroniclers confirm the presence of the cross: Diego Fernández el Palentino, *Primera y segunda parte de la historia del Perú,* BAE 164–165 (Madrid, [1571] 1963), 2:83 (pt. 2, bk. 3, chap. 6); and Pedro Gutiérrez de Santa Clara, *Quinquenarios o historia de las guerras civiles del Perú,* BAE 166–168 (Madrid, 1963), 2:253 (bk. 3, chap. 64).

59. Santacruz Pachacuti had a special interest in Tupac Amaru. He describes the celebrations for his birth during Capac raymi, when his father came back to Cusco from conquest (*Relación de antigüedades,* 242). Later, Huayna Capac could not succeed his father until Tupac Amaru, his uncle, had died (ibid., 254–255). Tupac Amaru was the inventor of the *collca,* "storehouse" (245–247), and the palace of his wife Curi Ocllo in Cusco was located on the hill of Collcapata. See Bernabé de Cobo, *Historia del nuevo mundo,* BAE 91–92 (Madrid, 1956), 2:171 (bk. 13, chap. 13). Molina, *Fábulas y ritos,* 49, mentions how, during the initiation rituals in Capac raymi, close relatives of the boys would wear a *colca uncu,* which name is a synonym of that of *collca pata.* But it is difficult to claim that they occupied the same third place as Tupac Amaru in relation to the initiator of a boy and the latter himself.

60. Pablo José de Arriaga, *Extirpación de la idolatría del Pirú,* BAE 209 (Madrid, 1968), 213, refers to the *huallca* as *huacra* or *tamta.* He mentions that it was worn around the neck. I draw the conclusion that *sipi* in Quechua was a synonym of *huallca.*

61. Bartolomé Arzáns de Orsúa y Vela, *Historia de la Villa Imperial de Potosí* (1702–1735), edited by Lewis Hanke and Gunnar Mendoza (Providence, R.I., 1965), 1:99 (pt. 1, bk. 1, chap. 2), describes the *sipi* as "a collar, or more like a tippet (although shorter), [which] was woven of beautiful green, white, and red feathers."

62. The astronomical reason the month of November was chosen for the Itu implied a longer period of the year: that from the first passage of the sun through zenith (30 October) to its second passage (14 February). Then the sun passes to the southern side of the sky, opposite where it normally is. South was the direction from which the royal ancestors had come and to which the dead returned; thus the whole period from 30 October to 14 February was considered a time when the initiates were brought into contact with the ancestors. Today, a similar interest of contact with the dead is defined as the period going from All Souls' Day (2 November) to the end of Carnival (a movable feast from the

beginning of February to the end of March); see Zuidema, "The Pillars of Cuzco," and idem, "The Moieties of Cuzco." Nevertheless, the Itu was celebrated not only in November but also, with some changes, at other times of the year when there was a special royal reason for doing so, such as a calamity affecting the whole kingdom or the king personally going to war. While during the last occasion it was celebrated only by the highest nobility, in November young men played a special role in it. R. Tom Zuidema, "The Lion in the City: Royal Symbols of Transition in Cuzco," in *Animal Myths and Metaphors in South America,* edited by Gary Urton (Salt Lake City, 1985), 183–250.

63. J. H. Rowe, "Standardization."

64. A. P. Rowe, "Technical Features."

65. Two other standardized types studied by Rowe are the *t'oqapu* (*tucapu*) waistband, discussed here, and the diamond waistband. There is no example of the latter in Guaman Poma.

66. J. H. Rowe's evidence comes from a controlled excavation where two tunics, an example of each type, were found together (Rowe, "Standardization," 245, 248, 259). Similar evidence comes from a cache of three male figurines, two of gold and one of silver, found in Pachacamac together with their miniature *uncus* (Site-Museum, Pachacamac). One of these is of the first type and two are of the second. Against the suggestion that Guaman Poma may have distinguished both types in his drawings goes the fact that he shows the first official of the king in Inca raymi with the checkerboard pattern and two alternating *tucapus* in the lower part, while no actual *uncu* exists with such a combination (fig. 8b).

67. Smithsonian Institution, Washington, D.C., no. 307655 (fig. 9b) and Peabody Museum, Harvard University, Cambridge, Mass., no. 46.77.30/7684.

68. Guaman Poma, *Nueva corónica,* 113.

69. The *uncu* has only three stripes in the lower part instead of the six of the Inca key checkerboard pattern. If the same checkerboard pattern had been applied to all of its quarters, then there would have been ten squares in a row and eight in a column, equal to the numbers as regularly shown in the Inca key checkerboard *uncu*. Two of the opposite subquarters repeat the same kind of checkerboard pattern as found in the two other main quarters, while the other subquarters have starlike objects. The stars are not organized in a checkerboard pattern but in diagonals.

70. Guaman Poma and other chroniclers specifically identify the places visited by these officers. Some of these were even called "surveyors," and clearly the stories about them express an intimate and precise interest in the geography of the empire (Zuidema, "El Ushnu"). The actual *uncu* reflects this type of interest; it combines the motif of *collcapata,* "storehouses ordered in rows forming a checkerboard pattern," with that of *casana,* referring with its four quarters to the political ideal of "four *suyus*." The *suyus* in Cusco were not of equal rank: in the council of the king two (I and II) were represented by four councillors each, and the other two (III and IV) by half that number. The higher ranking of the

first two *suyus* may have been replicated in the actual *uncu* by the quarters where a second-level quartering was applied.

71. John H. Rowe convincingly argues that the second and third pieces are heirlooms, made in colonial times. Rowe, "Standardization," 243–244.

72. While the numbers of twenty-three and twenty-two columns seem odd, they make sense if we consider them in relation to two numbers concerning the *ahuaqui*. Going from the left outermost to the right outermost *tucapu* on the shoulders, there is space for twenty-three columns of *tucapus* on each side of the *uncu*, but there are 2 × 11 = 22 *tucapus* in the two outer rows on the front and back halves. Clearly, the two numbers of columns in the waistband were chosen in relation to the design of the *ahuaqui*.

73. Cieza de León, *El señorío*, 21 (chap. 7); Murúa, *Historia general del Perú* 1:35 (chap. 9); Garcilaso, 56 (bk. 1, chap. 23), 267 (bk. 5, chap. 20).

74. The numbers of the diagonals in the *ahuaqui* (eighty) and of all the *masca paychas* (twenty-four) are double those of most interest in the political organization of Cusco and its province. The province was defined as a political unit of forty thousand families; the *ceque* system was based on the number of forty *ceques*, although here, for calendrical reasons, the number was changed to forty-one; twelve political divisions in the valley (ten *panacas* and two other groups) were in charge of the calendrical rituals, each in its own month; see Zuidema, *Inca Civilization in Cusco*; and idem, "The Moieties of Cuzco."

75. Juan Ruiz de Arce, *Advertencias que hizo el fundador del vínculo y mayorazgo a los sucesores en él*, reproduced in *Tres testigos de la conquista del Perú*, edited by el Conde de Canilleros (Buenos Aires, 1953), 73–119.

76. Thomas B. F. Cummins, "Abstraction to Narration: Kero Imagery of Peru and the Colonial Alteration of Native Identity" (Ph.D. diss., University of California at Los Angeles, 1988).

77. For the wooden beaker from Ollantaytambo, see Luis Llanos, "Informe sobre Ollantaytambo," *Revista del Museo Nacional* 5, 2 (1936): 123–156; Cummins, "Abstraction to Narration," 131, 134–136, pls. 51, 72; color photograph in Hans Horkheimer and F. Kauffmann Doig, *La cultura incaica* (Lima, 1965), 81.

For a study and illustrations of the Huari *uncus*: Ann P. Rowe, "Textile Evidence for Huari Music," *Textile Museum Journal* 18 (1979): 5–18. The face-neck jars, some twenty-two to twenty-five, belonged to an offering found in 1977 in Conchopata, a neighborhood of the city of Ayacucho, and are attributed to the Middle Horizon Epoch 1B; Anita G. Cook, "The Politico-Religious Implications of the Huari Offering Tradition," *Diálogo Andino* 4 (1985): 203–222; William H. Isbell, "Conchopata, Ideological Innovator in Middle Horizon 1A," *Ñawpa Pacha* 22/23 (1984/1985): 91–126; William H. Isbell and Anita G. Cook, "Ideological Origins of an Andean Conquest State," *Archaeology* 40, 4 (1987): 27–33, 74. The shoulder and body sections are decorated with the painted design of a shirt. The front part on the shoulders has any one of three possible designs, while braided hair is depicted on the back. The design of interest to us consists of two large humped animals that Cook interprets as felines. She compares them to the felines found in the yoke part of the Huari tunics mentioned.

78. Cieza de León, *El señorío*, 152 (chap. 45); Betanzos, *Suma y narración*, 81 (pt. 1, chap. 17). Also, Zuidema, "The Lion in the City," and idem, "The Moieties of Cuzco."

79. See Mary Hunt Kahlenberg, *Fabric and Fashion: Twenty Years of Costume Council Gifts* (Los Angeles, 1974), cover and fig. 4; Mary Jean Thomas, "The Reconstruction and Analysis of a Peruvian Middle Horizon Tapestry Fragment," *Syracuse Scholar* 4, 2 (1983): 24–42; fig. 2. One of the fragments still has a border showing a repetition of the Huari-Tiahuanaco staff god in a frontal position (ibid., 24–29). A third similar piece, mentioned by Thomas (fig. 4), consists of only one square of the feline head.

80. A remarkable and perhaps important feature is that none of these *uncu* examples includes the Inca key *tucapu* in its repertoire. As this *tucapu*-sign was of such importance in Huayna Capac's *uncu* and in the extant *uncu* compared to it, we may wonder whether there was not an exclusive choice of *tucapu* related to the use of the different types of *uncu* for purposes of rank and the calendar.

81. Teresa Gisbert, *Iconografía y mitos indígenas en el arte* (La Paz, 1980): 98–99, 77–78, figs. 96–97, 66–69, color plates facing pp. 80, 94. A painting from the eighteenth century and belonging to the Museum de Osma in Chorrillos, Lima, Peru, shows the whole procession with a view of three sides of the plaza of Cusco and with two Inca royal descendants reviewing the procession.

82. The Juli painting was made by Diego de la Puente (1586–1663) and the Ilave painting by an anonymous artist in 1680; see Gisbert, *Iconografía*, 77–78, figs. 66–69, and color plate opposite p. 80. The *tucapus* of the second painting are placed in the diagonal direction of the border, thus discarding the Inca convention of a stepped pattern.

83. Santacruz Pachacuti, *Relación de antigüedades*, 231, 242, already had made such kinds of connections between Capac raymi and the birth of two crown princes.

84. Further evidence for this suggestion may be found in a painting representing the Inca kings and the Spanish viceroys found in the Beaterio de Copacabana in Lima and belonging to one series with two other similar paintings. See Gisbert, *Iconografía*, 128–135, fig. 118; and Jaime Mariazza F., "Los Incas y los reyes españoles en la Catedral de Lima," *Boletín de Lima*, no. 51 (mayo 1987): 11–26. They all date from the eighteenth century and continue a tradition of Guaman Poma in their representation of Mama Huaco as the queen of Manco Capac and in their representation of the five ages. Only in this painting, however, are the Inca kings represented with the same *masca paycha* as found on the Corpus Christi paintings from Cusco. They combine, moreover, the feather necklace with the presence of the *ahuaqui* in the *uncu*.

85. In one of the Corpus paintings, the lion heads are missing. Another discrepancy here is that the "king" does not have the *masca paycha* on his head, but carries it in front of him. The two facts may have been related. Arzáns de Orsúa

y Vela (1:96, 99 [pt. 1, bk. 4, chaps. 1, 2]) mentions in his history of Potosí (1702–1735) a procession held in 1555 which also included men representing the Inca kings. Their royal insignia included the golden puma heads, which first he describes as "pomares and *licras*, which were some masks of puma heads, made of fine gold and that they placed on their shoulders, knees, and insteps of the feet" and then as "large masks of puma heads, called in the Indian language *puma*, which their kings used of pure gold." We do not know, however, from which early source, if at all, he might have derived this knowledge. See also Manuel Burga, *Nacimiento de una utopía: Muerte y resurrección de los Incas* (Lima, 1988), 378–384.

86. Myths of female ancestors were attached to the feasts of Inca raymi and Coya raymi. Mama Anahuarque, related to Coya raymi, was a very fertile woman and ancestress of the conquered pre-Inca population in the Cusco valley. Mama Huaco was the ancestress of the Inca conquerors; she was represented as a virile woman and conqueror and was honored during the harvest and immediately after, in the first ritual plowing by the king of Inca raymi.

87. We might suggest that the *Capac uncu* combined, and brought to a higher plane of integration, the concepts of the *collcapata* and *casana uncu*. On the one hand, the dispersed pattern of the *tucapus* on the *Capac uncu* corresponds to the checkerboard pattern of *collcapata*. The *ahuaqui* motif of the *Capac uncu*, on the other hand, is found most frequently in combination with *casana*. While the leading captain in September does not have it, representing a female design, the two other warriors and the king in August do. None of these men, during plowing and planting or during harvest and postharvest, has a waistband featuring *tucapus*, but the king in Capac raymi uses it together with the *ahuaqui* and dispersed patterns. The simple way to represent the king in the other months was with the *tucapu* waistband only.

88. R. Tom Zuidema, "La quadrature du cercle dans l'ancien Pérou," *Signes et Langages des Amériques: Recherches Amérindiennes au Québec* 3, 1/2 (1973): 147–165.

89. Juan de Matienzo, *Gobierno del Perú* (1567), edited with a preliminary study by Guillermo Lohmann Villena (Paris, 1967), 55 (chap. 14).

90. Guaman Poma, *Nueva corónica*, 366–369, 442–445, 451–452. Guaman Poma depicts the *uncu* as similar to the one of Viracocha Inca (eight). Thomas S. Barthel, "Viracochas Prunkgewand (Tocapu-Studien 1)," *Tribus* 20 (1971): 63–124, studied an *uncu* in the Museum of Dumbarton Oaks as belonging to this type and suggested an interpretation. It does not use the *tucapu* in the regular diagonal pattern as shown by Guaman Poma. The problem of *uncus* with irregular distribution of *tucapus* might be approached, including in the sample the American Museum of Natural History *uncu*, already mentioned, which in the waistband only has one diagonal repetition of a *tucapu* and no others. As far as I know, there are no actual *uncus*, as shown by Guaman Poma, that organize the whole field of the *uncu* with diagonals of *tucapu*.

91. Guaman Poma, *Nueva corónica*, 2, 33–43, 839.

SEVEN

We Are the Other: Peruvian Portraits of Colonial *Kurakakuna*

Thomas B. F. Cummins

> *Phrases such as, "I know them," or "that's the way they are," show the maximum*
> *objectification achieved. . . . Exoticism is one of those forms of simplification. It*
> *allows no cutural confrontation. There is on the one hand, a culture in which*
> *qualities of dynamism, of growth, of depth can be recognized. As against this,*
> *we find characteristics, curiosities, things, never a structure.*
> FRANZ FANON, *Toward the African Revolution*

When, after nearly five hundred years, we turn to look for representations of Andeans in colonial society, we are met with only a handful of
images in costume, most of which simply reflect our gaze. These are portraits of Inca kings and colonial *kurakakuna,* the traditional leaders of
Andean society, and we recognize ourselves in these images because they
are oil portraits of men and women rendered in European techniques
of modeling, color, and pose, richly painted on canvas, placed in frames,
and ready to be hung on walls (figs. 1, 2, 3, 4). This is an emphatically
different means of representation than was traditional in Peru. Nonetheless, by what they depict, these paintings hearken to the traditional
authority of Peru and its continuation into the colonial period. And this
is the problem that we face when looking at these paintings, because although we see familiar forms, they represent people who are different.

As colonial paintings, it is the presence of difference or "otherness"
in these portraits which is at issue, because not only did the European
colonialists topple and superimpose themselves on the elite who are here
depicted but they also consistently tried to eradicate almost all indigenous representations that reminded colonial Indians of their Andean
heritage.[1] Why then, we may ask, did the colonialists permit idealized
portraits of Inca kings? Why were there portraits of colonial *kurakakuna*
which, in varying degrees of iconographic detail, asserted their colonial
status in pre-Hispanic terms?

Admittedly, these paintings belonged to the elite of native and
Spanish colonial society, and they were meant for the interiors of buildings that had limited access for the majority of the pauperized native

Figure 1. Engraving in Antonio de Herrera y Tordesillas's *Historia general* of Inca kings by Juan Peyrou, after a colonial oil painting, c. 1611.

Figure 2. *Portrait of Don Marcos Chiguan*, c. 1745, oil on canvas.
Museo de Arqueología, Cusco.

Figure 3. *Portrait of Don Alonso Chiguan,* c. 1710, oil on canvas.
Museo de Arqueología, Cusco.

Figure 4. *Portrait of Unknown Female*, c. 1690, oil on canvas.
Museo de Arqueología, Cusco.

population.[2] Nonetheless, there is a direct relation between the privileged world of the colonial elite and the native population of Peru which is forged in part by these paintings. It comes through the public sphere of ritualized interaction between Spaniards, *kurakakuna*, and peasants, in which these pictorial images were brought to life so as to codify the status of sociopolitical relations. These paintings were an integral part of the acculturation process that permitted Peruvians to celebrate their "otherness" as it were, their Indian heritage in such a way as to inculcate passive acquiescence to Spanish rule and relentless economic exploitation.[3]

Beginning with the conquest, Peru's successful colonization would not have been possible if the Spaniards had not been able to rely on the help of the *kurakakuna*. They were the hereditary leaders who, because of their traditional authority within their own communities, had been important members of the Inca's bureaucratic machine, which changed the reciprocal village-based economy into an imperial state economy based on limited redistribution. *Kurakakuna* provided the nexus between the Inca ruling class and the pool of Andean labor, because they maintained their status as leaders of their traditional ethnic group as they became members of the Inca imperial hierarchy. Pre-Hispanic *kurakakuna* were therefore not actually of Inca lineage themselves; yet because of their traditional sociopolitical status, they were culturally integrated into the empire. They were required to live for a period of time at Cusco or some other Inca center, where they learned Quechua, Inca law, and Inca religion.

Kurakakuna essentially occupied a similar position for the Spaniards. They were required to learn the Spanish language and Spanish law, and to become Christians.[4] By this acculturation, they served to implement the rule of the new state structure. Most important, the *kurakakuna* class used the authority conceded to them by their native communities to implement Spanish taxation and to organize the *mit'a*, or *corvée*, system that helped to sustain colonial Peru economically by providing cheap labor for mines, textile sweatshops, and agricultural production. The Spanish colonial regime recognized almost immediately the necessity of maintaining these community leaders, even as the imperial structure of the Inca was systematically dismantled.

Due to historical events and political debates, however, the exact position of the native elite was not universally recognized until near the end of the sixteenth century, when the colonial administration decided that *kurakakuna* should be confirmed as legitimate leaders whose position was based on heredity.[5] They thus were accorded a number of privileges

that distinguished them from the rest of the native population. Most significantly, the *kurakakuna* were exempt from tribute and *mit'a* labor and
received a salary from the taxes collected. They also were given honors
similar to those of Spanish *hidalgos,* such as having a preferential place
next to the priest and holy image in any church procession.[6]

With these material and honorary benefits, the *kurakakuna* actively
entered into Spanish colonial society. Because they learned Spanish and
Spanish legal procedures, the *kurakakuna* were able to negotiate with the
Spaniards on their own behalf, and to act as intermediaries and guaran-
tors in almost all legal contracts between Spaniards and members of a
kuraka's community.[7] These honors and rights signified the distinction
between the active role of the *kurakakuna* and the passive participation
of the majority of native Peruvians (*indios tributarios*), who were merely
a source of labor for colonial society.

The distinction between participant (*kuraka*) in Spanish culture and
observer (*indio tributario*) of that culture thus was structured by the
privileges given to the former. Participation meant, in terms of art, that
one was in the painting, a subject who took part in cultural experience
rather than being the passive viewer of it.[8] This is made clear in the formal arrangement and subject matter of a remarkable series of paintings
of the Corpus Christi celebration executed in Cusco around 1675 (fig.
5). In one picture, a *kuraka* from San Sebastián, depicted in a mixture
of Incaic and Spanish costume, precedes the saint's carriage. In the
foreground, at the bottom of the canvas, there are busts of Indians
turned to look at the procession. Their bodies are conceived as being
outside the frame of the picture, which removes them from active participation in the event. They occupy the same external space as the
viewer of the painting and have the same status as an outside observer.
The pictorial space therefore establishes the social distance between
the *kuraka* and his community. These images, unlike the portraits of
kurakakuna and Inca kings, were publicly displayed in Cusco's Indian
parish of Santa Ana. The natives who attended mass, therefore, not
only saw an image of a liturgical procession but also twice became inac-
tive or passive observers to the primary procession of Corpus Christi.
The paintings offered a model of correct native behavior in these processions.[9] The natives' only access to participation was indirect, through
their relationship to the *kuraka,* who as their leader was granted the
privilege of a cultural participant.[10]

Essentially, the Spaniards transformed the ancient rights and privileges of the *kuraka* into a native version of lower Spanish nobility. Aside
from whatever other sociopolitical purposes this transformation had, it

Figure 5. *Procession of Corpus Christi, San Sebastián,* c. 1675, oil on canvas.
Museo Virreinal, Cusco.

allowed the Spaniards to recognize the *kurakakuna* and deal with them not as a distinct "other" who culturally confronted them but rather as a reasonable semblance of the colonists themselves.

The portraits of pre-Hispanic kings and colonial *kurakakuna* are an integral part of this transformation of social and cultural identity. The eighteenth-century portrait of Don Marcos Chiguan, *kuraka* of Huay-llamba and Colquepata, is perhaps the best example (fig. 2). It is the painting of an individual whose removal from office was sought in 1738 by the Marqués de Alcanizes y Oropesa; he complained that the *kuraka* had, among other abuses, branded his Indians like mules.[11] The portrait, painted two to five years after this event, displays a confident, almost arrogant Don Marcos who does not question his inalienable right to be *kuraka*. It asserts his position both visually and textually. The cartouche lists the honors bestowed on him by a number of viceroys and names him as a descendant of the third ruler of the Inca empire. Visually, Don Marcos strikes the pose of a Spanish noble, or more precisely, an *alférez real*, or royal standard bearer. Above his left shoulder is a coat of arms that originally had been granted to Paullu Topa Inca by Charles V in 1545.[12]

Thus, Don Marcos' costume, his coat of arms, and the standard all reiterate what is claimed in the text. It is not just the Spanish-style clothes, coat of arms, and cartouche, however, that assert Don Marcos' position within a transformed and coopted elite. This painting belongs to a colonial tradition of portraiture of both male and female native elite.[13] In some of these portraits, the figures are dressed almost exclusively in traditional Incaic clothes, as in the portraits of an unknown female and Don Alonso Chiguan Inca, an ancestor of Don Marcos (figs. 3, 4).

We therefore can see that there is a variety of possible costumes worn in these portraits and that the dress of the sitter is not the unqualified pictorial signifier of the position of the *kuraka* within Spanish society.[14] In fact, it is the portrait form itself that codifies this status, since all these figures strike a similar pose. They are placed in an interior space and stand in the foreground, filling the pictorial surface. They confidently confront their viewers and are immediately accessible to them. These are the pictorial conventions that articulate the world of Spanish colonial power, and they assert that these native leaders have a place in it. This is so because these poses, gestures, and formal arrangements are taken directly from the portraits of the Spanish colonial elite. We need only look at two paintings of some of Peru's most illustrious Spaniards to see the connection that was sought by these *kurakakuna*. One is a mid-seventeenth-century portrait of Doña Juana de Valdés y Llano, and the other is a mid-eighteenth-century portrait of the Archbishop of Arequipa (figs. 6, 7). These figures strike the same pose, fill the canvas in the same way, and are placed in the same kind of interior setting. In turn, these portraits derive from the aristocratic portraiture of Spain itself. Diego Velázquez's paintings of Philip IV and Queen Mariana suffice to make the connection (figs. 8, 9).

In short, these formal similarities mitigate the "Indianness" of these Peruvian figures and place them within the descending hierarchy of Spanish power and wealth, beginning with the King of Spain and ending with these native lords.[15] The portraits can be seen as an extension of the colonial procedure leading to a high-ranking *kuraka*'s investiture. The whole hierarchy of descending power was legally and ceremonially called into play so as to demonstrate that the authority of the new *kuraka* ultimately came from the King of Spain. Testimonies and other documents concerning the case were gathered and then were sent to Lima, where the viceroy or Audiencia judged the merits of the presenter's claim. Following a favorable decision, the presenter was installed in the presence of his community in a ceremony called *toma de posesión*. The new *kuraka* appeared in the central plaza dressed in Spanish-style clothes. The viceroy's representative, a *corregidor* or lieutenant, then raised the *kuraka*'s right hand, saying, "I give you possession and favor of the *kuraka*ship . . . *and I place you in it in the [name] of his majesty.* And in this I give you the investiture of said *kuraka*ship" (italics mine).[16]

The portraits of the *kurakakuna* are, however, more than mere reflections of this political hierarchy codified in investiture ritual. The portraits are different in form and content from traditional Andean imagery. The portraits reveal the epistemological shift in the native lords' understanding of the ways and means by which the new imagery could signify in relation to the terms of their colonial legal and political status. That is, these are not merely an extension into the colonial period of a pre-Hispanic artistic structure. The portraits in no way correspond to traditional Andean votive icons or abstract designs symbolizing rank or ethnic identity.[17] These are images of specific individuals that have meaning because they formally reproduce the likeness of that individual. And this is where we see the epistemological shift.[18] These portraits, including those of past Inca kings, have a Western evidentiary value. They signify mimetically the historical presence of the subject in a Western teleological sense. More important, these portraits "prove" not only the *kuraka*'s existence as an individual but also his right to be a *kuraka*.

Figure 6. *Portrait of Doña Juana Valdés y Llano,* c. 1650, oil on canvas.
Museo de Historia, Lima.

Figure 7. *Portrait of the Archbishop of Arequipa,* c. 1750, oil on canvas.
Museo de Historia, Lima.

Figure 8. Diego Velázquez. *Portrait of Philip IV*, c. 1625, oil on canvas. Museo del Prado, Madrid.

Figure 9. Diego Velázquez. *Portrait of Queen Mariana*, c. 1652, oil on canvas. Museo del Prado, Madrid.

This evidentiary quality is made clear by the relation between the image (figure and pictorial symbols) and text in these paintings.[19]

The text is the necessary diachronic element that substantiates the synchronic image. Through its historical narrative, the text asserts and attempts to authenticate that the image that is presented to the viewer is what it claims to be. This reciprocity between image and text is fictive in that both the image and the text are the artifice of the painter, conceived as a single compositional unit. Visual image and verbal text work independently because each appeals to different external referents (individual and document) through two different codes (pictorial and written). Together they give the illusion of being two independent sets of proof that corroborate each other.[20]

This understanding by the native elite that such images and texts constituted a form of document dates to the late sixteenth century, when such paintings were admitted as legal evidence to support claims. In 1586, for example, Leonor de Soto, daughter of an Inca princess and Hernando de Soto, appealed to a 1571 painting done in Cusco as part of her evidence that her father took part in the conquest of Peru and that she was entitled therefore to a land grant (*repartimiento*). The court scribe entered into the testimony of the case:

> I, said notary, give faith that *I saw* on said cloth a gentleman in the dress of [the order of] Santiago which *says* above his head in the painting, "Soto had seized and [had] under arrest Atahualpa," who there seemed to be painted, and he [de Soto] had [Atahualpa] under arrest.[21]

Here image and word are recognized legally as authenticating each other and are used as evidence of an historical event upon which a legal claim is presented.

More important, perhaps, in terms of an epistemological shift, is the fact that one of the first references to colonial portraits of past Inca kings occurs as evidence in another suit. In 1603, El Inca Garcilaso de la Vega received in Madrid a painting of the bust portraits of Inca kings arranged on a genealogical tree. The painting was sent from Cusco by descendants of the Inca and was to be used on their behalf at court, in solicitation of an exemption from tribute.[22] By having their ancestors depicted in Western portrait form, these members of the native colonial elite acknowledged both a different relationship to their ancestors and the representation of them. These painted figures are not actually claimed to be their ancestors. They contain no supernatural aura.[23] Rather, through analogy, these mimetic images assert the historic relationship between the litigants and their ancestors, by which they press their legal claim.[24]

Not every portrait of an individual *kuraka* or Inca king was brought into court as a legal document. These two examples, however, demonstrate that the acceptance by members of the native elite of Western portraits brought with it a different set of relations to portraits, which was predicated upon their position in colonial society rather than their place in traditional society.[25] Individual portraits asserted one's place in the world of colonial power, and portraits of past Inca kings came to stand for a *kuraka*'s distinct right to that power through his noble Andean heritage. Most claims by eighteenth-century *kurakakuna* to descent from the ten Inca dynastic kings could not have withstood close legal scrutiny. Moreover, the pretense of heredity was a fiction, since *kurakakuna* were often displaced or confirmed through Spanish manipulation of the investiture process, regardless of their legal right to the post. This fiction was necessary if there was to be any semblance of continuity in traditional leadership, even though that leadership was now defined through European criteria rather than Andean custom.[26] The possession of portraits gave a quasi-legal status to such claims of native authority. Antonio de Areche observed in 1780, for example, that the portraits of Inca kings "abounded in the extreme in the houses of Indians who take themselves to be nobles in order to sustain or boast of their descent."[27]

The individual portraits, in relation to the Inca portraits, show that members of the *kurakakuna* class were beholden still to their patrimony in order to confirm their status. Their contemporary social and political position was predicated on the Western concept of the historical past, even though that past was non-European. This is why, although Don Marcos Chiguan wears a thoroughly Hispanicized costume, it includes a bastardized version of the traditional Inca head ornament, of which the only authentic parts are the tassel (*maskha paycha*) and the headband (*llawt'u*), embellished with colonial jewels and two feathers.

These details are the unique or particularizing element of the paintings which sets them apart from the otherwise conventional format of Spanish portraiture. They depict graphically that the authority of the *kuraka* was based on his Indian heritage and that this lineage had to be proved before the Spaniards would recognize him legally as a *kuraka*.[28] These unique iconographic elements and their manipulation allow us to trace how the signs and symbols of the acceptance of Spanish rule by the *kuraka* were transmitted to the rest of the native population, in order to assure their acquiescence to it.

The rich dress found in these portraits alludes to the often fictive descent of the *kuraka* from one of the twelve Inca dynastic rulers. The crown, however, is the only element common to all these portraits. Originally, the headpiece was the attribute of the Inca emperor only; by the seventeenth century, however, all Incaic elements had lost their specificity and stood as general signs of the *kuraka* class. We can see this generalization most clearly in the lintel decoration of the Colegio de Caciques de San Borja in Cusco (fig. 10a). Opened in 1621, the school taught the sons of the ethnic lords so that when they succeeded their fathers they would be well "trained in . . . religion and good government."[29]

The lintel dates to after 1650, when Cusco was flattened by an earthquake. It displays the coats of arms of Spain and the Jesuit order, and a hybridized shield representing the *kuraka*.[30] Two elements of this shield are of particular interest. On the upper part of the escutcheon are two antithetically posed felines, with rainbows coming out of their mouths (fig. 10b). Below the rainbow is the Inca crown, the *maskha paycha* and *llawt'u*, and feathers. In 1582, this composition had been used as the exclusive emblem of the Inca dynasty in a painting of Inca and Spanish kings.[31] Less than one hundred years later, it appears as the general sign of a class of nobles who, for the most part, did not descend from these imperial monarchs.

Below and to the left of the rainbow motif is a tower with banners, which represents Cusco. By the seventeenth century, the tower and the rainbow were included within the bastardized crowns worn by *kurakakuna* and pictured in their portraits. Two points are crucial about this heraldic sign. First, it asserted that every *kuraka* was a direct inheritor of Inca dynastic rule, whether or not there was a blood descendant of the Inca. Second, it was repeated on such lintels of individual *kurakakuna*'s homes as the eighteenth-century example from Maras.[32] It is also possible that this image returned to the principal native communities emblazoned on the tunics of San Borja's students.[33] The founding rules for both San Borja and a similar school established in Lima stipulated that students should appear in public wearing a uniform that bore the heraldic signs found on the schools' lintels.[34] Thus, one can be fairly sure that most Indians in the southern sierras were aware of this iconography and its relationship to the *kurakakuna*.

The meaning of the image was known, however, through the seventeenth- and eighteenth-century images painted on *keros* (*qiru*), the ceremonial drinking cups. These vessels were used in Indian villages for feasts that, among other things, validated by traditional means the right of the *kuraka* to organize *corvée* labor to serve the Spaniards. The images on the colonial vessels are a synthesis of Western form and Andean spatial symbolism which, in relation to the vessel's ritual use, concep-

(b)

Figure 10. (a) and (b) *Lintel and Detail from the Colegio de Caciques de
San Borja,* c. 1670. Cusco.

tualized the traditional authority of the *kuraka*.[35] It is not by chance that
the feline rainbow motif is the most frequent design found on colonial
keros (*qirukuna*) (fig. 11a).[36] On *keros* (*qirukuna*), however, the Inca crown
below the rainbow of the lintel is replaced by the idealized figures of an
Inca and his wife (fig. 11b). The equation between the colonial *kuraka*
and the Inca king is thus more direct. There is at least one parallel to
these *kero* (*qiru*) figures in the oil portrait of an unidentified female. She
reaches toward the colonial version of the Inca crown, in the center of
which is a tiny Inca figure, holding a *tupa yauri,* or royal scepter (fig. 4).
The figure is identical to those found on *keros* (*qirukuna*), and it is

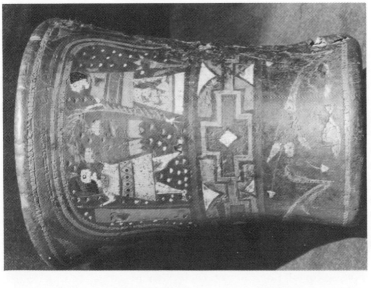

(b)

(a)

Figure 11. (a) *Figure of Feline with Rainbow on Kero* (Qiru), c. 1700, gum-based paint on wood. Museo de Antropología, Cusco. (b) *Figure of Inca and Female under Rainbow on Same Kero* (Qiru), c. 1700, gum-based paint on wood. Museo de Antropología, Cusco.

undoubtably a reference to her direct descent from one of the Inca monarchs.

Both figures relate to a tradition of idealized portraits of the dynastic Inca kings. The tradition dates at least to the late sixteenth century, and the figures are found in the only two early Peruvian illustrated manuscripts made at the beginning of the seventeenth century.[37] Throughout the seventeenth and eighteenth centuries, Inca dynastic portraits were owned by *kurakakuna* and Spaniards alike and also hung in official buildings or appeared as murals, as in the Colegio de San Borja.[38] While most Peruvians could not have seen these images, they certainly saw them on *keros* (*qirukuna*), and they also saw their *kurakakuna* dressed in Inca costume at events such as the procession of Corpus Christi.

In the constellation of all these images (portraits, lintels, *qirukuna*, and processions) there is an insistence on the Inca dynastic rulers that goes beyond merely asserting the aristocratic heritage of the *kurakakuna*. There are, however, different audiences for these various representations. It was one thing for the colonial regime to permit the ethnic lords to have themselves painted in variations of archaic costumes or tolerate their own possession of portraits of their ancient kings. It was quite another to allow such imagery to circulate freely among all levels of Andean society. After all, rebellions were not uncommon in Peru, and many were decidedly messianic.[39]

Part of the answer can be found in the comments of the French eighteenth-century traveler Amédée Frézier. Frézier writes about his visit to Peru in 1711 and tells how, during the festival of the Virgin Mary, the Indians paraded in the ancient costume of the Incas in all the Peruvian cities. They also reenacted Francisco Pizarro's execution of Atahualpa. About the reenactment Frézier says, "The Indians have not forgotten him [Atahualpa]; the love they bore their native kings makes them still sigh for those times. . . . [T]he Spaniards are not safe at this time and the prudent shut themselves up in their houses."[40]

The critical phrase is "still sigh for those times." It is a phrase used almost verbatim thirty years later by the Viceroy José Manso de Velasco, who wrote of a celebration in 1748 that

> the Indians have a separate celebration, and they reduce it to a representation of a series of their ancient kings, their dress, custom, and retinue; the memory saddens them, and some do not take off the clothes and insignia without tears.[41]

The two passages denote the European belief that these reenactments instilled a sense of resignation in the face of an irretrievable past and

that they permitted an acceptable form of sentimental expression toward that heritage.[42] In this sense, these comments also capture exactly
what Inca portraits are about. In fact, Frézier's passage accompanies a
drawing he made from a series of Inca portraits, painted by native artists
in Cusco. But, as already noted, even Don Marcos Chiguan's portrait
makes a direct allusion to the ancient kings for whom "the natives
sighed."[43] These allusions were necessary because the *kurakakuna* had an
active, if unknowing, part in the colonial pageantry that manipulated
and played upon nostalgia.

Beginning in 1555, there are detailed descriptions of Spanish festi-
vals, held in Cusco, Potosí, and Lima, which celebrated important events
such as the marriage or coronation of the Spanish king. Part of the public spectacle was a procession that wound through the city's streets. The
single consistent native contribution to this spectacle from 1555 to 1756
was the procession of the twelve Inca kings, who were impersonated by
kurakakuna or their children.[44] The last Inca to be represented was either
Huayna Capac, who ruled just prior to the arrival of the Spaniards in
Peru, his rightful heir Huascar, or Atahualpa, who met and was captured by Pizarro in 1532.[45] Like the portraits, lintels, and *keros*, these
impersonations legitimized and even aggrandized the authority of the
kuraka by their reference to history. However, these impersonations had
a deeper, teleological significance. They paraded the Andean heritage
before the native spectators as part of a constructed historical narrative
that not only legitimized the authority of the *kurakakuna* but also justified
all native subservience to Spanish authority.

First of all, even though the procession of past rulers stemmed from
an Andean tradition of ancestor worship, it was now subsumed within
a European celebration of religious and political importance. Second,
the parades often included the reenactment of specific events that occurred during the reign of each Inca. These often ended with Atahualpa's execution, and they were followed almost invariably by men
bearing the portraits of Spanish kings, beginning with Charles V and
ending with the reigning monarch.[46] Finally, the costumed *kurakakuna*
bowed in front of the impersonator/portrait of whomever was the highest Spanish authority present.[47]

There are a number of eighteenth-century paintings still surviving
that show this historical progression, but their precedent was set in the
late sixteenth century.[48] These impersonations and portraits all contributed to establishing a clear historical sequence that acknowledged the
Andean past but at the same time showed it to be conclusively severed
from the present by the juxtaposition of the last Inca ruler and the first

Spanish king under whom Peru was colonized.[49] Inca history and an independent Andean identity were, therefore, carefully relegated to a nos-
talgic period that existed only before the Spanish arrival. The present
allowed no place for an independent Andean identity or will. Rather,
all Andeans, even the *kurakakuna,* were subservient to the colonialists,
and any local ethnic lord who did not cooperate with the colonial administration was removed. This is why we find no paintings of the last three
Inca kings who succeeded Atahualpa. The first of these, Manco Inca,
revolted against the invaders. He retreated to the jungle refuge of Vilcabamba, from where he, and later his two sons Titu Cusi and Tupac
Amaru, waged guerrilla warfare for forty years—until 1571, when Viceroy Francisco de Toledo captured Tupac Amaru. All representations of
past Inca rulers carefully precluded reference to this dangerous model
of active resistance to Spanish claims. Tupac Amaru, the last truly Inca
emperor, also was executed by the Spaniards, but at no time was his
death reenacted by colonial natives.[50] Instead, it was Atahualpa's death
that was staged throughout Peru, just at it is today, because it served as
the permissible focus of an Andean identity in a Hispanic world.[51] It
marked the disjunction between past and present, and the unalterable
shift from native autonomy to colonial control. The masquerades and
portraits articulated a part of the imperial Spanish teleological justification of their rule.

   Thus, the "Indianness," the other, that is seen in these portraits, processions, and *keros* (*qirukuna*) was predicated on a nostalgia that was
meant to foster fatalism. It allowed Indians to sigh publicly for a past
represented in the dress and comportment of their lords, but which reduced them to being peasants. The "other" that is seen in these portraits
is therefore not Andean but Spanish. The pictorial language is itself
alien and so renders what appears to be native as exotic. It is a pictorial
language that was acquired by a class of individuals who had consciously
or unconsciously learned to objectify their own culture through two and
one-half centuries of acculturation. Thus, even though the rebellions of
the eighteenth century were based in part on an ideology that stressed
the Inca past so as to create a commonality between peasant and *kuraka,*
this shared identity was fictive.[52] A successful native revolt would not
have changed the social and economic differences that existed between
the native ethnic lords and the peasants of Peru.[53] Too many factors had
gone into the making of the colonial identity of the *kuraka* to allow him
to return to the set of sociopolitical relations that had existed before the
Spanish arrival.[54]

NOTES

1. Pierre Duviols, *La destrucción de las religiones andinas,* translated by Albor Maruenda (Mexico City, 1971, 1977).

2. For example, portraits of Inca kings were hung in the *cabildo* of Lima and were the subject of the murals in the *colegio* for the sons of *kurakakuna* in Cusco. Teresa Gisbert, *Iconografía y mitos indígenas en el arte* (La Paz, 1980), 127; Guillermo Lohmann Villena, "Noticias inéditas para ilustrar la historia de las bellas artes in Lima durante los siglos XVI y XVII," *Revista Histórica* 23 (1940): 29.

3. Only two studies have dealt with these paintings in any depth: John H. Rowe, "Colonial Portraits of Inca Nobles," in *The Civilizations of Ancient America: Selected Papers of the Twenty-ninth International Congress of Americanists,* edited by Sol Tax (Chicago, 1951), 258–268; and Gisbert, *Iconografía y mitos.* A debt is owed to each of these works, but this chapter departs from them, especially Gisbert, in that it analyzes these paintings as part of a colonial acculturation process. Gisbert's work is iconographic, and she (ibid., 152) treats this iconography as an autonomous native expression and as part of a growing independent native identity, which resulted in the rebellion of 1781. Native rebellions failed, in part, because many native leaders refused to participate and instead assisted in putting down insurrections. See Brooke Larson, "*Caciques,* Class Structure, and the Colonial State in Bolivia," *Nova Americana* 2 (1979): 203. It is true that most of these paintings were confiscated after the 1781 rebellion because part of the rebellion's rhetoric was based on an identification with the Inca past. What is of interest is why the Spanish colonial regime permitted their creation and distribution for almost two hundred years prior to that time.

4. See the essay of Rolena Adorno in this volume.

5. Many of the honors were first conceded to *kurakakuna* on an ad hoc basis, but were institutionalized by Viceroy Francisco de Toledo in 1571. It was not, however, until the beginning of the seventeenth century that the rules of inheritance finally were codified in Spanish law. Archivo General de Indias (hereafter cited as AGI), Lima, 274, Cédula, Lima, 12 February 1589; lic. Alonso de Bonilla to King, Lima, 25 May 1592; and AGI, Lima, 570, Cédula, Lima, 5 September 1598 and 22 February 1602; cited in Carlos Díaz Rementería, *El cacique en el virreinato del Perú* (Seville, 1977), 215–218.

6. Waldemar Espinoza Soriano, "Los señoríos étnicos del valle de Condebamba y provincias de Cajabamba," *Anales Científicos* 3 (1974): 131.

7. Karen Spalding, *De indio a campesino* (Lima, 1974), 37–38. Members of a native community often had individual work contracts with colonialists for up to a year's time. The individual *kuraka,* however, actually put his signature on the contract and guaranteed that the service that was contracted would be completed. Moreover, the *kuraka* often received a salary, usually in the name of the community. See, for example, Archivo Histórico del Cusco (hereafter cited as

AHC), registers of the notary Bastides 1645–1647, pt. 139A/592, fol. 681; and registers of the notary Gregorio Vázquez Serrano, 1700, pt. 2–228, fol. 151.

8. Graziano Gasparini, "The Colonial City as a Center for the Spread of Architecture and Pictorial Schools," in *Urbanization in the Americas from Its Beginnings to the Present*, edited by Richard Schaedel (The Hague, 1978), 270.

9. These paintings depict the ideal of native participation, which is very distinct from actual behavior. For example, a second painting from the 1675 series solemnly depicts the procession entering the cathedral while a group of Indian dancers in the lower left portion of the pictorial field reverently turns toward the procession. This 1675 depiction of correct behavior is quite distinct from a drunken brawl in which these same dancers were involved some twenty-five years later and which caused the prohibition of their participation in the 1701 celebration of Corpus Christi. See Diego de Esquivel y Navia, *Noticias cronológicas de la gran ciudad del Cuzco* (Lima, [1749] 1980), 2:183. Other accounts reveal that irreverent behavior during these ceremonies seems to have been the norm rather than the exception. The orderly and devout scene depicted in the painting represents the ideal.

10. The sociopolitical distinction between the *kurakakuna* and the *indios tributarios* also was seen clearly in the Catholic cult images, in which the donor portraits of *kurakakuna* vastly outnumbered even Spanish donor portraits. See José de Mesa and Teresa Gisbert, *Historia de la pintura cuzqueña* (Lima, 1982), 286–287. To my knowledge, there are no donor portraits of ordinary Indians. Just as in the paintings in Santa Ana, the nonelite's relation to these images was that of a passive worshiper.

11. Rowe, "Colonial Portraits," 267–268.

12. Ibid., 267.

13. John Rowe notes that Don Marcos Chiguan's portrait in particular stems from a colonial tradition of portraits painted of those who enjoyed the title of *alférez real de los Incas*. This prestigious elected position could be held only by descendants of the Inca. See John H. Rowe, "Genealogía y rebelión en el siglo XVIII: Algunos antecedentes de la sublevación de José Gabriel Thupa Amaro," *Histórica* 6, 1 (1982): 73. The first recorded portrait of one of these elected officials, Gil Pilco Thupa, is dated 1658. See Esquivel y Navia, *Noticias cronológicas*, 2:114. This information is found only in the New York Public Library's copy of the manuscript.

14. This is not to say that dress was not important. Clothing in pre-Hispanic and colonial Peru was always a critical ethnic and social signifier. Beginning in the sixteenth century, high-status *kurakakuna* wore Spanish items of clothes as symbols of prestige, and their access to this type of clothing was regulated by law. See Rolena Adorno, "On Pictorial Language and the Typology of Culture in a New World Chronicle," *Semiotica* 36, 1/2 (1981): 51–106; and Nathan Wachtel, *The Vision of the Vanquished: The Spanish Conquest of Peru through Indian Eyes, 1530–1570*, translated by Ben and Sian Reynolds (New York, 1977), 147–150. The wearing of both Spanish and Inca clothes by *kurakakuna* continued to

be an important issue in terms of social and cultural status throughout the colonial period.

15. For the strategies of Europeanizing self-representation of a seventeenth-century Peruvian lord, see Rolena Adorno, *Guaman Poma: Writing and Resistance in Colonial Peru* (Austin, Tex., 1986).

16. Espinoza Soriano, "Los señoríos," 131; italics mine.

17. See the essay of R. Tom Zuidema in this volume.

18. The noncorrespondence between traditional Peruvian imagery and Western imagery is evidenced by the differences between what happened in Mexico and what happened in Peru after the conquest. In Mexico, there was a tradition of figural imagery that was related to text and that was used as a type of record keeping. Because of this, aspects of Mexican imagery continued being used as evidence in Spanish colonial legal documents well into the eighteenth century. See James Lockhart, "Views of Corporate Self and History in Some Valley of Mexico Towns: Late Seventeenth Century and Eighteenth Centuries," in *The Inca and Aztec States, 1400–1800,* edited by George Collier, Renato I. Rosaldo, and John Wirth (New York, 1982), 367–393. Traditional Andean imagery at the time of the conquest did not have this quality. There is thus no known Peruvian colonial legal document that includes pre-Hispanic-based images. This accounts in part for the disparity in the visual records that exist between Mexico and Peru. See Thomas B. F. Cummins, "Realism versus Abstraction: Native Representation in the Americas and the Spanish Re-representation of the Inca," unpublished manuscript.

19. For the European tradition of painting as a document of an historical event, see Jan Panofsky, "Jan van Eyck's 'Arnolfini' Portrait," *Burlington Magazine* 64 (1934): 117–127. For a discussion of the Western relationship between text and image, see Norman Bryson, *Word and Image* (Cambridge, Eng., 1981), 1–28.

20. For further reflections on this relationship in the drawings of Felipe Guaman Poma de Ayala, see Rolena Adorno, "Visual Mediation in the Transition from Oral to Written Expression," *New Scholar* 10, 1/2 (1986): 181–196.

21. Enrique Marco Dorta, "Las pinturas que envió y trajo de España Don Francisco de Toledo," *Historia y Cultura* 9 (1975): 72.

22. El Inca Garcilaso de la Vega, *Los comentarios reales,* Biblioteca de Autores Españoles 134/135 (Madrid, [1609–1617] 1960), 384.

23. There is no evidence for portraiture from the time of the conquest. Mummies of important ancestors, including the Inca dynastic kings, were kept, venerated, and propitiated as living entities. Each Inca also was represented by a totemic image, *huaque,* but these were in the form of an animal or natural phenomenon and not in the likeness of the Inca.

24. This painting may also have had a more general form of evidentiary value. It is probable that it was used as a source for engraving the frontispiece that precedes the Peruvian section of Antonio de Herrera y Tordesillas's *Historia general de los hechos de los castellanos en las islas y tierra firme del mar océano* (Madrid,

[1610–1615] 1952), 10–11. See Marco Dorta, "Las pinturas," 72. In this case, the portraits stand as visual confirmation of the historical existence of the Inca dynasty in a sequential form understandable to Europeans. They also represent the impossibility of using pre-Hispanic Andean images to represent information to a European audience. See Thomas B. F. Cummins, "Realism versus Abstraction."

25. The tradition of presenting portraits in relation to legal procedures continued into the eighteenth century. See Gisbert, *Iconografía y mitos,* 151–152.

26. According to Díaz Rementería, the hereditary factors of the colonial institution of *kurakakuna* were basically recognized according to Las Leyes de Toro, 1505, which were written originally to codify the rules of Spanish nobility. See Díaz Rementería, *El cacique,* 165–166.

27. John H. Rowe, "Movimiento nacional del siglo XVII," *Revista de la Universidad del Cusco* 107 (1954): 30.

28. Lineage had to be proved in principle according to Spanish law. See Díaz Rementería, *El cacique,* 215–218. In reality, colonial officials often installed cooperative Indians as *kurakakuna* even though they did not meet legal criteria. Forged documents and false claims to heraldry were then used to sustain the appointment. María Rostworowski de Diez Canseco, *Curacas y sucesiones: Costa norte* (Lima, 1961), 147.

29. Francisco de Borja, "Provisión real," *Inca* 1 (1923): 71.

30. Gisbert, *Iconografía y mitos,* 168–169.

31. Diego Rodríguez de Figueroa, "Carta y memorial de Diego Rodríguez de Figueroa al Virrey Don Martín Enríquez sobre cosas tocantes a este reino de Potosí," in *Relaciones geográficas de Indias,* edited by Marcos Jiménez de la Espada, Biblioteca de Autores Españoles 184 (Madrid, 1965), 66.

32. Gisbert, *Iconografía y mitos,* 166.

33. The politics of the image of the rainbow in colonial Peru are extremely complex, because it was at once an idolatrous image associated with *amaru,* meaning serpent, and a legitimate part of Spanish colonial religious painting. As such, the presence of the rainbow in colonial imagery could have been read in various and contradictory ways, as suggested by Sabine MacCormack, "*Pachacuti*: Miracles, Punishments, and Last Judgment—Visionary Past and Prophetic Future in Early Colonial Peru," *American Historical Review* 93 (October 1988): 960–1006. This image of the rainbow therefore may very well have operated at a subversive level. But the scholarly ability to recover such meaning is dependent upon extant examples, which have survived because the rainbow appeared openly in a variety of colonial media. It did so in the examples discussed here because of the rainbow's heraldic associations, granted to the image as a legitimate sociopolitical sign within colonial Peru. One of the earliest examples is the coat of arms granted to the sons of Huayna Capac, Don Gonzalo Uchu Gualpa and Don Felipe Tupa Inca Yupanqui, by Charles V in 1545; see Santiago Montoto de Sedes, *Nobiliario hispano-americano del siglo XVI,* in *Documentos inéditos para la historia de Ibero-América* (Madrid, 1927), 2:300–305. Moreover, the rela-

tion between these coats of arms and Western-style portraits, such as can be seen in the painting of Don Chiguan, begins in the late sixteenth and early seventeenth centuries. For example, several of the watercolor illustrations that accompany Martín de Murúa's *Historia general del Perú, origen y descendencia de los Incas,* edited by Manuel Ballesteros-Gabrois, 2 vols. (Madrid, [c. 1613] 1962–1964), shows a full-length portrait of an Inca in a contrapposto stance with a coat of arms placed above the upper left shoulder. This relationship between portrait and coat of arms in Peru may have originated in documents granting the coat of arms. At least one sixteenth-century document existing in the Archivo General de Indias in Seville bestows a coat of arms to Inca nobility and has the shield illustrated on one page and a full-length portrait of an Inca on the other.

34. Borja, "Provisión real," 69–73.

35. The paintings on colonial *keros* (*qirukuna*) are based on European pictorial narrative imagery; however, the figures are arranged to the right or left of a central vertical axis according to Andean symbolic logic. See Juan M. Ossio, "Guaman Poma: *Nueva Corónica* o carta al rey, un intento de aproximación a las categorías del mundo andino," in *Ideología mesiánica del mundo andino,* edited by Juan M. Ossio (Lima, 1973), 155–213; Nathan Wachtel, "Pensamiento salvage y aculturación," in *Sociedad e ideología: ensayos de historia y antropología andinas* (Lima, 1973), 165–228; and Rolena Adorno, "Paradigms Lost: A Peruvian Indian Surveys Spanish Colonial Society," *Studies in the Anthropology of Visual Communication* 5, 2 (Spring 1979): 78–96.

The cups were used in colonial rituals in which members of an Andean community would, through the use of the cups, acknowledge their social identity as well as the authority of the *kuraka*. See Thomas B. F. Cummins, "Abstraction to Narration: *Kero* Imagery of Peru and the Colonial Alteration of Native Identity (Ph.D. diss., University of California at Los Angeles, 1988).

36. Gisbert has noted the correspondence between the iconography of these lintels, paintings, and *keros* (*qirukuna*) but draws no conclusions from it. See Gisbert, *Iconografía y mitos,* 168.

37. Marco Dorta, "Las pinturas," 67–68; and Rodríguez de Figueroa, "Carta y memorial," 62–67.

38. Gisbert, *Iconografía y mitos,* 127.

39. The largest native rebellion until 1780 was the Taki Unquy (c. 1560–1580). We recall that its proponents advocated a return to traditional ways and condemned the use of Spanish-style clothes and the Spanish language. Luis Millones, ed., *Las informaciones de Cristóbal de Albornoz: Documentos para el estudio del Taqui Ongoy* (Cuernavaca, Mex., 1971).

40. Amédée F. Frézier, *Relations du voyage de la Mer du Sud aux côtes de Chili et Pérou fait pendant les années 1712 et 1714* (Paris, 1716), 249.

41. José Antonio Manso de Velasco, "Relación que escribe . . . ," in *Memoriales de los virreyes que han gobernado en el Perú durante el tiempo del colonaje español, impresas de orden supremo,* edited by Manuel Atanasio Fuentes (Lima, [1756] 1859), 98.

42. As early as 1555, colonists noted the reverence that natives paid to the representation of past kings, especially Atahualpa, in portraits and masquerades. See Bartolomé de Arzáns de Orsúa y Vela, *Historia de la villa imperial de Potosí* (Providence, R.I., [1736] 1965), 1:244. This reverence could produce spontaneous rioting, such as Frézier says occurred after the reenactments. However, as spontaneous outbursts, they were momentary cathartic expressions of a much greater hostility and resentment that only organized resistance could overcome.

43. The iconographic connection between the impersonations and portraits has been made by Gisbert, *Iconografía y mitos,* 142.

44. The most comprehensive account of one of these masquerades is Jerónimo Fernández de Castro's description of Lima's 1725 celebration of the abdication of Philip V for his son Luis. See Carlos Romero, "Una supervivencia del Inkanato durante la colonia," *Revista Histórica* 10 (1936): 76–94. Most of the twelve Incas were impersonated by *kurakakuna* from all the major coastal communities. However, the third Inca, Lloque Inca, was impersonated by the son of a *kuraka* family from Jauja, which had sought legally to prove its direct descent from the Incas. See Ella Dunbar Temple, "Los caciques Apoalaya," *Revista del Museo Nacional* 2, 2 (1942): 165.

45. There is one exception to this. In the 1600 procession of Potosí celebrating the marriage of Philip III, each Inca king up to Huascar was represented by an impersonator who rode in a richly decorated carriage. The last carriage carried the Spanish kings who had ruled Peru: Charles I, Philip II, and Philip III. Seated below these monarchs were the Inca kings who ruled after the Spaniards had entered Peru. These included Manco Capac II, Sayri Tupac, Titu Cusi, and Tupac Amaru. These were Inca kings who revolted against Spanish rule and were not usually included in these processions. They occurred in the 1600 procession because they had received baptism and had thus acknowledged the authority of Christ, through whom the Spanish monarchs ruled. See Arzáns de Orsúa y Vela, *Historia de la Villa,* 1:244.

46. The meaning of these processions as a theatrical form of demonstrating the definitive end of Inca rule seems to have remained constant for at least 125 years. In a procession in Potosí in 1600, the carriage of the King of Spain immediately followed that of the last independent Inca (see note 45 above). In the 1724 Lima celebration of Philip V's abdication, the procession of Inca kings was preceded by Taunapa, ambassador and interpreter of the Incas. He paraded around the plaza, stopping before the viceroy to read a poem of the Incas' submission to him. Three days later, the *kurakakuna* again impersonated the Inca. This time they were not preceded by Taunapa; rather, they were followed by a carriage decorated in the form of a boat. It represented the ship that had brought the first thirteen *conquistadores* to Peru. On the quarterdeck was someone dressed as Pizarro, and images that represented the theological and cardinal virtues of Catholicism were on the foredeck. Finally, a young boy under an arch represented the King of Spain. See Romero, "Una supervivencia del Inkanato," 92–93.

47. Carlos Romero, "Festividades del tiempo heróico de los Incas," *Inca* 1, 2 (1923): 451.

48. Rodríguez de Figueroa, "Carta y memorial," 63–67.

49. The use of theater as a means of fixing into native consciousness the "correct" or Spanish view of conquest history was also used in Mexico. See Richard Trexler, "We Think, They Act: Clerical Readings of Missionary Theater in Sixteenth-century New Spain," in *Understanding Popular Culture,* edited by Stephen Kaplan (Berlin, 1984).

50. The only possible reference to Tupac Amaru in the reenactments of Atahualpa's death is the means of execution. Atahualpa was actually strangled, whereas Tupac Amaru was beheaded. Therefore, the colonial representation of Atahualpa's death by decapitation in the plays could suggest a reference to Tupac Amaru. However, it is more likely that Atahualpa's death is portrayed by the act of decapitation because this was a traditional Andean metaphor for defeat.

51. Natives were allowed to look to the past or to the future for their rightful place in Peru. The intent was to avoid claims in the present which would articulate native identity in distinction to those who governed them. (See Adorno, *Guaman Poma,* for how one Andean articulated the claims of the present and the needs of the future on the basis of retelling the past.) This identity would truly be the identity of Peruvian as "other," and this potentially revolutionary identity was to be avoided at all costs. This is as true today as it was in colonial Peru. It is not a matter of chance that a great deal of literature has focused on native revivalism in millenarian terms, such as the Inkarrí myths that posit a return of the Inca and a future that will be a true native world. Andeanists see this as a form of autochthonous resistance and describe the abundant existing variants of this myth. However, the Inkarrí myths and the millenarianism of the twentieth century are neither true myth nor millenarian; they are only cruel illusions perpetuated in the twentieth century on the basis of colonial-period beliefs. For the cynical use of Inkarrí ideology by the Velasco regime in the 1970s, see Rosalind Gow, "Inkarrí and Revolutionary Leadership in the Southern Andes," *Journal of Latin American Lore* 8, 2 (1982): 218–219.

52. Spalding, *De indio,* 186–193.

53. Ibid., 53–55.

54. I would like to thank Kyle Huffman, Joan Weinstein, Cecilia F. Klein, Rolena Adorno, Jane Williams, Emily Umberger, Ju-Hsi Chou, and Donald Rabiner, all of whom in one way or another contributed to this chapter.

EIGHT

Images of *Indios Ladinos* in Early Colonial Peru

Rolena Adorno

INTRODUCTION

In 1563, on his return to Spain after some twelve years as a judge of the Audiencia of Lima, the Licentiate Hernando de Santillán responded to King Philip's 1553 questionnaire on the customs of the Incas and, in the course of it, offered many opinions on contemporary colonial affairs.[1] After discussing Inca succession, he remarked on the current problems of succession in rule among *kurakakuna* (local ethnic lords). He noted that some had become "so *ladino*" (acquainted with Spanish language and customs) and familiar with the entanglements and disputes carried out among Christians that they no longer proceeded with the simplicity and rectitude by which they had been governed on these matters in Inca times. Instead, on taking office the new *kuraka* commonly took for himself the wealth of his predecessor, without leaving anything to the rightful heirs. Filing suit, the heirs would go to court to seek redress with the following result: "Everything is lost in lawsuits with lawyers [*letrados*] and litigation officers [*procuradores*], such that, at the end, both parties end up without anything except for being very clever at tricks and lies, as is seen every day in the Audiencia."[2]

The solution proposed by this defender of the Indians and harsh critic of colonialist abuses was to provide Indian courts and judges, governed by "those who understand their controversies and disputes, without the intervention of those lawyers and officials who are a pestilence upon the natives." This reform would be beneficial because, under present circumstances, "some who are *ladinos,* knowing that they won't get

232

caught in the lie because they are not understood by the judges, dare to perpetrate many deceits, for which there are Spaniards who incite them, in order to take advantage of them."[3] Santillán thus presents the paradoxical plight of the natives who knew Hispanic customs and language (*indios ladinos*) and were able to use the colonial legal system but still were thwarted by it. His view was echoed some fifty years later by the testimony of an Andean, Felipe Guaman Poma de Ayala, who was himself *ladino*.[4] Guaman Poma sarcastically remarked that to file petitions was to render losses (*peticiones/perdiciones*). Licentiates should be called "licentiate-asses," and *procuradores* "procurers of thieves."[5]

Although the puns do not translate from Spanish, the passions that produced them do so readily. *Indios ladinos* constituted a flashpoint of Spanish/Andean interaction. In this paper, I would like to consider what we can learn about that experience, mostly from two such individuals, who were unusual not in their occupation (as interpreters) but in how they played the role (having become writers in their own right).

The term itself presents a problem. While referring to natives who learned the Europeans' language and made possible transactions and negotiations of all sorts between Spanish colonial and native Andean societies,[6] it did not refer to a homogeneous group. Instead, it brought together under a single rubric a diverse constellation of social types.[7] *Indio ladino* was a common form of identification in colonial documentation. As an external designation originating in the foreign, Spanish community, it was not used by natives for self-identification except when dealing with Spanish-speaking outsiders. The sources considered here represent both the internal and the external perspectives: the European looking at the Hispanized Indian and the latter describing his own outlook to a European audience. This investigation elaborates the image of the *indio ladino* as perceived *by* outsiders and the self-image produced *for* outsiders to the indigenous world. It does not take into account topics of much more difficult access: their linguistic activity, their day-to-day lives, Spanish–*indio ladino* interactions, or the view of the *indios ladinos* which we might get from documents in which they communicated among themselves in their native languages.[8] Ironically, the *indios ladinos,* ever-present in the documentary records of colonialism as interpreters, translators, and scribes, most easily remain perpetually hidden within it.

Antecedents to the present inquiry include the 1965 Lima symposium on *mestizaje* sponsored by the National Academy of History of Peru under the leadership of Aurelio Miró Quesada, James Lockhart's 1968 discussion of Hispanized Indians (mostly interpreters) in daily contact with Spaniards in *Spanish Peru,* and John Hemming's consideration of native *lenguas* or interpreters in his 1970 *The Conquest of the Incas.*[9] The most complete story of one of the lives of the early interpreters is Antonio del Busto's 1965 study of Martinillo de Poechos (Don Martín de Pizarro).[10] In 1975, Francisco de Solano called attention to the importance of native interpreters (*ladinos*) as "one of the axes of acculturation" and created a typology, extending from conquest to colonial society, that included guides in exploration and discovery, "political interlocutors" in the negotiations of conquest, and official translators in investigations of civil officers (*residencias*), tours of civil and ecclesiastical inspection (*visitas*), and courts of civil and criminal justice (*audiencia*).[11] While some of the first native Americans who became *indios ladinos* were captured and taken to Europe (Don Diego Colón, captured by Columbus on his first voyage; Don Martín de Pizarro, taken to Spain by Pizarro in 1528)[12] or captured and imprisoned in America so that they could learn Spanish,[13] the later generations of *indios ladinos* who worked as *lenguas* or interpreters seem to have been recruited voluntarily, not always by force. The difficulty on this point is that native testimony prepared for a European audience hides the potential coercive dimension. At the same time, legislation against coercion and effective enslavement of intepreters indicates that such problems continued to exist throughout most of the sixteenth century.[14] The rebellion of *indios ladinos* via their participation in revitalist movements thirty years after the Spanish conquest of Peru suggests that coercion might have been a significant aspect of their early Hispanization.

Mestizos as well as ethnic Andeans were referred to as being *ladino,* and the term was applied to such diverse groups as the first natives who faithfully served the Spanish during the conquest (such as Felipillo and Don Martín Pizarro, mentioned above), the *kurakakuna* or ethnic lords, who were the points of contact between native and colonial societies, and the *yanakuna* or native servitors who, detached from their *ayllu* of origin, worked for nominal wages in the private employ of colonists.[15] Women as well as men were implicated.[16] Although the term was used in colonial times to stereotype and unify a wide range of experience, the emphasis on *indio ladino* as a category of analysis must be on the diversity it covers. Since the *indios ladinos* did not constitute a single social stratum, occupational group, or gender, taking up the topic of *ladinidad* involves choosing one among many possible sites of interaction. But first it will be useful to consider the origin of the term.

Indio ladino was used from the very beginning of Spanish colonial times in Hispaniola, Mexico, and Peru, and it had been imported from

Spain in one of its standard usages. According to the 1611 Castilian dictionary of Sebastián de Covarrubias, *ladino* had referred originally to those inhabitants of the Iberian peninsula who had mastered the language of the colonizing Romans and used it with elegance. Unlike the common and barbarous people who stumbled in the use of the Romans' language, those who became expert at it "were taken to be ingenious, men of great reason and merit, whence it came to be that this name was applied to those who are skilled and sagacious in any dealing."[17] That the connotation was positive (*solerte* as sagacious rather than cunning) is borne out by Covarrubias's other reference to the term: the man who had mastered the Latin language in Gothic and Alfonsine times was considered prudent and wise, "whence it has come about that to call a man *ladino* today means that he has great understanding and ratiocination, that he is sagacious, astute, and courteous [cortesano]."[18]

While *ladino* had originally referred to the common Romance vernacular of Spain excluding Catalunia, Roger Wright recently has studied the relationship of the concepts *latín* and *ladino* in medieval Spain to explain the latter's subsequent meaning with reference to the Sephardic Jewish cultural tradition.[19] This provides the missing link between the universal use of *ladino* to refer to the language of vernacular Romance and *ladino* to refer to any nonnative speaker of Castilian ("al morisco y al estranjero," according to Covarrubias) who became expert in the Spanish language.[20] Beyond its reference to polyglot achievement, the term had connotations, as we have seen, of prudence and sagacity of the individual referred to as *ladino*. With this meaning, the term was imported to Spanish America as a way of referring to those natives who were competent (speaking, and possibly reading and writing) in the language of the colonial overlords. Apart from today's use of the term in some areas of Latin America (such as Guatemala) to mean "Hispanized," the negative connotations it carries in other areas (such as Colombia) lead us to speculate on the colonial origins of these negative values. Some of them will become apparent in the following discussion; most of the colonial sources considered here, however, present neutral to positive values of the term.

A single *indio ladino* was likely to be active in a variety of social milieus. This is suggested both by the testimony of those who had such experiences and by the accounts of Europeans. In his *Coloquios de la verdad* (1562), for example, Pedro de Quiroga, Spanish canon of the Cusco cathedral and one of the viceroy Francisco de Toledo's inspection tour officers, dramatized the figure of the *indio ladino* as one who lived many such lives.[21] Tito, the native interlocutor in Quiroga's dialogues, described himself as having lived in various conquest and colonial settings and as having had as many masters: a Spanish captain during the war of conquest of Peru, a Spanish soldier during the civil wars among the Spanish, and subsequently a merchant, followed by a religious hermit.[22]

Among these various scenes of interethnic action, that of the missionary church provides the most accessible glimpses of *indios ladinos*. In fact, Pierre Duviols' *La destrucción de las religiones andinas* was the first study to isolate "los ladinos" as a category of analysis in his discussion of indigenous assistants to the offices of inquisition and extirpation of idolatries. These *indios ladinos,* commoners or even *kurakakuna* (the latter of whom tended to be little Hispanized), served as sacristans, chantres, parish secretaries, and *fiscales* or "employees of extirpation."[23] Significantly, sometimes individuals occupied these positions without the required linguistic competency, but they too came to be known as *indios ladinos.* Thus, as used within the Church, this very elastic term often indicated persons who maintained more or less close ties with ecclesiastics but who did not necessarily have a great knowledge of Spanish.[24] The sixteenth-century account of Pedro de Quiroga corroborates this view.[25] Quiroga criticized harshly the incompetence of some native interpreters and teachers (*maestros de la doctrina*) for not understanding the Spanish language or the doctrinal lessons they were expected to be teaching.

The use of native lay assistants in the tasks of evangelizing and extirpating "idolatries" was widespread in the face of a shortage of Spanish church personnel, and testimony from Spanish and native sources indicates that *indios ladinos* were of crucial assistance in the greatest discoveries of native ritual practices and cult objects made by the church inspectors.[26] Those *indios ladinos* who worked for the Church as *alguaciles, fiscales,* or *coadjutores* gathered information for the local priests and carried out their orders. As outlined in the provisions of the Second Provincial Council of Lima in 1567, the duties of these individuals included informing the priests of new births so that the infants could be baptized, of illnesses so that the victims could receive the sacraments, of drunkenness or *waqa* worship so that offenders could be punished, and of absenteeism from Mass so that the truants could be corrected.[27] From these *indios de confianza,* as they were called in the constitutions of the Council, emerged informants and interpreters, able copyists and, in two cases that we know—Felipe Guaman Poma de Ayala and Juan de Santacruz Pachacuti Yamqui—independent writers. The importance of the Church to the dissemination of *ladinidad* is apparent from the fact that these two rare native colonial sources—Guaman Poma and Santacruz

Pachacuti—are the fruits of their authors' experiences with Hispanic written and religious culture.

Such cases, however, cannot be considered individually without reference to the complex webs of relationship which constituted the conditions of their emergence. Given the sources examined here, the institutions and officers of the Church provide the most pertinent points of reference. Institutions such as the *visita* and activities such as the suppression of native cults and nativist movements gave the *indios ladinos*, of the type cited here, their most sharply defined features. Thus, the testimony of Christian clergy, working at the Cusco cathedral, as parish priests (*padres doctrinantes*) in local Andean communities, or as church inspectors (*visitadores*), provides necessary data.

Seen as the loose set of general policies and local practices that constituted it, the Church as a social and political institution is the axis on which much of the testimony turns, with natives and priests alternately acting as agents and objects of observation. These "images" are the recuperable resonances of the intercultural relationships that gave them life and that will be glimpsed occasionally in this discussion. According to Solano's typology, the present inquiry falls under the rubric of "official translators" and similar activities. As a complement to the cases from contact and conquest cultures studied by del Busto, Hemming, and Lockhart, this discussion looks at the intermediaries in the more settled colonial culture of the years post-1600.

The terms *lengua* and *indio ladino* appear frequently in colonial Spanish sources, but they are best foregrounded by the colonial native writings of Guaman Poma and Santacruz Pachacuti. In his *Nueva corónica y buen gobierno* (1615), Guaman Poma used the term *indio ladino* with great frequency and made dozens of comments on *indio ladino* experience. In spite of his intentions to cast his own social role as one much higher, he interpreted the *indio ladino* experience "from within," autobiographically. Although not focusing on colonial affairs as Guaman Poma did, Santacruz Pachacuti's *Relación de las antigüedades deste reyno del Pirú* (1613) offers illuminating insights on the consequences of *ladinidad*.

The dynastic claims of both individuals were not based on Inca lineage; being separate from the native elite most recognized by outsiders, the *indio ladino* tag might have rested heavily on these descendants of the Yarovilca of Allauca Huánuco and of the *kurakakuna* of the Canchis in Collasuyo. Guaman Poma did not call himself *indio*, but rather *qhapaq churi* (the son of the most powerful lord, *qhapaq apu*); he was not a commoner but a lord who was *ladino*.[28] He considered *indio ladino* a

cultural and class designation to which he was superior. Thus, on using
the term, he referred to persons of lower status than himself as he conveyed that he and they would be subject to the same common identification by outsiders.

Juan de Santacruz Pachacuti Yamqui was descended from the *kurakakuna* of the region of Collao in Collasuyo, an area associated with
Cusco from the origins of its state expansion and today among the provinces of the Department of Cusco.[29] He bore a title of prestige, "Yamqui," which had mythical origins and was given to the most noble of the
early inhabitants of the area; it would be the equivalent of *apu* (powerful lord).[30] According to Jan Szemiński, Santacruz Pachacuti seemed to
know Cusco and also Lima and its environs. Szemiński suggests that Santacruz Pachacuti's low opinion of "the priests of today" indicates that
the latter probably worked as an interpreter, an *indio ladino*, for inspectors of idolatries, although he mentions only one priest by name,
Fray Vicente de Valverde, who accompanied Pizarro in the conquest
of Peru.[31]

Santacruz Pachacuti concluded his *relación* with reference to Valverde's evangelizing activities in Cusco. Since he made note of the fact
that the Dominican's efforts would have been much more effective if he
had known the language instead of relying on interpreters, he suggests
his own familiarity with the difficulties of verbal translation of Christian
theology for one not schooled in that tradition. In offering a preamble
to his *Relación de las antigüedades deste reyno del Pirú*, Santacruz Pachacuti
not only proclaimed his own Christian faith but also cast his ancestors—some four generations of them—in the role of extirpators of idolatry.[32] Szemiński has analyzed Santacruz Pachacuti's genealogical account and discovered that he would have belonged to the fifth or sixth
postconquest generation of his family, thus making his perspective that
of a later generation than Guaman Poma's, even though their writing
was contemporaneous.[33]

Apart from Guaman Poma and Santacruz Pachacuti as Andean
sources, European ones such as Cristóbal de Albornoz, the witnesses in
Albornoz's *Informaciones de servicios,* Pedro de Quiroga, and the decrees
of the Second and Third Provincial Councils of Lima (1567, 1583–1584)
offer valuable insights on the perception and self-perception of *indios
ladinos.* To orient this discussion, four aspects of the complex and contradictory collective portrait of *indios ladinos* from the turn of the seventeenth century will be considered. The categories of this provisional
typology have been suggested by the native sources themselves and consist of (1) the leader and participant in messianic movements, (2) the as-

sistant to the church or civil inspector, (3) the plaintiff-petitioner against colonial abuses, and (4) the chronicler-historian.

THE *INDIO LADINO* AS MESSIANIC LEADER

One of the first major notices drawn by *indios ladinos* in the viceroyalty of Peru was for Taki Unquy, the Andean movement that preached the triumph of Andean gods over the Christian and advocated rejection of all that was European.[34] Discovered by Luis de Olivera in the early 1560s, Taki Unquy had roots that sank deep into native tradition at the same time as it incorporated elements from the culture it combated.[35] Coinciding with Titu Cusi Yupanqui's plans for armed struggle from Vilcabamba in 1565, Taki Unquy was spread from Huamanga in central Peru to Lima to the west, Cusco to the east, and as far as La Paz to the south. Adherents were warned to avoid contact with Europeans, on the claim that the latter desired to kill Andeans in order to extract strength-giving fat from their bodies. European testimony tells of the movement's contagion among all social groups, "*caciques* as well as common Indians and old people as well as boys and girls and all other age groups."[36]

The key role of *indios ladinos* (and mestizos) as preachers and dog-matizers in this and other messianic movements seems indisputable,[37] yet at the same time we know too little about them. In his *Instrucción para descubrir todas las guacas del Pirú y sus camayos y haziendas* (1581–1584), Cristóbal de Albornoz pointed to "the *indios ladinos* raised among us" as those who were responsible for disseminating the Taki Unquy movement all over Peru.[38] Male and female, the *takiunquero* leaders preached the victory of non-Inca divinities, such as Pachacamac and Titicaca, over the Christian god and dissuaded their compatriots from the use of European clothing or food under pain of punishment by the *waqakuna* (Andean divinities).[39] Two witnesses testified to the fact that some female leaders on Juan de Mañusco's *repartimiento* called themselves "Santa María" and "Santa María Magdalena" in order to be honored as saints as they preached the doctrine of their sect.[40] At the same time, the Andean divinities became internalized and incarnate in the Taki Unquy leaders themselves.[41] The *Informaciones de servicios* of Albornoz contain testimony by Cristóbal de Molina and Luis de Oliviera to the effect that the *takiunqueros* took on supernatural powers, painted their faces red, and claimed that the *waqakuna* spoke through them.[42]

Two aspects of Taki Unquy, as well as other Andean movements of the sixteenth century (Yanahuara and Muru Unquy), reveal the role played by leaders who had been indoctrinated, to greater or lesser degrees, in European Christian culture. First, these movements were prophetic if not messianic, implying the coming or return of liberating supernaturals;[43] on this point, the influence of Christian preaching seems evident.[44] Second, the redeeming forces would not be the Inca or his solar god, Inti, but rather regional or ethnic Andean gods. It seems clear that Taki Unquy did not invite the return of the Inca, nor did the elite solar cult of the Incas play a role.[45] The European observers who linked the Incas at Vilcabamba with Taki Unquy did so mistakenly or opportunely; Franklin Pease suggests that it would have been advantageous for Albornoz to relate the armed religious movement "rooted out" by him with the political victory of Toledo over the rebel Incas at Vilcabamba.[46]

The role of Hispanized Andeans is crucial to understanding these revitalist movements. Yet the European sources concentrate on the achievements of the extirpators rather than on the practices of the leaders, thus leaving little information (or information not yet deciphered) about these key participants. Still, some deductions can be drawn about the importance of their role. First, their Christianization would have made imaginable the notion of the coming of a redeemer in a new age and, second, their status as non-Incas (either as elites of other dynastic traditions or as commoners) would have made the absence of the Inca plausible and attractive. Within a line of activities that Christianized Andean situations, the *takiunqueros* heralding the redeeming return (but with a difference) of the Andean gods and a Guaman Poma or a Santacruz Pachacuti proclaiming himself the herald of a new coming of Christ are not so very different. Evangelization in the Andes makes possible both prototypes of the *indio ladino*—the loyal Christian and the advocate of a rival messianism.

The tension between the two is most clearly drawn out by Guaman Poma's discussion of Taki Unquy. Key to Guaman Poma's assessment is the fact that he called its dogmatizers *falsos hechiceros*. Given his use of the term *hechicero* for all the specialists in traditional spiritual and medicinal practices, *falso hechicero* is not a redundancy but a separate category. For example, in his *Buen gobierno* discussions of colonial times, he opens his chapter on *visitadores* or church inspectors with a portrait of his former employer, Cristóbal de Albornoz.[47] The Andean author declares that Albornoz "broke and burned the *waqas* and crowned the male and female *hechiceros* with the hat of humiliation and punished the false *hechicero* and *taki unquy*."[48]

Looking back into Guaman Poma's *Nueva corónica* descriptions of Inca and earlier times, we find in his chapters on spiritual practices several references to *falsos hechiceros* and Taki Unquy, again in the context of his employment by Cristóbal de Albornoz. Of these false religious specialists, Guaman Poma declared:

> Other *hechiceros* speak with demons and suck and say that they remove sicknesses from the body and that they take out silver or stones or sticks or worms or toads or straw or corn from the bodies of men and women. These said individuals are false healers, they deceive the Indians and the devil, all with the sole objective of deceiving them to get their wealth and teaching them to be Indian idolaters. They say that there is a sickness called *taki unquy*.[49]

What made the *takiunquero* a *false* shaman, in Guaman Poma's view? He cited, after all, a traditional basis for the phenomenon. He noted that *taki unquy* was a sickness to be eradicated, in Inca times and after. He described the month of September in the ancient ritual calendar as the time when the Inca rid settlements of illness; there were many ceremonies for doing so, including "other ceremonies to banish *taki unquy, sara unquy, pukyu unquy, pacha panta*," and several others.[50] The dancing sickness and the corn sickness described as traditional, pre-Hispanic phenomena by Guaman Poma were also named together in Polo de Ondegardo's account, in which Polo[51] referred to "a dancing sickness that they call *taki unquy* or *sara unquy*, for whose relief they call the sorcerers."[52]

Taki Unquy clearly seems to have been mounted on annual ceremonies for the expulsion of sicknesses of pre-Hispanic times, when the Pleiades, Onccoi Ccoyllor or Collca, considered sacred (*waqa principal*), appeared in the sky.[53] This colonial version of the traditional healing of sickness persisted at least until the second decade of the seventeenth century.[54] Thus, Guaman Poma's repeated references to *taki unquy*—not tied to a specific decade or movement—make sense.[55]

According to Guaman Poma, who as an Andean knew Taki Unquy's traditional origins, and as a *visitador*'s assistant observed its current practices, Taki Unquy was exploited by its leaders for their own devious purposes—namely, for their own personal gain. This image of the religious charlatan who deceived others for his own profit characterizes Guaman Poma's view of the *takiunquero*, and it corresponds to that offered in the *Informaciones* testimony by the mestizo priest Cristóbal de Molina.[56] Nevertheless, while Molina and others viewed this exploitation of native Andeans as economic, Guaman Poma saw Taki Unquy as a gross form of spiritual exploitation. These shamans were fraudulent, Guaman Poma asserted, because they cheated the Indians and the devil too. Let us see what he means.

Albornoz described how the *takiunquero* leaders enticed the traditional religious specialists (*kamayuqkuna*) to a meeting in order to kill them.[57] He explained that, in order to overpower other cults so that "there be no others who command nor preach any other religion," the *takiunqueros* gathered together the *kamayuqkuna* of traditional cults in other provinces. Bringing together their unsuspecting guests, having them dance and get inebriated, the *takiunqueros* were able to kill them all without any resistance. The *visitador*'s condemnation of this heinous act is predictable and self-evident, and Guaman Poma shared it. Yet this explanation does not fully account for the latter's reaction.

Whereas Albornoz and other European witnesses saw the movement as opposing Christianity and denying loyalty and obedience to the colonists, Guaman Poma viewed the cult as challenging the traditional salutary prerogatives of native society. As an Andean, he interpreted the consequences of the *takiunqueros*' actions as wrongfully usurping the position of the powerful *kamayuqkuna* or traditional priests of native society. That is, he saw Taki Unquy within the context of an Andean spiritual tradition, in which there were many types of "shamans and popes and bishops and priests, some good and some bad."[58] He explained: "The good ones they call servants of the spirits [*demonios*] who spoke with them, such as Mama Uaco, *quya* [the Inca's principal consort], and the bad ones deceive the devil and the Indians."[59] In Guaman Poma's typology, religious and medicinal specialists who ordered Andean society according to its traditional values were to be approved; he condemned only those "who deceive the Indians and the devil too," such as the *takiunqueros*. His statement invites comment on two counts: first, for condoning the activities of traditional religious specialists, and, second, for doing so for current times, not just the past. Notwithstanding his professed Christianity, his attitude toward Andean spirituality is much more complex and tolerant than that of his priest employers.

Thus, the dismantling of the striking elocution *falsos hechiceros* reveals more than Guaman Poma's condemnation of the Taki Unquy movement. It uncovers as well a sympathy for traditional religion which his other, too-loud protests would seem to reject outright. In this way, the enthusiasm of the *indio ladino* assistant for the eradication of the movement that went by the name of Taki Unquy was very different from that of his employer Albornoz. For Guaman Poma, Taki Unquy had a deep resonance in Andean experience which corresponded to the struggle between true and false cult practices—that is, between those capable of serving the needs of Andean society and those bent on destroying its traditional harmonies. Those "false healers" who came in for his greatest criticism were precisely the *indio ladino* apostates:

> that the said Indians are getting drunk: the most Christian, although he may know how to read and write, carry a rosary and dress like a Spaniard, . . . —he seems a saint—on getting drunk, he speaks with demons and worships the *waqakuna* . . . speaking of his ancestors, performing their ceremonies.[60]

In contrast to Guaman Poma's extended discussions, Santacruz Pachacuti's only allusions to Andean indifference to, or rejection of, Christianity are indirect ones. He concluded his narration by remarking that today's priests were not working hard, as had those of Valverde's generation, when "there had been much devotion among the Spaniards and the natives were exhorted with good examples."[61] Despite the difference between Guaman Poma's strident expression of wrath against *indio ladino* apostasy and Santacruz Pachacuti's silence on the subject, we shall see their mutual concern about the widespread phenomenon in their protestations of devout Christianity.

THE *INDIO LADINO* AS *VISITADOR*'S ASSISTANT

In Albornoz's *Informaciones de servicios* the native adjunct to the enterprise of cult suppression was referred to, as noted above, as an *oficial de confianza*.[62] Like the description of the *indio ladino* in the documents of the Second Provincial Council, this denomination became an assertion vigorously defended in the writings of the *indios ladinos* themselves. Santacruz Pachacuti is even more boastful than Guaman Poma on this score. Newly Christian, the ancestors of Santacruz Pachacuti, the "adoptive children" of Jesus Christ as he called them,[63] proved themselves to be the enemies of all idolatries and ancient rites by "pursuing the *hechiceros*, destroying all their *waqakuna* and idols, showing them to be idolaters, and punishing them before their vassals and subordinates all over the province."[64] Santacruz Pachacuti's notion that religious loyalty was to be expressed not only by professing the faith but also by claiming participation in opposing and exposing the practitioners of traditional rites again suggests that he worked with the Catholic clergy. More than attesting indirectly to his own experience, however, his remarks reveal the importance he attached to communicating the notion that participation in extirpation activities was a "proof" of the Christian fervor of himself and his forebears.

The *indio ladino* as fervent New Christian was both a self-image and a representation by others. It was the view foregrounded in the *Tercero catecismo y exposición de la doctrina christiana por sermones*. Published in 1585 after the conclusion of the Third Provincial Council of Lima and approved by metropolitan ecclesiastical rather than conciliar authorities,[65] the *sermonario* of the *Tercero catecismo* was an influential if not repeatedly disseminated tract.[66] In its sermons, the *indio ladino* was frequently cited as an example for the neophytes to follow: "Have you not seen good *viracochas* [Spaniards] confess and many *indios ladinos* who are good sons confess many times during the year, and pray, and discipline themselves? These are the blessed of God, and the priests love them very much."[67]

Whatever the range of their personal views of Christianity might have been, the *indios ladinos'* active collaboration in eradicating traditional ritual practices made them indispensable to church officials. There is significant testimony from European colonial sources on the willingness of native Andeans to expose traditional religious specialists to the *visitadores*. Cristóbal de Molina made the point, and many witnesses in the *Informaciones de servicios* of Albornoz testified to the same. In his *Ritos y fábulas de los Incas*, Molina asserted:

> There are a great number of male and female natives who, because of understanding the offense done to our Lord by this [Taki Unquy], in no way permit its practice but rather reveal to their priests its practitioners so that they may be punished.[68]

Native collaboration in extirpation activities was not, however, a simple question of voluntarily coming forward to serve. Some of Albornoz's witnesses revealed, unwittingly no doubt, the coercion of native assistants when they noted that such denunciations and self-denunciations often were due to fear produced by intimidation rather than Christian zeal: "Y prestó a los yndios terror y espanto."[69] The acknowledgment of native fear as a cause for denouncing others is a rare yet significant occurrence in the *Informaciones de servicios*. As we shall see later, Guaman Poma gave this interpretation full expression in his commentary on the extirpation-of-idolatries activities he came upon at Huarochirí on his final trip to Lima.[70]

Apart from whether native service in the campaigns against traditional beliefs was forced or voluntary—and both Guaman Poma and Santacruz Pachacuti claim that theirs was the latter, undertaken out of zeal—Guaman Poma's discussions of native idolaters reveal many facets of the *indio ladino*-as-extirpator experience that are left in silence behind

Santacruz Pachacuti's proud proclamation that he and several generations of his family had participated in the extirpation of idolatries. When
one examines Guaman Poma's account in detail, Santacruz Pachacuti's
ardent defense of his *kuraka* ancestors as extirpators of idolatries becomes more resonant, both because the *kuraka* class was generally responsible for the maintenance of traditional ritual practices and because
both our informants had a stake in convincing their readers that their
own collaboration was motivated by religious zeal rather than greed.
Ironically, the policies of reward that were to ensure native collaboration
in such activities made suspect the motives of those very *indio ladino*
collaborators.

First of all, the works of Guaman Poma and Santacruz Pachacuti were
written when the extirpation-of-idolatries campaigns in Peru were in
full swing, and this accounts for the character of their works and the
inspiration under which they were written. For instance, while Guaman
Poma stated that his work was produced over a period of twenty to thirty
years, the entire *Nueva corónica y buen gobierno* as we know it today was
written down in 1612 and 1613 and revised in 1614, possibly extending
through the first months of 1615.[71] What is most striking regarding the
potential impact of *visita* activity on the *indio ladino* is the degree to which
Guaman Poma's chronicle follows the substance and format of the *visita*
report. Beyond the description of native practices "so that the good can
be spared, the evil ones eradicated," he made the categories of *visita*
commentary his own model of description for the *Buen gobierno*. He did
so by replacing the settlement-by-settlement description of *visita* reports
with his exhaustive survey of the ethnic and/or vocational groups and
social ranks that made up colonial society. Descriptions like the following
one seem to come straight from a church inspector's report, rather than
an Andean chronicler:

> Don Francisco Alcas is described as an "Indian . . . who never con-
> fesses . . . and lives in concubinage with his brother's wife, all of whom
> never go to mass. . . . He had some old shrines in the mountains where
> interments took place at the time of the Incas with the ceremonies that
> here have been described. . . . As he is a rich Indian, he bribes the *corre-
> gidores* and the priest of the village to remain silent on the location of the
> burials."[72]

Guaman Poma tells how, on the basis of this report from a mulatto informant, he went to witness the ceremony and write about it "so that these
practices may be corrected in this kingdom in all the settlements and
cities and villages and that it be punished, an example."[73]

Furthermore, he repeatedly insisted that his work would be useful in inspection tours, particularly those of the Church.[74] To the very last additions he made to his work in the systematic revision he undertook in 1614, he reiterated his concern for continuing inspections of native settlements, and he suggested imposing such scrutiny vigorously on the parish priests as well. In these final textual emendations, he repeated his earlier recommendations concerning the suppression of certain rituals.[75] Many such examples could be cited as testimony to the influence of the church inspector on the *indio ladino* who served as his adjutant. The assistant's adherence to his employer's judgments appears time and time again in Guaman Poma's work.[76]

In a similar manner, Santacruz Pachacuti's work was designed as an auxiliary report on native beliefs, their "histories and barbarisms and fables," which would be used like the materials gathered at Huarochirí by Francisco de Avila for the eradication of native beliefs and practices. The annotations in the hand of Francisco de Avila in Santacruz Pachacuti's manuscript, alongside the Huarochirí manuscript with which it was bound, offer compelling material evidence on this point.[77]

The crucial issues, however, center on those areas in which the outlooks of church inspector and native assistant converge and, more important, differ. Guaman Poma offers considerable insight into this problem. Many of his seemingly anticolonialist opinions actually coincide with an internal Spanish critique of colonial practices made by Albornoz himself.[78] First, we find in Albornoz as in Guaman Poma the conviction that the weight of colonial society was wrongly and exclusively borne on the shoulders of the natives.[79] According to Albornoz, the bishops were too powerful and unaccountable in their self-interest. The corruption of church inspectors was a cause of inadequate advancement in the Christianization of the population, and those appointed as parish priests were of low quality and qualifications.[80] Guaman Poma voiced the same complaints, recommending that the bishops and archbishops, as well as all other offices and stations, be held accountable by the mechanism of the *visita*:[81]

> The following should be inspected: archbishops, bishops, cathedral chapters and collegiate churches, vacant sees and clergy, friars, convents, nuns, hermits, and secular officials of justice, Indians, blacks, Spaniards in this kingdom, and the said churches and chaplaincies and collections of income, works, images, ornaments, alms, dowries, and donations, all that which the holy mother church in this kingdom contains.

Another shared concern revealed in the citation above—one that may partially explain Guaman Poma's own later emphasis on visual communication in his writing—is the state of repair of religious images and statues in the parishes. Guaman Poma's insistence that the adornments of the church be inspected corresponded to Albornoz's complaint that "all is fallen to the ground": broken and fallen to pieces are the ornaments of the church; "there is no place on which to focus one's gaze." [82] Guaman Poma's concern for *imágenes* and the visual stimulants to worship are best recalled in his drawing of native artisans refurbishing a life-size crucifix and in his recommendations[83] for such religious representations:

> And thus in the churches and temples of God there should be objects of interest and many paintings of the saints. And in each church there should be a painting of the Last Judgment. It should depict the coming of the Lord to the Last Judgment, the heavens and the world and the agonies of hell, so that it be a witness to the Christian sinner.[84]

Another area where the *indio ladino* and internal Spanish critique of colonial practices merge is the workings of the church councils. The presence of *indios ladinos* in the provincial councils seems assured, yet we do not have information concerning their participation, even from Guaman Poma. At best, the familiarity of this *indio ladino* informant with the dictates of the provincial councils is revealed through the frequency with which Guaman Poma cited their policies.[85] The conciliar concern to educate the native community in Spanish literacy (seeing education as part of Christianization) was a central theme of Guaman Poma, who may have been attracted to the idea through his service at one or another of the councils. Conciliar warnings that native ritual and belief were so powerful that their adherents and dogmatizers could destroy in a day what took a year to build[86] were insights probably gained from *indios ladinos* such as Guaman Poma, who made the same point.

This *indio ladino* revealed his most profound knowledge of conciliar decrees on some of the specific recommendations he gave for the reformation of the clergy, which he presented as his own. Hand in glove are the assessments by the Third Church Council and Guaman Poma on priestly shortcomings: sexual corruption, flamboyant attire, gambling, business transactions, and extraeconomic activity, not to mention the excesses perpetrated by *visitadores*.[87] "Instead of souls for the Lord they earn silver [for themselves]" ("En lugar de ánimas sacan reales y plata") sums up his eternal lament.[88]

How common, among *idios ladinos*, was Guaman Poma's view that it was the Church's agents, rather than the institution itself, who were to be criticized? To the very end of his writing, Guaman Poma expressed an attitude in favor of the ecclesiastical *visita* but critical of the practicing *visitador.* As Duviols concluded, Guaman Poma did not criticize the institution of extirpation itself but rather the abuses perpetrated under its protection.[89] He recommended the royal provision and selection of inspectors as a measure designed to curb the abuses that he detailed in his chapter on *visitadores,* and he insisted on the need of such officials to interrogate the activities of the priests, not only the natives in their charge.[90] If Santacruz Pachacuti's family beyond his great-grandparents were involved in *visita* activities as he claimed, then it must not have been uncommon for generations of a single family to create a tradition of working in the Church's employ.

Yet for all the coincidences of viewpoint of church inspector and native adjunct, Guaman Poma reveals that the lay assistant also exhibited a strong independence of criteria. One such example is the subject of the *takikuna,* the ritual dances of the Andean communities and a key feature of traditional Andean culture until today.

In his *Instrucción,* Albornoz advised that the dances or *takikuna* of the natives be monitored, for the participants became inebriated on going out of their villages and then turned to *waqa* worship.[91] His experience with Taki Unquy no doubt made him wary of all ritual dancing. Guaman Poma saw it differently. The dances formerly performed for the *waqakuna* ("dioses falsos, demonios por mandado de los pontífises *layqhakuna,* hichiceros") were now to be performed for "the true God and all that the holy Roman church demands." Without drinking ("Con ello dansen y baylen hasta caer con todo su seso; cin pecado, se huelgue"[92]), the ritual dances were a splendid and Christian thing. Furthermore, Guaman Poma argued, they would be the very means by which the people would be able to abandon their idolatrous customs. He recommended that the priests should allow and encourage these dances and that the natives should be punished if they failed to perform them.[93] Guaman Poma took his justification for this apparently novel program from Scripture itself: "They are to do it because King David himself danced and played before the sacrament of the Ancient Law."[94]

Guaman Poma reiterated his own position on ritual dances on two other occasions, stating that, when not accompanied by ritual drinking, these practices should be permitted by colonial officials: "That is why I described the idolatries that they had, so that the bad practices might be punished, the good preserved."[95] The construction of his work on the model of a *visita* report is again apparent.

Santacruz Pachacuti's *kuraka* clan serves as counterpoint to a problem raised by the *visita:* the collusion between priests and native communities outlined in detail by Guaman Poma. The tension between the *kuraka,* on one hand, and the *visitador* and his native assistant, on the other, are revealed by juxtaposing Guaman Poma's account to that of Albornoz. The correspondence between names of persons mentioned in Albornoz's *Relación de amancebados, hechiceros, y guacas* (1584) and Guaman Poma's *Nueva corónica* suggests that the latter probably worked for the former on the *visitas* to Lucanas, Soras, and Apcara.[96] The clan and personal names of many of the offenders listed in Albornoz's report, as well as that of Don Juan Cocha Quispe, Albornoz's *fiscal*, appear in the *Nueva corónica y buen gobierno*.[97]

Overall, Guaman Poma's account reveals an alienation from the local native communities and their hierarchies. First of all, as an itinerant *indio ladino*, he would be jealous of their local control, which he condemned as the usurpation of the prerogatives and positions of legitimate lords. We recall that Guaman Poma claimed himself to be not of the *kuraka* class but rather *awki qhapaq churi*, the son of great and powerful princes. The individuals whom he criticized, then, would be, according to his own self-definition, inferior to his own inherited rank even though, in the colonial administration, they might serve in the same office, such as that of *gobernador de indios*. His condemnation of *kurakakuna* as impostors and usurpers stems from his view about the disintegration of Andean society after the conquest: the usurpation of the ethnic lords' prerogatives by *yndios bajos*, who became the new *falsos caciques prencipales*, was the source of ruin of Andean society. His assessment was anticipated in the 1560s by Pedro de Quiroga,[98] who put his criticism of the colonial empowerment of lowly Andeans in the words of the fictional Tito:

> When one *kuraka* dies, you install as our master and lord the worst Indian and greatest thief that you have in your house and employment. . . . Be assured that the greatest oppression, the greatest harm and tribulations that these kingdoms suffer today, come from these *caciques*.[99]

These testimonies best reveal the extent to which the *kuraka*, with a power base in both the societies of his *ayllu* and the municipal district, could manipulate both to his own advantage.

Second, as a church inspector's assistant, Guaman Poma would be at odds with the local *kurakakuna* because of their "idolatry." His chapter on *principales* is devoted entirely to the native rituals that he recommended be abolished and the Christian rites that should replace them. He summed up the character of the ethnic lords or those serving as such, as follows: "And every day they are gambling, drunk; they worship *waqakuna*, idols, and with the demons, being drunk, they return to their ancient law."[100] In fact, the portraits of particular *kurakakuna* he chooses

to paint in this chapter are just those whom he describes as *hechiceros*.[101]
Here it becomes apparent that the *indio ladino* held as a weapon against
his enemies the opportunity to betray them to the church inspection
officials.

Given the overwhelming emphasis Guaman Poma placed on idolatry
in his discussion of native lords, it comes as no surprise that he modified
his own self-identification from *cacique prencipal* to *capac ques prencipe*.[102]
The collective portrait that he had painted of the *kuraka* class made it
essential that he distance himself from them in the eyes of his readers.
In this context, we look again at his attitude toward Albornoz and his
other native assistants. By examining Guaman Poma's views on Albornoz
and his activities, we can begin to elucidate the apparently contradictory
views on extirpation and extirpators held by Christian *indios ladinos*.

In spite of Guaman Poma's partial agreement with the *visitador*'s outlook, we may ask if he admired Albornoz as he seems to state. The question has recently been raised by Sabine MacCormack,[103] who suggests
that, although Guaman Poma mentioned Albornoz with respect as a
"Christian judge, who punished all alike, whether hur.:ble or exalted,"
he also "did not fail to notice that the man was caught between spiritual
interests of the missionary church and his own and the viceroy's material
interests." In reviewing the pertinent evidence on this issue, we note that
many suits were brought against Albornoz by native communities. Re-
grettably, the veracity of the charges and results of the suits are not
known,[104] and Guaman Poma's silence on the subject is of no help.

Guaman Poma accused Albornoz's *fiscal* Juan Cocha Quispe—but not
Albornoz—of gaining profit from the confiscations that accompanied
the practice of extirpation:[105]

> At the command of Cristóbal de Albornoz, he destroyed all the *waqas* and
> idols [of others], while concealing his own. And because of it, he became
> a *kuraka* and carried away great bribes. And thus, he came out very rich;
> the judge [Albornoz] came out poor. And, with it, he [Cocha Quispe][106]
> became a *kuraka*, *principal*, and all the Quichiuas and settlers from other
> areas [*mitmaqkuna*] obeyed him. And his children remain at the head of
> the said Quichiua *ayllu*.

Guaman Poma here offers an implicit criticism of Albornoz, not to
the effect that he profited by these activities but rather that he supported
and encouraged his assistants in doing so. Again, the viewpoints of
church inspector and Andean assistant diverge. In his *Instrucción*, Albornoz recommended that the extirpations be carried out by "clerics of
good judgment and without greed" and that these officials reward their

helpers and informants, promoting some with offices and riches, giving *cacicazgos* to others.[107] Guaman Poma, meanwhile, registered disgust at this practice through his criticism of Juan Cocha Quispe, whom he condemned not only because he received a *cacicazgo* that was still (in 1613) under the control of his heirs but also because he had been a commoner.[108] Furthermore, Guaman Poma declared, Cocha Quispe destroyed the sacred objects and places of others but had managed to hide and keep his own.

Overall, Guaman Poma's testimony reveals that the *indio ladino* was perhaps the most universally hated member of the church inspection tour, reviled by both the native community and its parish priest. The contempt in which the local priest and native parishoners held the *indios ladinos* was centered not on the struggle between Christian and Andean beliefs, but rather on the tug of war over who would have access to native wealth, the local priest or the inspector's retinue. Obviously, the confiscation of native goods by the church inspector would remove these properties from the reach of the local priest. For this reason, the self-interested collusion between the parish priest and the native community is the source of Guaman Poma's repeated criticism:

> And in some places, the parish priest knows about it [traditional religious practices]. In the interest of his own wealth and gain, he consents and allows it as well as for other arrangements that he has among the Indians, which are known only among them in this kingdom.[109]

> With the drunken feasts, the said priest indulges himself and those who do not participate are banned from the *pueblo* so that the excesses of the priest—as well as of the Indians of this kingdom—are not seen.[110]

> All that I have said I have seen with my own eyes, and the parish priests consent to it because they care more for their private gain than for any other thing. After first telling the priest about these practices, the *indio ladino* is later cast out of the village.[111]

Here the *indio ladino* is the persecuted witness, as his ability to recognize practices forbidden by the Church was both exploited by the inspection team and despised by the local community.

The role of the *indio ladino* as accuser had other facets. Feared also because of their ability to participate in the colonial legal system, *indios ladinos*, according to Guaman Poma's repeated testimony, were thrown out of local jurisdictions not only by priests but also by *corregidores* who feared that they would make trouble and file charges of misconduct.[112]

This brings us to another facet of *indio ladino* experience, discussed at the outset by Santillán, that of plaintiff and petitioner.

THE *INDIO LADINO* AS PETITIONER

The *pleito* was the only recourse that the native communities had for defending themselves against the abuses of the clergy and other colonial authorities, and this type of suit existed in great numbers.[113] The role of *indio ladino* as petitioner and plaintiff against the colonial establishment and its personnel appears consistently in both European and Andean sources.[114] The sermons of the *Tercero catecismo,* the chief source and model of sermons for the rural clergy in the first decades of the seventeenth century,[115] offer information in this regard, if we assume that the behaviors they warned against were precisely the ones most commonly practiced. These sermons consistently emphasized the themes of the proper moral, social, and political comportment of the local community. In this corpus we find many priestly admonitions and warnings against the practice of natives' filing of complaints.

With regard to protesting or petitioning against colonial authorities, or giving testimony against them, the sermons spoke plainly to the Andean population: the natives were admonished to bear the suffering caused by negligent or malevolent colonial authorities—priests as well as *corregidores*—because the offenders' punishments would be meted out by the Almighty.[116] The Andean neophytes were urged to refrain from denouncing their colonial overlords or giving testimony—described as false testimony—against them; the sermons offered fierce warnings about the temporal consequences of doing so.[117] At the same time, and even as the Andeans were entreated to remain silent regarding the abuses perpetrated by the colonists,[118] they were urged to inform their priest and the *visitadores* about the proscribed activities of the local *kurakakuna*. Thus was issued a general invitation to become informers against the local *kuraka*.

The real concern of the sermon authors is revealed on this latter point, when they complain that the natives always tend to do just the reverse: communicating among themselves, covering up for one another, refusing to cooperate as informers with the church authorities, and yet being talkative and noisy when gathered together and commanded to be silent.[119] The sheer number of times the sermons admonish the natives *not* to present grievances against the colonial authorities and *not* to file complaints against the parish priests reveals that the Andeans' reputation for doing so was well established by 1585. One sermon sums up the oft-repeated warning: "Watch your tongue, brothers and sisters, and you will protect your soul" ("Guardad vuestra lengua, hermanos, y tenéis guardada vuestra ánima").[120]

This external, colonial view of the *indio ladino* as a real or potential troublemaker is corroborated by Guaman Poma's testimony. He expressed with bitterness the hatred that he felt that colonialists had for the *indios ladinos*. Citing the terms *ladinejo* and *santico ladinejo* as derisive descriptions applied, Guaman Poma revealed that the *indio ladino* often was scorned as a self-righteous and zealous convert.[121] He harangued about those who would keep *indios ladinos* away from their appointed colonial offices.[122] In one of his diatribes against local colonial authorities for trying to keep the natives from learning Castilian, Guaman Poma declared:

> They do not want to see Christian *ladino* Indians speaking in Spanish. It frightens them, and they have me thrown out of the village. All collude in the effort that they [we] all be ignorant, asses, to end up by taking all one has, property, wife, and daughter.[123]

In the *Nueva corónica y buen gobierno,* the stigma associated with being a *pleitista* comes into full view in Guaman Poma's angry retort to a Spaniard who suggests that Guaman Poma should go to Spain to air his complaints against the colonists. Guaman Poma replied:[124] "I am not going to present complaints, but rather to advise the King and unburden his royal conscience."

In searing satirical dialogues, the Andean author placed on the lips of Spaniards the advice to one another of either coopting *indios ladinos* or punishing these "great complainers." The fictional Spanish voices scorned the *indios ladinos,* on one hand, as "pusillanimous" and "incompetent," as individuals who, when threatened, fainted and fled.[125] On the other hand, the *indios ladinos* were derided as *bachilleres,* that is, great and impertinent talkers, who were also scoundrels.[126] Here *ladino,* with reference to linguistic ability and astuteness, had a decisively negative and derogatory connotation. This view from outside, reported by Guaman Poma, had been noted in Quiroga's *Coloquios de la verdad.* Being a troublemaker and talkative (*malo y bachiller*) were colonialist perceptions of the vocal and articulate *indio ladino* which went hand in hand.[127] Quiroga criticized this view by having the *indio ladino* Tito utter the complaint that if an Indian showed good reasoning or good judgment, that is, if he "talks like a man, complains like a man, and asks to be treated like a human being, he is called a lousy troublemaker." "Do you want us," asks Tito, "to behave like beasts so that you could treat us as such?"[128]

The opposite side of the coin of Andean speech was colonial silence, and both Quiroga and Guaman Poma commented on it. Guaman Poma condemned the silence of *indios ladinos* which resulted from cooption and bribery. In spite of knowing the law and being able to bring complaints, Guaman Poma complained, many *indios ladinos* were easily persuaded not to do so: "All they want to do is drink until they fall down; invited to a Spanish table, with a little wine they will content themselves to keep silent."[129] The Spanish priest Quiroga had observed a different type of Andean silence; it signified not acquiescence but its opposite: "You are silent because of rage and being offended, because we contradict your idolatrous beliefs. Your silence is of the one who would avenge himself."[130] This is the native silence also observed in the *sermonario* of 1585.

The tension between noncompliant silence and the threat of bringing complaints constituted the heart of the controversy surrounding Francisco de Avila. Looking at it closely, we may see more clearly why a lordly, self-professed Christian *indio ladino* like Guaman Poma would have been so appalled at this particular case. In this regard, Antonio Acosta has recently brought to full light what Pierre Duviols suggested about the well-known extirpator of idolatries Francisco de Avila some time ago.[131] According to Acosta, the natives of San Damián de Huarochirí brought their suit of over one hundred charges against Avila the year *before*—not after, as Avila claimed—the priest began his self-appointed campaign against idolatry in his parish. In meeting the women of Huarochirí in Jauja on his way to Lima, Guaman Poma surely would have learned about Avila's conduct and how it had provoked the community to bring suit against him.[132] The nature of the charges made against Avila were precisely those that Guaman Poma condemned throughout his book, namely, the blackmail of parishioners by the local priest after they had colluded in maintaining and covering up the practice of traditional rituals, sexual relations, and extralegal economic arrangements.[133]

In his narration of the Huarochirí case in the last chapter ("Camina el autor") added to his book, Guaman Poma focused only on the cruelties wreaked on the natives by Avila's later, vindictive campaign, not the earlier collusion and resultant antagonism that had developed between them. In an entirely different case from his own locale of Lucanas he had described the type of charge-and-countercharge antagonism that had developed in Huarochirí and about which he surely would have been told. Describing this local instance is pertinent to understanding why Guaman Poma could commend Cristóbal de Albornoz and condemn Francisco de Avila. The case is that of a *kuraka,* Don Juan Capcha, and a local parish priest called Antón Fernández de Peralta.

Guaman Poma described the relationship between them as intimidation on the part of the *kuraka,* fear on the part of the *padre.* According to Guaman Poma,[134] Capcha was a *pleitista* who always filed charges against the priests. In order to tell his story of Capcha, Guaman Poma copied into his own manuscript two letters, one presumably from the priest Antón Fernández de Peralta to Capcha, expressing great fear at Capcha's boldness ("I am shocked that a *kuraka* as honorable as you would do such a bad thing as flee when I visit and then file charges of lies against your priest"). The other, from Capcha to Guaman Poma, begins with the salutation "A mi señor, don Felipe de Ayala, príncipe" and warns that Don Juan will throw the priest out of the parish.[135] Here is the stalemate: the priest charged Capcha with keeping the natives under his jurisdiction from hearing Mass or saying confession; Capcha accused the priest of doing violence against them.

This is the type of situation which also developed between Avila and his parishioners in Huarochirí. From his familiarity with such cases, we may surmise that Guaman Poma's ire against Francisco de Avila arose from the latter's activities not only as an extirpator of idolatries but also as a parish priest. Such an assessment would ring true to all the accusations that he had made against local priests throughout his work. Thus, the deep and bitter condemnation of Avila that Guaman Poma expressed concerns not only the recent tortures that Avila mandated and the suicides that he provoked but also his long-term deceit and exploitation of the local community. Guaman Poma accused Avila of torture and terror, while he ascribed to Albornoz only punishments that he considered proper and just. It would be revealing to know where an *indio ladino,* working between two cultural traditions, would draw the line between just corporal punishment and torture.

I would also argue that the difference in Guaman Poma's assessment of Albornoz and Avila had to do with the degree to which the latter's local corruption, once the relationship with the community soured, destroyed the community that he had been so eager to exploit. Albornoz was spared the wrath reserved for Avila because he had not compromised himself and local *ayllu* communities through the means of the *doctrina.* While Avila combined the worst possible patterns of church activity as corrupt priest and brutal inspector, Albornoz, removed from the local

setting, represented the comprehensive, high-minded approach to colonial society that Guaman Poma admired and in part emulated through
his writing. Santacruz Pachacuti's few remarks about his family's extirpation activities suggest that he too stood on the side of the vigorous
repression of native practices when he understood that repression to be
carried out with high moral purpose. The anonymous *indios ladinos* of
the Huarochirí community who helped bring suit against their parish
priest surely paid the ultimate price for exercising the legal right of the
pleito.

THE *INDIO LADINO* AS WRITER

The *indio ladino* as informant is glimpsed in only a few works, such as
the manuscript of Huarochirí,[136] and the case of *indios ladinos* as writers
is equally rare. Yet the native's move from informant to writer fore-
grounds in another way the relationship between the Spanish clergy and
the *indio ladino.* Santacruz Pachacuti said nothing on the subject, although the creation of his history of the Incas and account of their "barbarisms and fables" is a testimony to that experience. As indicated above,
he may have been ordered or commissioned to write his *relación* about
ancient Peruvian history and beliefs as part of the information-gathering
for the campaigns against Andean religion. While he was schooled in
traditional, oral Andean history and religion, he interpreted the Spanish
Christian image of the cosmos according to ancient Andean molds.[137]
The views that he shared with Guaman Poma suggest a common or similar experience with missionary evangelization: the creation of the world
and Adam and Eve (Adaneva, in Santacruz Pachacuti's case) as the pro-
genitors of humankind, the appearance of a Christian apostle in Inca
times and the partial acceptance of the evangelizing mission, and, finally,
the arrival of a new, different era of time with the Spanish invasion.[138]

To sketch out some variations on the theme of the tutorial relationships between missionary clergy and *indios ladinos,* we turn again to
Guaman Poma's explicit commentary. His admiration for the Franciscans, the Jesuits, and religious hermits, contrasted to his harsh criticisms
of other orders, reveals the subtleties of *indio ladino* loyalties and aver-
sions. One type of relationship between the *indio ladino* and the regular
clergy of negative stripe is told by Guaman Poma about the Mercedarian
friar Martín de Murúa. He described Murúa in the most unkind terms
and satirized his pastoral (or antipastoral, in Guaman Poma's view) outlook in a sermon in Quechua.[139] In this case, familiarity bred contempt;

Guaman Poma assured his readers that if he were to try to write about the life of Murúa, it would take him at least a year to put together an account of all his wrongdoing.[140] However, what Guaman Poma did not reveal was the working relationship that he had with Murúa in writing and illustrating the life of the Incas. Manuel Ballesteros Gaibrois and Emilio Mendizábal Losack have presented convincing visual evidence and textual comparisons to the effect that Guaman Poma's hand contributed drawings to Murúa's historical works.[141] Although the specific character and length of that relationship remain to be discovered, Guaman Poma's case points to one type of clergy–*indio ladino* relationship that must have been common.

Guaman Poma revealed a relationship of a different type in his unmitigated admiration for Fray Luis Jerónimo de Oré, a Franciscan friar from Huamanga and author of works of religious devotion for Andeans. Guaman Poma cited him as "one of the learned men who composed books"[142] and paid him the honor of copying portions of Oré's work into his own.[143] Like Oré, Guaman Poma took seriously the type of social action which had the written word as its outcome.[144]

For the *indio ladino* coming into a written culture when his parents and grandparents had known exclusively the oral, there was no question about the relationship of word—particularly the written word—and deed. The corpus of writings of early colonial Peru on the problems of evangelization and extirpation, particularly the sermons and catechisms produced in bi- and trilingual editions for the native populations and the *visita* accounts of Andean ritual practices written by and for the clergy, had as their goal to change the way people thought and behaved. At the conclusion of his *Ritos y fábulas de los Incas,* for example, Cristóbal de Molina spoke of the *visita* as the written report that he held in his hands, "la visita que entre manos tengo."[145] In this case the actual inspection tour and its written report bear the same name, and both are aspects of a single action: the survey of native religious practices needed to instruct church personnel in their eradication. Participating in the activities that led to and included the production of these works, the natives skilled in Spanish would have seen the word that interpreted action and the word that mandated action as inextricably intertwined. They would have understood that linguistic activities—from the creation and conservation of oral traditions to the production of written texts—were not separate from social practices but in fact constitutive of them.[146] Writing was an institution of colonization, the *indio ladino* quickly understood, and to enter into its use ultimately became an anticolonialist stance.[147]

CONCLUSION: IDENTITY AND ALTERITY

The testimony of the *indio ladino* brings forward the complexity of inter- and intracultural perceptions that accompany colonialism. The *indio ladino* turned messianic leader is, from the European perspective of the *visitador*, the lapsed Christian reverting to former beliefs. This charismatic figure is also marked with betrayal by the Christian Andean, but from a slightly different perspective, as an impostor who betrays traditional practices and usurps the role of the traditional priest-practitioner. The *kuraka* is seen by the *visitador* as a betrayer of Christian trust in concealing *waqakuna* and their own *waqa*-related practices. This same *kuraka* is seen as false by the native elite for usurping positions of authority rightfully belonging to others and as a betrayer of his own vassals by working in collusion with colonial authorities for his self-interest. The viewpoints of *visitador* and *indio ladino* converge in the condemnation of collusion between parish priest and *kuraka* in hiding sacred objects and practices from the church inspectors for their mutual self-interest. The *indio ladino* himself is seen by the *visita* officials as faithful adjunct to their mission but as troublemaker by local officials for whom the native *pleito* was a source of conflict and harassment.

This dizzying summary of cross-cultural viewpoints of and by the *indio ladino* reveals the complexities of that experience in colonial society. The self-representation of the *indio ladino* is that of an isolated figure, suspected by natives and colonizers alike as being a potentially subversive cultural "half-caste." Given this self-perception, the strident insistence of Guaman Poma and Santacruz Pachacuti on their positions as Christians and collaborators with the evangelizing mission becomes a more intelligible, more compelling testimony. Considering the single stereotypical label of *indio ladino,* in spite of the range of caste and class concealed thereby, the individuals so identified constantly had to adjust their positions as subjects. The search for and adjustment to various models of identity belie the multiple subject positions that the colonial subject seemed destined to take, not merely sequentially but most often simultaneously.[148]

The fact that the *indio ladino* commonly stood outside the various constituencies and alliances that made up colonial society is best revealed by Guaman Poma. It consists not in one of his self-serving self-portraits as social outcast but in one of his statesmanlike governmental recommendations. In each pueblo, he advised, there should be an *indio ladino* as *veedor*, as overseer, whose job would be to monitor the activities of all the groups that made up local colonial society: priests and *corregidores, encomenderos, kurakakuna,* and "yndios mandoncillos."[149] The suggestion that there be *indio ladino* inspectors to monitor the activities of Europeans and *criollos* on one hand and the native communities on the other admits a view of the *indio ladino* as being external to all social and ethnic groups. As Guaman Poma and Santacruz Pachacuti revealed, the identity of one who was a cultural mestizo was constantly challenged, whether by Andean commoners and elite or by Spanish priests and *corregidores.* One of the most compelling versions of the history of colonialism would be that which the lives of *indios ladinos* could reveal. Such an examination would surely give the lie to the simplicity of patterns of accommodation and resistance so easily constructed to explain Andeans' lives after the Spanish invasion of Tawantinsuyu.

NOTES

1. Lic. Hernando de Santillán, *Relación,* in *Colección de libros y documentos referentes a la historia del Perú,* 2d ser., edited by Horacio H. Urteaga and Carlos A. Romero (Lima, 1927), 9:1–124.

2. Santillán, *Relación,* 25.

3. Santillán, *Relación,* 26.

4. Raúl Porras Barrenechea, *Los cronistas del Perú (1528–1650) y otros ensayos,* edited by Franklin Pease G. Y., Biblioteca Clásicos del Perú 2 (Lima, 1986), 326, compares Santillán's *alegato* in favor of the Indians with Felipe Guaman Poma de Ayala's *Nueva corónica y buen gobierno.*

5. Felipe Guaman Poma de Ayala, *Nueva corónica y buen gobierno* (1615), edited by John V. Murra, Rolena Adorno, and George L. Urioste, 2d ed., rev. (Madrid, 1987), 411, 918. Pagination from the 1987 edition corrects Guaman Poma's original numbering. Translations of all Castilian texts into English are my own.

6. See Pierre Duviols, *La destrucción de las religiones andinas (conquista y colonia)* (1971), translated by Albor Maruenda (Mexico City, 1977), 284; and Frank Salomon, *Native Lords of Quito in the Age of the Incas: The Political Economy of North Andean Chiefdoms* (Cambridge, Eng., 1986), 239.

7. I am grateful to Jan Szemiński for his helpful commentary on an earlier version of this paper, which was read at the symposium "In Word and Deed: Interethnic Encounters and Cultural Developments in the New World," 9–14 October 1988, Albany, New York.

8. These dimensions of colonial interactions are called to mind by James Lockhart in *Charles Gibson and the Ethnohistory of Postconquest Central Mexico,* Institute of Latin American Studies Occasional Paper 9 (Melbourne, Aust.: La Trobe University, (1988), 15; and idem, "Postconquest Nahua Society and Concepts Viewed through Nahuatl Writings," *Estudios de Cultura Nahuatl* 20 (1990): 117–140.

9. The papers from the Lima congress were published in *Revista Histórica* 28 (1965); see also James Lockhart, *Spanish Peru (1532–1560): A Colonial Society* (Madison, Wisc., 1968), 199–220; John Hemming, *The Conquest of the Incas* (London, 1970), 82, 281–282.

10. José Antonio del Busto Duthurburu, "Martinillo de Poechos," *Revista Histórica* 28 (1965): 86–101. See the last will and testament of Martinillo in "Algunos documentos inéditos sobre el Perú colonial," *Revista Histórica* 16 (1943): 124–137.

11. Francisco Solano, "El intérprete: Uno de los ejes de la aculturación," *Terceras jornadas americanistas de la Universidad de Valladolid: Estudios sobre política indigenista española en América* (Valladolid, 1975), 265–278.

12. Bartolomé de las Casas, *Historia de las Indias*, in *Obras escogidas de Fray Bartolomé de las Casas*, edited by Juan Pérez de Tudela Bueso, Biblioteca de Autores Españoles 95 (Madrid, 1957), 1:250, 269, 274, cited by Solano, "El intérprete," 267; Hemming, Conquest of the Incas, 281.

13. Solano, "El intérprete," 268, cites Gonzalo Fernández de Oviedo (*Historia general y natural de las Indias*, bk. 10, chap. 7) on the incarceration of natives for the purpose of teaching them Spanish and training them as interpreters.

14. Solano, "El intérprete," 269–271.

15. I have followed Salomon's *Native Lords of Quito,* 241, definition of the colonial *yanacona.*
The following studies offer additional insights into the *indio ladino* experience: Manuel Burga, *Nacimiento de una utopía: Muerte y resurrección de los incas* (Lima, 1988); Luis Miguel Glave, *Trajinantes: Caminos indígenas en la sociedad colonial, siglos XVI–XVII* (Lima, 1989); George Kubler, "The Quechua in the Colonial World," in *Handbook of South American Indians,* edited by Julian H. Steward (1963), 2:354–359; Karen Spalding, *De indio a campesino: Cambios en la estructura social del Perú colonial* (Lima, 1974), 61–87; Steve J. Stern, *Peru's Indian Peoples and the Challenge of Spanish Conquest: Huamanga to 1640* (Madison, Wisc., 1982), 167–187, 255; Rafael Varón Gabai, *Curacas y encomenderos: Acomodamiento nativo en Huaraz, siglos XVI y XVII* (Lima, 1980).

16. See José Antonio del Busto Duthurburu, "Una huérfana mestiza: La hija de Juan Pizarro," *Revista Histórica* 28 (1965): 103–106; idem, "La mestiza del capitán Hernando de Soto, su familia, y los lienzos del Virrey Toledo," *Revista Histórica* 28 (1965): 113–117; María Rostworowski de Diez Canseco, *Doña Francisca Pizarro: Una ilustre mestiza (1534–1598)* (Lima, 1989).

17. Sebastián de Covarrubias Horozco, *Tesoro de la lengua castellana o española,* edited by Martín de Riquer (Barcelona, 1943), 747.

18. Covarrubias, *Tesoro,* 753.

19. Roger Wright, "Early Medieval Spanish, Latin, and Ladino," *Litterae Judaeorum in Terra Hispanica,* edited by I. Benabu and J. Yahalom (Jerusalem, in press); idem, "El latín y el ladino en los siglos once y doce," *Papers of the Nineteenth International Conference of Romance Linguistics and Philology* (La Coruña, Spain, in press). See also Manuel Alvar, "Aceptaciones de *ladino* en español," in

Estudios de lengua y literatura, vol. 2 of *Homenaje a Pedro Sáinz Rodríguez* (Madrid, 1986), 25–34.

20. Covarrubias, *Tesoro,* 747.

21. Pedro de Quiroga, *Coloquios de la verdad,* edited by Julián Zarco Cuevas (Seville, [1562] 1922), 63.

22. Guaman Poma, *Nueva corónica,* 716, states that he has dealt with *visitadores,* "ciruiendo de lengua y conuersando, preguntando a los españoles pobres y a yndios pobres y a negros pobres," that he has seen church inspectors and civil inspectors of *visitas, revisitas,* and *composición de tierras* and has dealt with them as a poor man. Since his work on the *composición de tierras* is confirmed by an external source, it behooves us to try to document his other associations. See Juan C. Zorrilla A., "La posesión de Chiara por los indios Chachapoyas," *Wari* 1 (1977): 49–64; and Steve J. Stern, "Algunas consideraciones sobre la personalidad histórica de Don Felipe Guaman Poma de Ayala," *Histórica* 2, 2 (1978): 225–228.

23. Duviols, *La destrucción,* 284–285.

24. Duviols, *La destrucción,* 284.

25. Quiroga, *Coloquios,* 117, 122.

26. On the native role in extirpation activities, see Duviols, *La destrucción,* 280–289; Karen Spalding, "Social Climbers: Changing Patterns of Mobility among the Indians of Colonial Peru," *Hispanic American Historical Review* 50, 4 (1970): 657–660; idem, *Huarochirí: An Andean Society under Inca and Spanish Rule* (Stanford, Calif., 1984), 217–218; and Guaman Poma, *Nueva corónica,* 298, 908.

27. Enrique T. Bartra, ed., *Tercer Concilio Limense: 1582–1583* (Lima, 1982): 177–178.

28. Guaman Poma, *Nueva corónica,* 754, 755; on 75, he claimed descent from the Yarovilca Allauca Huánuco dynasty that predated the Incas:

> To say Yaru Willka is to refer to that very very much higher lord of all the nations. . . . These were kings and emperors over all the rest of the kings and absolute lords in all their kingdoms of the ancient Indians from their nation, although there were many other kings of the various fortified settlements. But this one had the highest crown since before the time of the Inca, and afterward he was feared by the Inca and thus was the 'second person' [viceroy] of the Inca.

Guaman Poma identified his grandfather as *Qhapaq apu* Guaman Chaua, *segunda persona del Inca* (the Inca's viceroy). See José Varallanos, *Historia de Huánuco* (Buenos Aires, 1959), 77–82, for the relation of the Yarovilca polity to the Inca state.

29. Franklin Pease G. Y., "El mestizaje religioso y Santa Cruz Pachacuti," *Revista Histórica* 28 (1965): 125, 131; Jan Szemiński, *Un kuraca, un dios, y una historia: Relación de antigüedades deste reyno del Pirú por Don Joan de Santa Cruz Pacha Cuti Yamqui Salca Maygua,* Antropología e Historia 2 (Jujuy, Argentina, 1987), 4.

30. Szemiński, *Un kuraca,* 4; Marcos Jiménez de la Espada, ed., *Tres relaciones de las antigüedades peruanas* (Madrid, 1879), 231.

31. Szemiński, *Un kuraca,* 2–3.

32. Juan de Santacruz Pachacuti Yamqui, *Relación de antigüedades deste reyno del Pirú*, in *Colección de libros y documentos referentes a la historia del Perú*, 2d ser., edited by Horacio H. Urteaga and Carlos A. Romero (Lima, 1927), 9:127–128.

33. Szemiński, *Un kuraca*, 4–5.

34. Luis Millones's discovery of Albornoz's *Informaciones de servicios* and many subsequent studies have elucidated the structure, organization, and meaning of the movement. See Luis Millones, "Un movimiento nativista del siglo XVI: El Taki Onqoy," *Revista Peruana de Cultura* 3 (1964): 134–140; idem, "Nuevos aspectos del Taki Onqoy," in *Ideología mesiánica del mundo andino*, edited by Juan M. Ossio (Lima, 1973): 97–101; idem, "Taki Onqoy," *Cielo Abierto* 10, 28 (n.d.): 9–15; Luis Millones, ed., *Las informaciones de Cristóbal de Albornoz*, Sondeos 79 (Mexico, 1971); Marco Curatola, "El culto de crisis del Moro Oncoy," in *Etnohistoria y antropología andina: Primera jornada del Museo Nacional de Historia*, edited by Marcia Koth de Paredes and Amalia Castelli (Lima, 1979); Duviols, *La destrucción*; Juan M. Ossio, ed., *Ideología mesiánica del mundo andino* (Lima, 1973); Sabine MacCormack, "*Pachacuti*: Miracles, Punishments, and Last Judgment— Visionary Past and Prophetic Future in Early Colonial Peru," *American Historical Review* 93, 4 (1988): 960–1006; Bruce Mannheim, "The Virgin and the Pleiades: Poetic and Religious Syncretism in Colonial Peru," unpublished manuscript; Franklin Pease G. Y., *El dios creador andino* (Lima, 1973); Stern, *Peru's Indian Peoples*; Nathan Wachtel, *Los vencidos: Los indios del Perú frente a la conquista española (1530–1570)*, translated by Antonio Escohotado (Madrid, 1976); Abdón Yaranga Valderrama, "Taki Onqo ou la vision des vaincus au XVIe siècle," *Les Mentalités dans la Péninsule Ibérique et en Amérique Latine aux XVIe et XVIIe siècles— Histoire et problématique: Actes du XIIIe Congrès de la Société des Hispanistes Français de l'Enseignement Supérieur, Tours 1977* (Tours, 1978).

35. The following paragraph summarizes Wachtel, *Los vencidos*, 282–295.

36. Millones, *Informaciones*, document 2, p. 54; cited by Stern, *Peru's Indian Peoples*, 55.

37. Millones, "Un movimiento," 138; Stern, *Peru's Indian Peoples*, 51–67.

38. Pierre Duviols, "Albornoz y el espacio ritual andino prehispánico," *Revista Andina* 2, 1 (1984): 215.

39. Millones, *Informaciones*, document 1, p. 17.

40. Millones, *Informaciones*, document 2, pp. 46, 62.

41. Wachtel, *Los vencidos*, 288.

42. Millones, *Informaciones*, document 1, pp. 18, 37. Luis de Olivera testified:

They [*waqakuna*] entered the bodies of the Indians and made them speak, and from there they began to tremble, saying that they had the divinities in their bodies and that they took over many of them and they painted their faces with red coloring and they put them in some enclosure and the Indians went there to worship them as such divinities and idols that were said to have entered their bodies.

43. Guillermo Cock and Mary Eileen Doyle, "Del culto solar a la clandestinidad de Inti y Punchao," *Historia y Cultura*, no. 12 (1979): 51, point out the absence of any clear notion of a liberator in Taki Unquy, noting that it would

later be explicit in the myths of Inkarrí. With the limitations that the concepts imply, they consider that Taki Unquy could be called revitalist or prophetic.

44. Franklin Pease G. Y., "Felipe Guaman Poma de Ayala: Mitos andinos e historia occidental," *Caravelle* 37 (1981): 25–26.

45. Franklin Pease G. Y., "Las versiones del mito de Inkarrí," *Revista de la Universidad Católica,* no. 2 (1977): 29–30; Cock and Doyle "Del culto solar," 51.

46. Pease, "Las versiones," 30.

47. Guaman Poma, *Nueva corónica,* 689.

48. Guaman Poma, *Nueva corónica,* 690.

49. Guaman Poma, *Nueva corónica,* 282. Guaman Poma went on to mention several other practices and ended this page and the chapter by stating that he knew everything that he had written about these "popes" (*pontífices*) because he was serving Cristóbal de Albornoz, "inspector general of the holy mother church who destroyed all the *waqakuna,* idols, and *hechicerías* of the kingdom. He was a Christian judge." I shall return later to Guaman Poma's assessment of Albornoz.

50. Guaman Poma, *Nueva corónica,* 255.

51. José Polo de Ondegardo, "Los errores y supersticiones de los indios, sacados del tratado y averiguación," *Revista Histórica* 1, 1 (1906): 198.

52. Cited by Millones, "Taki Onqoy," 11.

53. Cock and Doyle, "El culto solar," 53, first made this assertion; see, more recently, MacCormack, "*Pachacuti,*" 982–987.

54. Millones, "Un movimiento nativista," 138; "Nuevos aspectos," 97.

55. It also leaves open the question of when Guaman Poma worked for Albornoz. Guaman Poma's is the only testimony on that employment, and he gives no information as to where or when it occurred. His familiarity with the personnel and practices of Albornoz's *visitas,* however, leaves little doubt that his claim was true.

56. In Albornoz's *Informaciones de servicios,* Cristóbal de Molina testified that, upon capture and trial in Cusco, two male and one female leaders confessed that they exploited their dogmatizing for material gain, collecting offerings given them for their preaching. Molina testified on a second occasion (in 1584) that, when punished in Cusco, one of the leaders of the movement, Juan Chocne, confessed to preaching the Taki Unquy doctrine for purposes of personal reward. According to Millones, "Taki Onqoy," 12, Chocne was regarded by Albornoz as the most blameworthy of the thirteen offenders he sent to Cusco for punishment; at the end, Chocne "proclaimed repentance and asked public pardon." See Millones, *Informaciones,* document 1, p. 22; document 3, pp. 28–29.

57. Duviols, "Albornoz y el espacio ritual," 216.

58. Guaman Poma, *Nueva corónica,* 267.

59. Guaman Poma, *Nueva corónica,* 267.

60. On haranguing against such individuals who died from alcoholic consumption, "without confession, like horses and brute animals," Guaman Poma, *Nueva corónica,* 877, picked up the language of the first collection of bilingual Spanish-Quechua sermons published in Peru in the colonial period. Sermon 23

of the *Tercero catecismo* was devoted to the theme of drunkenness. However, Guaman Poma's concern was not, as was the sermon's, the problem of death without spiritual salvation of filial inheritance but rather death intestate and the consequent loss of Andean wealth and goods to European and creole owners. See *Tercero catecismo y exposición de la doctrina christiana por sermones* (Lima, [1585] 1773), 311–331. See Spalding, "Social Climbers," for other evidence of persistent *indio ladino* proselytizing for native religions around 1611.

61. Santacruz Pachacuti, *Relación*, 235.

62. Millones, *Informaciones*, document 2, pp. 115, 151.

63. Santacruz Pachacuti, *Relación*, 129.

64. Santacruz Pachacuti, *Relación*, 129.

65. Javier Castillo Arroyo, *Catecismos peruanos en el siglo XVI*, Sondeos 1 (Mexico, 1966), 46.

66. It was the only collection of sermons in a bilingual Spanish-Quechua edition published in the Peruvian viceroyalty in the sixteenth century; it was not reprinted until the eighteenth century (Duviols, *La destrucción*, 342).

67. *Tercero catecismo*, 141; see also 170. Guaman Poma, *Nueva corónica*, 637, corroborates this view, declaring that pious priests held devout *indios ladinos* in high regard.

68. Cristóbal de Molina, *Ritos y fábulas de los Incas* (Buenos Aires, [1575] 1959), 104. See also Millones, *Informaciones*, document 2, pp. 37, 47, 63, 69, 70, 74, 89, 90, 112.

69. Millones, *Informaciones*, document 2, p. 84; see also document 2, p. 37.

70. Guaman Poma, *Nueva corónica*, 1111, 1114, 1122.

71. These dates were generally known and accepted by scholars since Pietschmann. See Richard A. Pietschmann, "*Nueva corónica y buen gobierno* de Don Felipe Guaman Poma de Ayala," in Felipe Guaman Poma de Ayala, *Nueva corónica y buen gobierno (codex péruvien illustré)*, Travaux et Mémoires de l'Institut d'Ethnologie 23 (Paris, 1936), vii–xxviii. However, by scrutinizing the physical evidence of the autograph manuscript in 1977, I was able to confirm these assertions. See Rolena Adorno, *Cronista y príncipe: La obra de Don Felipe Guaman Poma de Ayala* (Lima, 1989), 54–61.

72. Guaman Poma, *Nueva corónica*, 908.

73. Ibid.

74. Guaman Poma, *Nueva corónica*, 1, prefaced his book by declaring that it would be useful for general inspection tours of native settlements and also for inspections conducted by the Church. With reference to his chapter on *hechiceros*, he declared expressly: "This is written to punish and inquire about the idolaters against our holy Catholic faith" (*Nueva corónica*, 280).

75. The practices of *ruthuchiku* and *warachikuq* are such examples. In his *Instrucción*, Albornoz had cited *ruthuchiku* and *warachikuq* as widespread practices to be rooted out by the *visitadores*. *Ruthuchiku*, the first cutting of the hair of male children, was accompanied by offerings, ceremonies, and naming the celebrants for ancestors or *waqakuna*. See Duviols, "Albornoz y el espacio ritual," 202. *Warachikuq*, the ceremonial girding of male children, was another rite of passage

which Albornoz considered idolatrous. Guaman Poma, *Nueva corónica*, 285, 585, 615, 795, insisted that both practices, continuing to his day, deserved to be punished throughout the kingdom.

76. See Rolena Adorno, "Las otras fuentes de Guaman Poma: Sus lecturas castellanas," *Histórica* 2, 2 (1978), and Duviols, "Albornoz y el espacio ritual," for the coincidence of Albornoz's and Guaman Poma's descriptions of ritual practices. However, the differences between the Andean native and the European inspector are made apparent by the greater detail of Guaman Poma's accounts. On practices about which Albornoz gave simple warnings, we find Guaman Poma consistently discussing and detailing them in much greater depth. Burial customs, ritual dances, and practices such as the Inca-style perforation of the ears, all cited for vigilance and prohibition by Albornoz, in Duviols, "Albornoz y el espacio ritual," 202–203, are given their greater due by Guaman Poma. The detailed burial customs that Guaman Poma discussed according to the divisions of the Inca empire are commentaries on contemporary practice. Again, he describes them as "idolatry," stating that he was an eyewitness to them, that the Spanish priests often consented to their observance, and that the devout *indio ladino* was a persona non grata on such occasions.

77. Szemiński, *Un kuraca*, 2.

78. See Duviols, "Albornoz y el espacio ritual," 180.

79. To place Guaman Poma's remarks in their appropriate context, we can examine a letter that Albornoz wrote to Philip III in 1602 from Cusco; it is reproduced in Millones, *Informaciones,* document 6, pp. 1–8. This letter was called to my attention by Duviols, "Albornoz y el espacio ritual," 180–182, who remarked on its relation to the outlook of Guaman Poma. Albornoz expressed the following view of the dependence of the colonizers on the Andeans in his letter to the king in 1602:

> The bishop and the cleric and the religious and the nun and the viceroy and the judge and the *corregidores, vecinos* and soldiers—we all depend on them [the natives] and we treat them like slaves, and what is most regrettable is that all the measures that Your Majesty takes on their behalf are subverted and end up causing them harm and further hardship.

See Millones, *Informaciones,* document 6, p. 6. Guaman Poma, *Nueva corónica,* 1065, expressed the same critique and raised it to a higher magnitude: "The pope is pope and the king is king because of the Indians of Peru."

80. Condemning the corruption of the inspectors, Albornoz, in Millones, *Informaciones,* document 6, p. 5, lamented that the worst aspect, since the officials attended to their own gain, was that the natives remained as idolatrous in their ways as in pre-Columbian times, because they were not taught Christian doctrine by the distracted and greedy *visitadores*. Furthermore, Albornoz continued, the *doctrinas* were manned by the most clever candidates but not by the most able: "the worst of it is that clever negotiating for parish posts is more important than the merits of those who seek them." The *doctrinas* were thus occupied by those who negotiated best, while older and more worthy priests were passed over.

81. Guaman Poma, *Nueva corónica,* 699.

82. Millones, *Informaciones*, document 6, p. 3.

83. Guaman Poma, *Nueva corónica*, 687, 688.

84. Guaman Poma, *Nueva corónica*, 688.

85. See Guaman Poma, *Nueva corónica*, 232, 528, 579, 585, 586, 600, 604, 612, 622, 654, 656, 665, 673, 674, 679, 693, 701, 702, 892, 895, 987, 999, and 1089. Since he usually mentioned them in general references, it is difficult to tell whether he had in mind specific actions of the Second or the Third Council or the common dispositions of both.

86. Bartra, *Tercer Concilio*, 80.

87. Guaman Poma, *Nueva corónica*, 30, 31, 74–76, 79, 95, 97, 98, 150.

88. Guaman Poma, *Nueva corónica*, 914.

89. Duviols, "Albornoz y el espacio ritual," 180.

90. Guaman Poma, *Nueva corónica*, 711.

91. Cristóbal de Albornoz, "Instrucción para descubrir todas las guacas del Pirú y sus camayos y haziendas," in Duviols, "Albornoz y el espacio ritual," 202.

92. Guaman Poma, *Nueva corónica*, 796.

93. Guaman Poma, *Nueva corónica*, 798.

94. See also Guaman Poma, *Nueva corónica*, 988: those who labored in the mines should be given a month off to divert themselves, to sing their songs and dance their dances with their wives and relatives, because they might die in the mines and never see their wives and children again.

95. Guaman Poma, *Nueva corónica*, 317, 330.

96. José Varallanos, *Guaman Poma de Ayala: Cronista, precursor, y libertario* (Lima, 1979), 22, 38–39, has discovered that many of the names of *kurakakuna* mentioned by Guaman Poma in the *Nueva corónica* are also found in the *Relaciones geográficas de Indias* (1586) and Albornoz's *Relación de amancebados, hechiceros, y guacas* (1584).

Albornoz's *Relación de la visita de Hatun Lucana* and Guaman Poma's *Nueva corónica y buen gobierno* have in common the names of many native lords. Don Juan Guancarilla, cited for "concubinage" in Albornoz's *Relación* in 1584 (Millones, *Informaciones*, document 4, p. 34), is named by Guaman Poma as the father of a *kuraka*, Don Felipe Guancarilla, who is not obeyed by his current, opportunistic subordinates (Guaman Poma, *Nueva corónica*, 792). Don Juan Guancarilla appears in the *Relaciones geográficas del Perú* of 1586 as a *kuraka* on the *repartimiento* of Hatun Lucanas, and he is so identified by Albornoz. See Marcos Jiménez de la Espada, *Relaciones geográficas de Indias*, edited by José Urbano Martínez Carreras, Biblioteca de Autores Españoles 103, (Madrid, 1965), 1:226.

Guaman Poma mentions Don García Mullo Guamani as the *segunda persona* of Don Diego Luca of the *ayllu* of Oma Pacha in Lucanas and as the father of Cristóbal de León, "decípulo del autor" (Guaman Poma, *Nueva corónica*, 499). In the *Relaciones geográficas del Perú* of 1586, García Mullo Guamani is listed as a *kuraka* in the *repartimiento* of Lucanas Andamarcas (Jiménez de la Espada, *Relaciones geográficas*, 237). In Albornoz's *Relación*, one Pedro Mollo Guamani, "indio del repartimiento de Hatun Lucana," was punished for *taki unquy*; "Mollo Guamani" of Lurin Lucana was punished as an *hechicero* (Millones, *Informaciones,* document 4, pp. 35–36).

In the section on the *waqakuna* of the *caciques* in Albornoz's *Relación de la visita de Apcara,* Pedro Pilconi is listed among the guilty; in Uchacayllo in Apcara, Cristóbal Pilconi is listed as punished among those who were "favorescedores y consentidores de la dicha seta" of Taki Unquy (Millones, *Informaciones,* document 4, pp. 44–45). Guaman Poma refers twice to a Don Juan Pilconc, *kuraka kamachikuq,* and cites him for collusion with the *corregidor*; he later draws a picture in which Pilcone files a complaint against the *corregidor* with the priest's help (Guaman Poma, *Nueva corónica,* 499, 602).

97. The *Relación de amancebados* consists of lists of names of (1) *kurakakuna* punished for concubinage, (2) "yndios" punished for Taki Unquy, (3) *kurakakuna* who maintained *waqakuna* and shrines on their lands for worship by them and their subjects, (4) the names of said *waqakuna,* and (5) the names of those *kurakakuna* and *principales* who were punished for worshiping the local divinities and for concealing and protecting the *takiunqueros.*

98. Quiroga, *Coloquios,* 93; see also 68, 95.

99. See Spalding, *De indio a campesino,* 31–87.

100. Guaman Poma, *Nueva corónica,* 788.

101. The rituals against which Albornoz and Guaman Poma separately warned are exactly those that the latter attributes to these *principales.* In fact, every native lord whom Guaman Poma mentions by name in this chapter is accused of some of the shortcomings singled out in Albornoz's *visitas.* Don Gonzalo Quispe Guarcaya, of the pueblo of Chuci in Lucanas, is an *indio tributario* turned *kuraka* and *principal* of Lucanas; he is cited by Guaman Poma, *Nueva corónica,* 780, for thievery and polygamy. Guaman Poma, ibid., 787, mentions Don Gonzalo again in the context of how the *kurakakuna* encouraged "adultery" (polygamy) and prevented their communities from performing Christian religious duties such as saying confession and offering alms for masses for the dead. He accuses the *kurakakuna* of forcing their subjects to stay in the *puna* to die without confession. He cites Quispe Guarcaya for stealing a beast of burden from a devout Andean woman who wanted to sell it to have a mass said for her deceased father (ibid., 787). These false lords do these things, Guaman Poma asserts, because they are *hechiceros.*

102. "*Qhapaq* ques prencipe" ("great, powerful," that is, a prince) was a late addition to the text in which the author had previously identified himself and his father as *caciques prencipales.* See Rolena Adorno, "The *Nueva corónica y buen gobierno*: A New Look at the Royal Library's Peruvian Treasure," *Fund og Forskning* (Copenhagen) 24 (1979/1980): 1–28.

103. Sabine MacCormack, "The Heart Has Its Reasons: Predicaments of Missionary Christianity in Early Colonial Peru," *Hispanic American Historical Review* 65, 3 (1985): 461.

104. See Duviols, "Albornoz y el espacio ritual."
105. Guaman Poma, *Nueva corónica*, 690.
106. Duviols interprets this passage as I do. See Duviols, *La destrucción*, 285.
107. Albornoz in Duviols, "Albornoz y el espacio ritual," 218.
108. Guaman Poma, *Nueva corónica*, 690.
109. Guaman Poma, *Nueva corónica*, 907.
110. Guaman Poma, *Nueva corónica*, 795.
111. Guaman Poma, *Nueva corónica*, 298; see also 294, 299.
112. Guaman Poma, *Nueva corónica*, 497, 609, 637, 728, 920.
113. Duviols, *La destrucción*, 406.
114. For a discussion of the use of the Spanish colonial legal system by native society, see Stern, *Peru's Indian Peoples*, 114–137.
115. Duviols, *La destrucción*, 342.
116. *Tercero catecismo*, 101, 298–307, 355–357, 361, 382.
117. *Tercero catecismo*, 177–178, 266–270.
118. *Tercero catecismo*, 199, 367.
119. *Tercero catecismo*, 367, 368.
120. *Tercero catecismo*, 368–369.
121. Guaman Poma, *Nueva corónica*, 733, 738, 796, 838.
122. Guaman Poma, *Nueva corónica*, 544, 586.
123. Guaman Poma, *Nueva corónica*, 920. For an analysis of Spanish colonial policies that had the effect of simultaneously restricting bilingualism in the administrative and legal domain and encouraging it among local *kurakakuna* in order to facilitate colonial rule, see Bruce Mannheim, "'Una nación acorralada': Southern Peruvian Quechua Language Planning and Politics in Historical Perspective," *Language in Society* (Cambridge, Eng.) 13 (1984): 291–309.

Studies noting the obstruction of Andeans' learning Spanish (Duviols, *La destrucción*, 411; Mannheim, "'Una nación acorralada,'" 304–305) usually cite Guaman Poma as their source. For a study of Guaman Poma's attitude toward literacy, see Rolena Adorno, "Writing about Reading: An Andean View of Literacy in the Early Spanish Colonial Period," *Yale Journal of Criticism* 2, 1 (1988): 197–203.

Such reticence about natives learning the colonists' language was not confined to Peru. For Yucatan, for example, Ralph L. Roys, introduction to *The Book of Chilam Balam* (Washington, D.C., 1933), 4–5, notes that the missionary Pedro Sánchez de Aguilar admitted to wanting to prohibit the natives from learning Spanish.

124. Guaman Poma, *Nueva corónica*, 1117.
125. Guaman Poma, *Nueva corónica*, 738.
126. Guaman Poma, *Nueva corónica*, 738.
127. Quiroga, *Coloquios*, 80, 84.
128. Quiroga, *Coloquios*, 80.
129. Guaman Poma, *Nueva corónica*, 733.

130. Quiroga, *Coloquios,* 112; see also 113.

131. Antonio Acosta, "El pleito de los indios de San Damián (Huarochirí) contra Francisco de Avila," *Historiografía y Bibliografía Americanistas* 23 (1979): 3–33; and Antonio Acosta, "Francisco de Avila: Cusco 1573(?)–Lima 1647," in *Ritos y tradiciones de Huarochirí del siglo XVII,* translated and edited by Gerald Taylor (Lima, 1987), 569–579.

132. Guaman Poma, *Nueva corónica,* 1120–1121.

133. For a description of the abuses for which Avila was charged, see Antonio Acosta, "Francisco de Avila," 572–575.

134. Guaman Poma, *Nueva corónica,* 791.

135. Guaman Poma, *Nueva corónica,* 793.

136. See George L. Urioste, "The Editing of Oral Tradition in the Huarochirí Manuscript," in *From Oral to Written Expression: Native Andean Chronicles of the Early Colonial Period,* edited by Rolena Adorno (Syracuse, N.Y., 1982), 101–108; George L. Urioste, *Hijos de Pariya Qaqa: La tradición oral de Waru Chiri (mitología, ritual, y costumbres)* (Syracuse, N.Y., 1983); Frank Salomon, "Chronicles of the Impossible: Notes on Three Peruvian Indigenous Chroniclers," in Adorno, *From Oral to Written,* 9–39; and Frank Salomon and George L. Urioste, *The Huarochirí Manuscript: A Testament of Ancient and Colonial Andean Religion* (Austin, Tex., forthcoming).

137. Szemiński, *Un kuraca,* 7.

138. Szemiński, *Un kuraca,* 7–9.

139. Guaman Poma, *Nueva corónica,* 625; see also 661, 662, 663, 920, 1090.

140. Guaman Poma, *Nueva corónica,* 663.

141. See Emilio Mendizábal Losack, "Las dos versiones de Murúa," *Revista del Museo Nacional* (Lima) 32 (1963): 153–185; Manuel Ballesteros-Gaibrois, "Estudio preliminar," in Fray Martín de Murúa, *Historia general del Perú, origen y descendencia de los Incas,* edited by Manuel Ballesteros-Gaibrois, Colección Joyas Bibliográficas, Bibliotheca Americana Vetus 1/2 (Madrid, 1962–1964); idem, "Relación entre Fray Martín de Murúa y Felipe Huamán Poma de Ayala," in *Estudios americanistas: Libro jubilar en homenaje a Hermann Trimborn,* edited by Roswith Hartman and Udo Oberem (St. Augustin, Germany, 1978); idem, "Dos cronistas paralelos: Huamán Poma y Martín de Murúa (confrontación de las series reales gráficas)," *Anales de Literatura Hispano Americana* 9, 10 (1981): 15–66.

142. Guaman Poma, *Nueva corónica,* 926, 1090.

143. Guaman Poma, *Nueva corónica,* 1, 1090. See ibid., 3:1317, 1358, for commentary.

144. On summarizing his own experiences, Guaman Poma, (*Nueva corónica,* 916) considered seeing, comprehending, serving, and writing (to the king) all of a piece.

145. Molina, *Ritos y fábulas,* 104.

146. For a discussion of language as social action (not as "talk about" but as "doing by saying") as well as an analysis of a single instance of language as social

action, see Bruce Mannheim, "Discursive and Presentational Form in Language: Subliminal Patterning in a Quechua Folksong," in *Through an Andean Kaleidoscope: The Making of Andean Texts,* edited by B. J. Isbell, forthcoming.

147. See Rolena Adorno, *Guaman Poma: Writing and Resistance in Colonial Peru* (Austin, Tex., 1986).

148. See Rolena Adorno, "El sujeto colonial y la construcción cultural de la alteridad," *Revista de Crítica Literaria Latinoamericana* 14, 28 (1988): 55–68.

149. Guaman Poma, *Nueva corónica,* 903.

QUECHUA GLOSSARY

Sources Cited

Acosta, Joseph de
1962 (1590)   *Historia natural y moral de las Indias.* Mexico City: Fondo de
                     Cultura Económica.

Bertonio, Ludovico
1984 (1602)   *Vocabulario de la lengua Aymara.* Cochabamba: Centro de Es-
                     tudios de la Realidad Económica y Social.

Cobo, Bernabé
1956 (1653)   *Historia del Nuevo Mundo.* Madrid: Editorial Atlas.

González Holguín, Diego
1989 (1602)   *Vocabulario de la lengua general de todo el Perú llamada lengua
                     Qquichua o del Inca.* Lima: Universidad Nacional Mayor de
                     San Marcos.

Hemming, John
1970   *The Conquest of the Incas.* New York: Harcourt Brace Jo-
                     vanovich.

Murúa, Fray Martín de
1946 (1590)   *Historia del origen y genealogía real de los reyes Incas del Perú,*
                     edited by Constantino Bayle. Madrid: Instituto Santo To-
                     ribio de Mogrovejo, Consejo Superior de Investigaciones
                     Científicas.

1962–1964 (1613)   *Historia general del Perú, origen y descendencia de los Incas . . . ,*
                     edited by Manuel Ballesteros-Gaibrois. Colección Joyas Bib-

271

liográficas, Bibliotheca Americana Vetus 1. Madrid: In-
stituto Gonzalo Fernández de Oviedo, Consejo Superior de
Investigaciones Científicas.

Salomon, Frank

1986   *Native Lords of Quito in the Age of the Incas: The Political Economy of North Andean Chiefdoms.* Cambridge, Eng.: Cambridge
University Press.

Szemiński, Jan

1987   *Un kuraca, un dios y una historia.* Jujuy, Argentina: Facultad
de Filosofía y Letras, Universidad de Buenos Aires.

Urioste, Jorge L.

1980   "Glosario índice del Quechua de Waman Puma." In Felipe
Guaman Poma de Ayala, *El primer nueva corónica y buen
gobierno,* edited by John V. Murra and Rolena Adorno.
Mexico City: Siglo XXI, 3:1075–1108.

aclla (variant *aqlla*)
  chosen, the chosen one (Urioste 1980:3:1076)

ahuaqui
  weaving; V-shaped and stepped yoke-design on *uncu*

amaru
  serpent, dragon (González Holguín 1989:24); mythical serpent often associated with rainbows

apu (plural *apukuna*, variant *apo*)
  great lord or highest judge (González Holguín 1989:31)

aucaylli (variant *auccay haylli*)
  triumphal song sung during harvest (González Holguín 1989:38)

awki qhapaq churi (variant *auqui capac churi*)
  son of a powerful lord (Urioste 1980:3:1077)

ayllu
  "localized kindred or larger localized group self-defined in kinship idiom"
  (Salomon 1986:237)

capac (variant *qhapaq*)
  king, royal (González Holguín 1989:135); powerful, one who has the support
  of many (Urioste 1980:3:1096)

casana (variant *caxane*)
  design of four squares within one larger square on an *uncu*

casay
  to pierce; *kassuni huypu huan* "to break the clods for sowing" (González Holguín 1989:127)

colca
the Pleiades

collca
"storehouse of walls; trox: walled granary" (González Holguín 1989:686). The walls were probably made of stone.

collcapata (variants *collca pata, colca pata*)
design of a checkerboard pattern as used on an *uncu* (Murúa 1946:21, 215)

coya (variant *quya*)
the Inca's queen consort

curaca
See *kuraka*

chacara
sown land, cultivated field; a small Spanish estate, usually supplying stable regional markets

champi
club (Cobo 1956:9, 14, 255)

chaqui taclla
Andean footplow

chaski (variant *ch'aski*)
post runner of the Inca empire (Salomon 1986:238); messenger

chumpi
waistband (González Holguín 1989:121)

chuñu
potato dried in the sun (González Holguín 1989:121)

chuspa (variant *chhuspa*)
shoulder bag worn by men (González Holguín 1989:125)

hanan
high, upper; term used for the upper half or moiety of the city of Cusco; "a high thing or above" (González Holguín 1989:148)

haravi (variants *haraui, arawi*)
love song (Urioste 1980:3:1081)

huaca
See *waqa*

huaka (Aymara)
waistband used by women, according to Bertonio (1984:143)

huallca
collar; "everything hung around the neck" (González Holguín 1989:173)

huaque

a statue of each Inca king's totem ("cada rey en vida hacía un ídolo o estatua suya, de piedra, la qual llamaba *guaoiqui,* que quiere decir hermano, porque a aquella estatua en vida y en muerte se le había de hacer la misma veneración que al propio Inga" [Acosta 1962:227])

huaricsa (variant *wariqsa*)

a dance (Urioste 1980:3:1105)

hurin

the lower half or moiety of the city of Cusco: from *ura,* "the low place" (González Holguín 1989:356)

kamachikuq

local or minor authority (Urioste 1980:3:1083)

kamayuq (plural *kamayuqkuna,* variants *kamayuj, camayo*)

"person specializing in the production of a good, or exploitation of a resource, as delegate of a community, political authority, or religious cult" (Salomon 1986:238)

kero

See *qiru*

khipu (variants *k'ipu, quipu, quipo*)

"mnemonic record, usually numerical, made of knotted cords" (Salomon 1986:238)

kuraka (plural *kurakakuna,* variants *curaca, kuraca*)

"native lord of a non-Inca polity" (Salomon 1986:238)

layqha (plural *layqhakuna*)

traditional religious specialist

llancapata

tunic

llawt'u (variant *llauto*)

cloth headband (González Holguín 1989:212)

masca paycha (variant *maskha paycha*)

red cloth tassel worn over the forehead as a crown of the Sapa Inca; "a fringe that the Inca used as a crown" (González Holguín 1989:232)

minga (variant *mink'a*)

grant of collective labor to an authority; a voluntary wage laborer at the silver mines (especially Potosí)

mita

"Spanish colonial reworking of Incaic cyclical corvée" (Salomon 1986:239); obligatory public service

mit'a
Incaic cyclical *corvée,* used for public works, infrastructures, and the military (Salomon 1986:239)

mitayu (variants *mitayo, mit'ayuq*)
a person fulfilling periodic obligatory service

mitmaq (plural *mitmaqkuna,* variant *mitmaj*)
person sent from place of origin to serve outside interests, usually of the Inca state (Urioste 1980:3:1090)

muru unquy (variants *moro unqoy, moro ungoy*)
Andean resistance movement (sixteenth century) based on traditional ritual practices

Onccoi Ccoyllor (see also *colca*)
the Pleiades

pacha panta
an illness to be expelled during the month of September (Guaman Poma 1980:255)

pachakuti (variant *pachacuti*)
the one who transforms the world, "the cataclysm" (Urioste 1980:3:1091)

panaca
a branch of the Inca nobility in Cusco; from *pana,* "sister of the man, or cousin or from his land, or lineage, or acquaintance" (González Holguín 1989:277)

paucar uncu (variant *pawqar uncu*)
a type of tunic

pincullu (variant *pinqullu*)
flute

pukyu unquy (variant *pucyo oncuy*)
an illness to be eradicated by the Inca during the month of September (Guaman Poma 1980:255)

qhapaq apu (variant *capac apo*)
powerful lord

qhapaq churi (variant *capac churi*)
son of a powerful lord

qiru (plural *qirukuna,* variants *qiro, kero*)
wooden drinking cup (González Holguín 1989:305)

quipu
See *khipu*

raymi
calendrical feast, especially where solar celebrations are involved

ruthuchiku
the first hair-cutting; ceremony of the life cycle (Urioste 1980:3:1098)

sara unquy
corn sickness; an illness to be eradicated during the month of September (Guaman Poma 1980:255)

sipi (Aymara)
feather collar (Bertonio 1984:319)

sucullo ccahua
black shirt

suntur paucar
royal standard with crown of feathers near the top

suyu (variant *suyo*)
one of the four divisions of the Inca empire

Taki Unquy (variant *Taqui Onqoy*)
Andean resistance movement (sixteenth century) based on the traditional ritual practice of eradicating the "illness of the dance" during the month of September; "he who becomes ill dancing" (Urioste 1980:3:1101)

takiunquero (Hispanicized Quechua)
participant in the Taki Unquy movement

tarco (Aymara; variant *tarcu*)
neck or the bone that is at the beginning of the neck (Bertonio 1984:338)

tinku (variant *tinkuq*)
confluence, convergence

tucapu (variants *tocapo, t'oqapu*)
various squares or rectangles, mostly abstract designs, used in combination on Inca *uncus*

tupa cochor
square golden plaque

tupa cusi
royal golden beaker (Murúa 1964:1:22, 54)

tupa yauri
royal scepter with the head in the shape of an ax carried by the Sapa Inca; royal insignia of the Inca (González Holguín 1989:347); a kind of royal halbard

uncu
tunic

usnu (variant *ushnu*)
ceremonial seat; "raised platform used as imperial judgment seat" (Hemming 1970:517)

Viracocha
creator god (Hemming 1970:517); applied to the Europeans after 1532

waqa (plural *waqakuna*, variant *huaca*)
the sacred; divine personages and sacred places

warachikuq
ceremonial girding of male children

Yamqui
an honorific title equivalent to *apu* (Szemiński 1987:4)

yana (plural *yanakuna*, Hispanicized Quechua *yanacona*)
"colonial servitor of a private person, treated as dependent and paid nominally" (Salomon 1986:241)

Yanahuara
Andean resistance movement (sixteenth century) based on traditional ritual practices

CONTRIBUTORS

Rolena Adorno, Professor of Romance Languages and Literatures, Princeton University.

Author of *Guaman Poma: Writing and Resistance in Colonial Peru* (1986); co-editor with John V. Murra of Felipe Guaman Poma de Ayala's *El primer nueva corónica y buen gobierno* (1980, 1987); editor of *From Oral to Written Expression: Native Andean Chroniclers of Early Colonial Peru* (1982); author of *Cronista y príncipe: La obra de Felipe Guaman Poma de Ayala* (1989); and co-editor of this volume.

Kenneth J. Andrien, Associate Professor of History, Ohio State University.

Author of *Crisis and Decline: The Viceroyalty of Peru in the Seventeenth Century* (1985), and several scholarly articles on Spanish colonial history; he is co-editor of this volume.

Thomas B. F. Cummins, Assistant Professor of Art History, University of Chicago.

Author of "Abstraction to Narration: Kero Imagery of Peru and the Colonial Alteration of Native Identity" (Ph.D. diss., 1988); "Kinshape: the Design of the Hawaiian Feather Cloak" (1984); and scholarly articles on pre-Columbian and Spanish colonial art of the Andes.

John F. Guilmartin, Associate Professor of History, Ohio State University.

Author of *Gunpowder and Galleys: Changing Technology and Mediterranean Warfare at Sea in the Sixteenth Century* (1974), and numerous scholarly articles on early modern technology and warfare in the Mediterranean and the Atlantic.

James Lockhart, Professor of History, University of California at Los Angeles.

Author of *Spanish Peru, 1532–1560* (1968) and *The Men of Cajamarca: A Social and Biographical Study of the First Conquerors of Peru* (1972); co-author with Frances Karttunen of *Nahuatl in the Middle Years: Language Contact Phenomena in Texts of the Colonial Period* (1976); co-author with Stuart B. Schwartz of *Early Latin America: A History of Colonial Spanish America and Brazil* (1983); co-editor with Frances Karttunen of *The Art of Nahuatl Speech: The Bancroft Dialogues* (1987); and author of the forthcoming *The Nahuas After the Conquest.*

John V. Murra, Professor Emeritus of Anthropology, Cornell University.

Author of *Formaciones económicas y políticas del mundo andino* (1975), *and La organización económica del estado Inca* (1978, 1980); editor of *Visita hecha a la provincia de Chucuito en 1567* (1964), and *Visita de la provincia de León de Huánaco en 1562* (1967, 1972); co-editor with Rolena Adorno of Felipe Guaman Poma de Ayala's *El primer nueva corónica y buen gobierno* (1980, 1987); co-editor with Nathan Wachtel and Jacques Revel of *Anthropological History of Andean Polities* (1986); and editor of the forthcoming house-to-house census of coca leaf growers in Bolivia, 1568.

Carla R. Phillips, Professor of History, University of Minnesota.

Author of *Ciudad Real, 1500–1750* (1979); *Six Galleons for the King of Spain* (1986); and numerous scholarly articles on early modern Spain.

William D. Phillips, Professor of History, University of Minnesota.

Author of *Enrique IV and the Crisis of Fifteenth-Century Castile* (1978); *Slavery from Roman Times to the Early Transatlantic Trade* (1985); and many scholarly articles on medieval and early modern Spain.

R. Tom Zuidema, Professor of Anthropology, University of Illinois.

Author of *The Ceque System of Cuzco: The Social Organization of the Capital of the Inca* (1964); *La Civilisation Inca au Cuzco* (1986); *Reyes y guerreros: Ensayos de Cultura Andina* (1989); *Inca Civilización in Cuzco* (1990); and many scholarly articles on the civilizations of the Andes.

INDEX

238; Gonzalo, 93, 121–123, 139, 142
n.3, 143 n.10; Hernando, 44, 46, 56,
58–59, 63 n.18, 64 n.20, 121; Pedro,
44, 46, 55, 57–59, 65 n.34, 67 n.56, 86
n.13, 121, 197 n.53
Pizarro, Don Martín de, 234
Pleiades, 170, 196 n.46, 241, 262 n.34
Pleito, 233, 239, 252–253, 255–256, 258,
269 n.131
Plowing rituals, 170
Poechos, Martinillo de. *See* Pizarro, Don
Martín de
Poli Collection, Lima, Peru, 176, 178–179,
182
Polo de Ondegardo, Juan, 79, 81–83, 85,
87 n.21, 88 n.28, 89 nn.43–44, 91 n.38,
92 nn.43–44, 183, 241, 263 n.51
Pontifical city, 190, 191
Pope Leo III, 191
Porras Barrenechea, Raúl, 85, 86 nn.11–
12, 87 nn.23–24, 259 n.4
Portugal, 13–14, 20, 24, 26, 29–34, 73, 90,
93, 100–101, 105; Portuguese Madeira,
31–33
Portuguese. *See* Portugal
Postan, M. M., 38 n.31
Potosí, Peru, 81, 83, 86, 97, 101, 109–110,
112, 114–115, 118 n.34, 123, 126–127,
132–134, 136, 140, 142 n.9, 143 n.20,
196 n.44, 202 n.85, 223, 230 nn.45–46
Prescott, William H., 44–45, 62 nn.12–13,
84, 88 n.42, 111, 118 n.36, 142 n.3
Procurador (litigation officer), 232–233
Puente, Diego de la, 201 n.82
Puma head and skin, 179, 182, 187, 202
n.85

Qhapaq apu, 237, 261 n.28, 267 n.102
Qhapaq churi. See Qhapaq apu
Quechua, 83, 120 n.48, 153, 174, 198 n.60,
256
Queen Mariana, 212, 216
Queija, Berta Inés, 147 n.56
Quipu. See Khipu
Quiroga, Pedro de, 235–236, 238, 249,
253–254, 261 nn.21,25, 267 n.98, 268
nn.127–128, 269 n.130
Quispe Guarcaya, Don Gonzalo, 267 n.101
Quisquis, 63 n.18

Quito, 59, 65 n.29, 78, 110, 121, 147
nn.60,61
Quizo Yapanqui, 57, 67 n.55

Ramírez, Susan, 114, 120 n.49, 146
nn.49,53,55, 148 n.60
Raua Ocllo, *coya*, 168–170
Raymi: Capac rami, 167, 171, 174, 179, 182–
183, 187–190, 197 n.53, 198 n.59, 201
n.83, 202 n.87; *Coya raymi*, 170, 175,
187–189, 192, 202 n.86; *Inca raymi*,
167–170, 175, 177, 187–188, 190, 192,
196 nn.45,48, 199 n.66, 202 n.86
Rebellion, of 1536–1537, 48, 50, 61; of
1539, 40, 45, 48, 60; of Hernández
Girón, 67 n.55
Reconquest, 13–16, 20, 30, 34 n.2, 49
Reducciones, 85, 125–243
Regalado de Hurtado, Liliana, 147 n.58
Relación, 238, 256
Remy, María Isabel, 146 n.49
Repartimiento, 125, 217
Residencias, 234
Ricard, Robert, 111, 118 n.36
Riel, Jacques, 63 n.16
Rivera C., Silvia, 148 n.60
Rivera Serna, Raúl, 148 n.61
Rodríguez de Figueroa, Diego, 228 n.31,
229 n.37, 231 n.48
Roman, 35 n.12, 235
Roman Law, 2, 21, 23, 34
Romero, Carlos, 230 nn.44,46, 231 n.47
Rostworowski de Diez Canseco, María, 76,
86 nn.7,14, 140, 146 n.55, 228 n.28,
260 n.16
Rowe, Ann P., 152, 175, 192 n.5, 192 n.6,
193 n.12, 199 nn.64–65, 200 n.77
Rowe, John H., 84, 88 n.42, 152, 174–175,
192 n.5, 194 n.20, 195 n.33, 197 n.53,
199 nn.63,66, 200 n.71, 225 n.3, 226
nn.11–13, 228 n.27
Roys, Ralph L., 268 n.123
Ruiz, Bartolomé, 75–76, 86 n.9
Ruiz, Teófilo F., 37 n.23, 38 n.31
Ruiz de Arce, Juan, 179, 200 n.75
Rumeu de Armas, Antonio, 39 n.36
Ruminavi, 63 n.18
Ruthuchiku, 264 n.75

Designer: U.C. Press Staff
Compositor: Prestige Typography
Text: 10/12 Baskerville
Display: Baskerville
Printer: Braun-Brumfield, Inc.
Binder: Braun-Brumfield, Inc.